Personal Effects

Personal Effects

WHAT RECOVERING

THE DEAD TEACHES

ME ABOUT CARING

FOR THE LIVING

Robert A. Jensen

with James Hider

ST. MARTIN'S PRESS

New York

First published in the United States by St. Martin's Press,
an imprint of St. Martin's Publishing Group

PERSONAL EFFECTS. Copyright © 2021 by Robert A. Jensen.
All rights reserved. Printed in the United States of America.
For information, address St. Martin's Publishing Group,
120 Broadway, New York, NY 10271.

www.stmartins.com

Library of Congress Cataloging-in-Publication Data

Names: Jensen, Robert A., author. | Hider, James, author.
Title: Personal effects : what recovering the dead teaches me
   about caring for the living / Robert A. Jensen with James Hider.
Description: First edition. | New York : St. Martin's Press, 2021. |
   Includes index.
Identifiers: LCCN 2021016221 | ISBN 9781250267993
   (hardcover) | ISBN 9781250268006 (ebook)
Subjects: LCSH: Disaster relief. | Jensen, Robert A.
Classification: LCC HV553 .J45 2021 | DDC 363.34/8—dc23
LC record available at https://lccn.loc.gov/2021016221

Our books may be purchased in bulk for promotional,
educational, or business use. Please contact your local
bookseller or the Macmillan Corporate and Premium Sales
Department at 1–800–221–7945, extension 5442,
or by email at MacmillanSpecialMarkets@macmillan.com.

First Edition: 2021

10 9 8 7 6 5 4 3 2 1

For Brandon

I hope the price was not too high

Contents

In Memoriam

What we do not know about
a missing loved one becomes all that we know

−T. S. ELIOT (Paraphrased)

Introduction

There are always shoes. No matter what the event—earthquake, flood, accident, fire, or bombing—the shoes are everywhere. Sometimes, they contain a foot—or part of a foot—because the dead are often separated not just from their clothes, but from their own extremities.

There are always treasures, too. In the case of Swissair Flight 111, insurers searched the bottom of the Atlantic for literal treasure: more than ten pounds of diamonds, rubies, and other precious stones that had been lying in the cargo hold alongside an original Picasso and fifty kilos of paper money. But the treasures I look for are far more valuable. They are the personal treasures: wedding rings, heirloom watches, and eyeglasses; passports and pictures; journals, books, toys, and favorite clothes that offer tangible proof people exist—or at least existed once—and were loved. They are the reminders of lives lived, the last glimpses of the people we knew, how they lived and how they died.

Most important, there are always those left behind. There are the spouses, the parents, the children, and the friends and other relatives who wait at home or come to the airport, expecting to see their loved one get off a flight. Instead they see a message on the arrivals board, asking them to contact an agent, or they get a text from a friend who sees something on the news. Then, if they are lucky enough to live in a country that has a response system in place, they find themselves shuttled to a somber hotel conference room, where they meet me, their guide to a new life they never expected to happen. If no such system exists, they then have to scramble to piece together what happened to their loved ones themselves, sometimes sifting through wreckage or mass graves or erecting impromptu memorials in the ruined homes or offices.

There are also the friends and coworkers who white-knuckle through every commercial flight they're forced to take for the rest of their lives, especially after the horror of the Boeing 737 Max Jet crashes in Indonesia and Ethiopia, which killed 346 people. Like so many other man-made disasters, these could have been avoided, except for the fact that we are all people and people make mistakes and will always continue to do so. The story of the loss of the 737 Max and the response by Boeing may seem shocking to us, but it is not the first time something like that has happened and unlikely it will be the last.

The aftershocks of tragedy reverberate for decades: grief, trauma, mental illness, lawsuits, bad press, lost revenue. Most of my life has been spent responding to those events. As the head of the world's leading disaster management company—on retainer with many of the world's airlines, national governments, maritime, rail companies, and others—I handle the dead, often literally.

My real purpose, though, is to help the living. I can't offer them closure, but I do offer them a way to manage their recovery and create the best chance for them to transition from what was normal to what will be, for them, the new normal.

From 9/11 and Hurricane Katrina to the 2010 Haitian earthquake and the 2004 South Asian tsunami, I've led efforts to recover and repatriate human remains, return possessions to families, and help governments and people go forward. If journalists write the first rough draft of history, I'm the one adding the footnotes, giving the dead their due, buried at the bottom of the page. In the lobby of my Houston offices hangs a Stars and Stripes flag; a flag that once flew over the New York City Medical Examiners Memorial Park, an area holding refrigerated trucks with human remains recovered from the World Trade Center. It is similar to the flag that hangs in the lobby of the United Nations headquarters in New York, which we recovered from the bombed-out UN offices in Baghdad, from where we returned those lost to their families. Flags, like bodies, are powerful symbols.

There are great lessons to be learned and shared from these events. What I've learned in life is that no one—businesses, governments, the media, even first responders or families—is ever quite prepared enough for these crises or disasters. Everyone will react differently, and I don't mean while the event is occurring, but after the danger has passed. Some will panic; others will shut down and pretend it did not happen. Others will want to watch, but not directly: they will peek between their fingers, horrified but unable to look away, knowing that nothing will ever be the same. I have never been one to turn away. When I was fourteen, I was in a car accident. My mom was driving. She was mad because my sister and I had missed the bus to school and she had called in sick to work, so she wasn't thrilled about taking us to school in a small town where people would see her. Distracted and then flustered, she hit the gas instead of the brakes, slamming into an old steel streetlight. It didn't move. As the car wrapped around the pole, my legs were pinned underneath the dashboard. That wasn't so bad. My head and face shattering the windshield was the bad part. The impact cut my forehead to ribbons and left my face and scalp full of small pieces of glass, some of which still now work their way out or have to be removed by doctors. When the firemen finally cut through the car to get me out and I could somewhat stand to get onto the stretcher, I'll always remember that many of the bystanders turned away, lowered their heads, or covered their eyes. Others just stared. The shock of how I looked was not something they were prepared for. They weren't involved, so they were lucky they could turn away.

Survivors—living people who have been directly affected by mass fatalities—can't turn away. Some try, but eventually they will have to deal with the consequences. For a period of time— for some it will be longer than others—these people will experience a life outside the ordinary. How the system responds to care for them will have a huge impact on how long or how hard that that period is. Hopefully they will have their world back. It will be different, but it will be theirs.

No matter where I am in the world, when I tell people what I do, it becomes a long conversation, one I repeat over and over. The fascination never goes away. It is a rare glimpse beyond the headlines and behind the yellow tape and barricades set up to isolate and protect the scene—in some ways, those barricades are meant to protect the living, because when people see what is behind them, their world changes forever. But what goes on behind those barricades, when done right, can be a masterpiece of coordination, exhaustive work, and finding a path through the worst that the world can throw at us.

It takes leadership to manage the unmanageable, to bring order to chaos. People in charge are not always rational when under huge pressure or wrestling with unbearable grief. They make bad decisions with far-reaching ramifications or make promises that can't be fulfilled. Sometimes, I have to say "no" to a bad decision. I was once asked to saw the body of a deceased Marine in half because his trapped body was partially visible in his dress uniform in the Oklahoma City bombing. I said "no" because it was a total lack of respect for the Marine and the life he gave.

Sometimes, I've had to say "yes" to requests that were difficult but necessary. I've had to negotiate my way through checkpoints manned by militiamen in war-torn countries; to tell family members that the DNA test we used to identify their late father's remains had, in fact, revealed that he was never actually their father in the first place. Before this, as a young Army officer in the last days of the Cold War, I was responsible to launch, when ordered, Pershing II Nuclear Missiles. Missiles that could have destroyed thousands of lives.

One thing I take away from the mayhem I have seen is an understanding that as people, we focus on the things we can't control while overlooking the many things we can. There are a lot of things we don't really control, and we forget that. We all get hints of this from time to time. Some are mere annoyances— canceled flights, rained-out events. Others shock us, with a threat of loss of life or actual loss of life, such as: aircraft accidents, terrorist attacks, school shootings, or natural disasters, like floods and storms that devastate farms and businesses. None of them new; we are just more aware of them. We will all live and we will all die. The key is to live well. Life should be about living, not dying.

I have dealt with sudden, unexpected, and often violent death most of my adult life on a scale few can fathom. Think about any major disaster over the past thirty years, and chances are I was there and personally involved. And not just a walk-through for a day, but for many days, months, or even years.

This book is about how to avoid being overwhelmed, to see

the good in situations, how to solve problems, and lead people from what their life was to what it will be.

For most people life is a routine, like traveling down a highway every day. Then all of a sudden that highway collapses in front of them and now, where once there was roadway, there is a huge, bottomless chasm. My job is to have a plan, the tools, and resources to build a bridge across that chasm. The survivors, the people we help, the families and friends of the deceased, their job is to cross that bridge and continue on with life. How well we build that bridge will for many determine how many cross that bridge. No matter how well we do, some will not. Building that bridge and the journey across is what this book is about.

It is also about the toll it takes on the bridge builder. A former colleague of mine, a British forensics expert, cannot hear the sound of ice cubes being dropped into a glass without instantly recalling the image of ice blocks being offloaded from trucks to refrigerate the thousands of bodies recovered in Thailand's trashed coastal resorts after the South Asian tsunami of 2004. Because I lead people, I am responsible for them. Therefore, a major part of my job is to make sure they know when they are hitting their limits, not to push people beyond what they can take, to teach them to recognize their own limits and to know themselves. After each event we are all a little bit different. How different is hard to tell and varies greatly from person to person. But always different.

That goes for me too, but who watches out for me and what will happen to me? To be honest, I don't really know. No one forced me into this job, I like what I do, and I am good at it. I think I have a pretty good outlook on life: chances are if you ever met me after hearing what I do, I probably wouldn't fit your expectations. But I am not normal; and someday I will stop and then I hope to find an ordinary world, one that must exist even for me. I've always been a fan of the '80s band Duran Duran, and often think of their song "Ordinary World" when I look back on the life I've lived.

> There's an ordinary world
> Somehow I have to find

This is a lot for a book, but then again, I have seen a lot.

1. The Opposite of Meaning

The front of the Alfred P. Murrah Federal Building had been sheared off as if it were a doll's house. A vast pile of shifting rubble reared up outside, the height of several floors. The stairs at the back of the building remained intact but unstable—you could still go in through the underground parking lot to access them, through a thick dust cloud faintly illuminated by the dying headlights of cars whose owners were never coming back. Overhead, you emerged into the pounding of jackhammers and the whir of metal grinders on jagged rebar, sending sparks flying through the dazzling glare of arc lights. The smell of death was there, but not overpowering; concrete is an endothermic material, meaning it absorbs heat, energy, and fluid. When it encases a body, it dries it out, almost like a mummy.

Oklahoma City taught me an early and important lesson about sudden, large-scale catastrophes: Don't expect wisdom at the moment of death. Don't expect anyone to know where they're going or even what they're doing: authority figures, first responders, loved ones, and sadly even the executive branches of government. While there are rare examples of standout leadership, usually politicians are more likely to be concerned with the political fallout. Death doesn't create meaning; it tries its best to *undo* meaning. Our work as the living is to build legacies and institutions that can hold fast in the face of death's assault.

By the time I arrived in Oklahoma City as the commander of the US Army's 54th Quartermaster Company (MA)—the main Mortuary Affairs unit—the search for the living was over. A makeshift mortuary had been set up in a damaged church right next to the destroyed federal building: not because it made a good mortuary, but because it was the first place that stunned police and firefighters had found to leave the bodies of those they couldn't save, while they hurried back inside to look for survivors. So that is where we set up shop: in any case, there are worse places than a church for the dead to pass through.

It was a chaotic scene. Oklahoma City had been used to the occasional tornado, but a devastating act of terrorism? No one had ever expected that. This was 1995, and America was living in a cozy bubble of what the political thinker Francis Fukuyama had mistakenly called the end of history. The Cold War was won, the economy was booming, and life was good. People can forget when times are easy that bad things sometimes just happen, or they start to believe that bad things only happen to bad people, people who somehow brought it upon themselves. And then, out of the blue, came the worst act of domestic terrorism the country had ever known.

People are paralyzed in the face of mass death: it's that place where we don't allow our minds to go. Officials don't know the rules and procedures of catastrophe, and few can bring themselves to look the survivors in the eyes. For most people, pretty much anywhere in the world, it is the first and last time in their lives they face horror on such a vast scale. They're lucky in that.

One of the first things people have to learn is no one is ever in charge. People may be in charge of one piece of the puzzle or another—and what they do will impact everyone else, and vice versa. But there is no one who has overall control—ever. This creates the opportunity for chaos to rule.

There was another problem particular to the Murrah building. In the United States (with few exceptions) dealing with the deceased falls within a state's rights. Each state or territory manages deaths differently; some have statewide systems while others have local or county systems. The exception is for deaths that occur on federal property—federal buildings, military installations. The Murrah building was a federal building, and therefore was not within the state jurisdiction. In the United States, regulations around which jurisdiction is responsible for conducting criminal investigations and death investigation are well regulated. The problem is the actual resources to do the work. Because there is no "Federal Medical Examiner," beyond the Armed Forces Medical Examiner, the recovery of the deceased is often accomplished by local or state governments. That is not normally a problem. However, in politically sensitive or mass fatality incidents that creates lots of problems. There are also systems to augment the local authorities, when they are overwhelmed, but the local authorities retain control. So, the jurisdiction of the Murrah building itself was not in question, but because of the event the jurisdiction and control of decisions with regard to the deceased was a nightmare. Clearly, because this was a federal building, the US Army could enter it and recover the deceased. (This led to an expectation that the US Army would then be able to do this again, such as in Hurricane Katrina or the pandemic, without the public's understanding Army personnel could not provide recovery in private residences or buildings not under federal ownership.) You'd be amazed at how often the question of jurisdiction—accompanied by the jockeying egos of officials, the agony of grieving relatives, and the sudden media spotlight—the whole bundle wrapped up in obscure bureaucratic red tape—simply overwhelms the efforts to recover the dead after a mass fatality.

So, when the Clinton administration called in the 54th, which at the time was the military's only active-duty Mortuary Affairs unit, these were the problems we would and did face. Today there are two military active-duty Mortuary Affairs units. Our everyday job was to receive the mortal remains of US servicemen killed in the line of duty from their units and get them to the Armed Forces Medical Examiner and back home.

Since taking charge of the unit as a thirty-year-old captain, after writing doctrine, studying, and seeing some pretty bad mistakes, I began pushing for a more proactive role for my troops, trying to get them forensic training. At the same time working with military leadership to change information flow, trying to impress on them the need for a faster flow of information from the battlefield to higher command levels and on to the families. I felt we could not only help relatives through the crippling pain of not knowing what had happened to their sons and daughters, but also smooth the decision-making process for the chain of command. Not knowing what happened to a missing person is the worst pain people can go through. Getting wrong information is even worse.

For example, in one operation, I received the body of a soldier who had been killed by a landmine. The division was planning for the death of "a hero." Frankly, he *was* a hero: he had volunteered to serve others and left his family to try and bring peace to the world. But he didn't die stepping on an unmarked landmine as reported. The blast pattern on the soldier's body—shrapnel peppering the inner thighs, chest, and face—suggested he had been squatting over the device. In a rather casual manner, I asked some soldiers from his unit if he'd had any nicknames. When they said "MacGyver"—the resourceful

TV secret agent who is always poking into mysteries—my suspicions grew.

Now, as a matter of course, when a dead US service member is flown home, the body has to be x-rayed to make sure there is no unexploded ordnance inside: it could go off on the flight or during the handling of the remains. In this case, I x-rayed the late soldier's body and found that his multi-tool, which was missing from his belt, was embedded inside his forehead. He had been attempting to defuse a well-marked landmine and accidentally detonated it.

I reported this to the commanding general so they could ensure the family received the truth and not create a media event that would later have to be changed, downplayed, or explained, as would later happen in the tragic case of Pat Tillman, the NFL star killed by friendly fire in Afghanistan. Being honest does not detract from the loss or the incredible value these people have: it simply prevents the pain, mistrust, and anger that follows when the truth comes out.

That was the kind of active investigative role I was trying to engender in my unit. I had been en route to a training session with reserve Mortuary Affairs units based in Puerto Rico when Timothy McVeigh set off his fertilizer-based bomb in the back of a Ryder rental truck. As I landed at Miami International airport, my beeper (this was the days before mobile phones) went crazy. I found a pay phone and called Washington. They said there had been a bombing. I asked how bad, and they said, "Beirut bad." That told me all I needed to know: the truck bombing of a US Marines barracks in Beirut in 1983 had killed in total 241 American service members, 58 French peacekeepers, and 6 civilians. Even though I had never dealt with such a massive attack before, at least I knew what we needed and what to expect. Or at least I thought I did.

There were plenty of senior officers who thought my soldiers were too dumb for anything more than "bagging and tagging." The Mortuary Affairs unit has the lowest entry level requirements in the whole Army, so people who had been busted from other units often ended up there, making it a classic bunch of misfits. In reality they are far from it. Some of them were misfits for unusual reasons—several of my soldiers had dropped out of highly demanding language courses in intelligence units, and the Army typically had no idea where to put them afterward. We had people who could speak Mandarin Chinese or Arabic searching through the pockets of the dead: I believed they could do much more.

We set up our mortuary tables inside the wrecked church next to the federal building. Out front, we stationed the refrigerator trucks—known for short as "reefer trucks"—to hold the bodies, until the state medical examiner would collect them. Our job after the recovery was to remove any personal items, which helped with a tentative identification but also needed to be preserved so they could be passed on to the families and to complete initial documentation. Anytime the firefighters were close to uncovering a body our teams would head out on to the "pile," as the ruined building quickly became known, carrying gurneys and digging equipment. Every so often, an air horn would blast out its warning: falling rubble or a slide of debris. You either had to stand still or, if one saw some obvious cover, take shelter. The rubble shifted treacherously underfoot, like mountain scree, and we were thirty to forty feet above the ground, which was itself covered in a mosaic of broken glass and the metal ribs of the building. We worked our way from bottom to top to avoid spilling debris onto people working below. It was dangerous, slow, arduous work.

For building collapses, if available we use a floor plan to work out where the offices were. From the outside, it was hard to tell one ripped-open, debris-choked space from another: what had been the neat offices of a military recruiting station, the Drug Enforcement Agency (DEA), or a Social Security office were now just hanging tangles of wires and sagging insulation, concrete and rebar, indistinguishable from the offices of the Bureau of Alcohol, Tobacco and Firearms (ATF) or the Internal Revenue Service.

Five days after the blast, we had a tentative list of the missing and where they were most likely to be found. The search plan was hardly definitive, though, since some people did not die in their offices. Some were killed instantly in the blast, some of them pinned under the rubble. Even compiling a list is fraught with difficulties: back in those days, there was no secure way to sign in, and people who had signed in might have already left the shattered building and gone home, where they sat in shock while worried relatives reported them missing.

Some of the dead were still trapped at the desks they had only just sat down behind at the beginning of their working day—the bomb went off at 9:02 a.m., just as people were settling in for a day's work. We recovered the body of a woman who was wearing two different shoes—a sneaker on one foot and a high-heeled shoe on the other: an odd pairing. She was clearly sitting down to change into her work shoes for the day when the bomb went off. Had she arrived a few minutes later, perhaps she might have survived. A matter of minutes meant she could have been coming up a back stairwell, somewhat shielded from the blast. Sometimes, it is simply your time.

Bombs can kill people in a number of different ways. The rapidly expanding gases traveling outward from the point of detonation have enough force to rip a person to pieces at close range or shred a body with shrapnel. The blast wave alone can rupture vital internal organs and kill a person even if there is no obvious external injury: most commonly, the lungs simply burst. But what happens most often in an attack like Oklahoma City is crush injuries, where collapsing walls or other structures fall on a person. Sometimes those injuries too are internal and barely visible at first glance, though many are more obvious. We also recovered a body whose dusty head had been crushed into a perfect triangle by a fallen pillar.

To complicate matters, we had been asked to find a single leg—a leg that had belonged to a woman who was luckily still alive but whose limb had been amputated in situ so she could be rushed to hospital for life-saving surgery. It was the only way for the rescuers to get her out of the building alive: an incredibly brave surgeon spent hours cutting through the trapped leg, breaking the blades of his saws until he was down to just a pocketknife, which he used to sever the final tendons. Our job is to locate and remove as much human tissue as is safely possible, both to allow it to be buried appropriately but also to avoid complex legal issues that may arise in the subsequent legal quagmire that inevitably follows such destructive events.

In fact, in Oklahoma one of the severed legs that was found was later misidentified and buried with a body that had two intact legs. There were eight bodies in total buried without their left legs after the bombing. The fact that there was a human leg unaccounted for had very real consequences: it allowed white supremacist Timothy McVeigh's defense lawyers to speculate that the "real" bomber had died in his own explosion, sowing doubt about the guilt of their client. But it also had a profound effect on relatives of the dead, because any trace of doubt creates enormous problems for those left behind, and who can be tortured by the thought that part of their beloved relative could be unaccounted for.

One of the dead who was buried without an intact left leg was a twenty-one-year-old service member from the US Air Force, Lakesha Levy. She had been a lab technician at the nearby Tinker Air Force Base and had gone in uniform to the Social Security offices to get a new social security number. After the trauma of losing Lakesha, her family then had to endure the further horror of seeing her body—which had been buried in a cemetery in her hometown of New Orleans—being disinterred and subjected to a DNA and footprint test to prove the suspected extra leg was hers.

The leg did in fact belong to her, the tests showed. But that still left the headache of the leg she had been buried with. That could have then been used as a defense tactic by McVeigh's lawyers. To make matters worse, the buried limb had been embalmed and could not be effectively DNA tested with the procedures that existed at the time. It was finally reburied, along with other unidentified remains of bone fragment and flesh, in a memorial garden on the city's capitol grounds.

Lakesha had been the last member of the armed forces to be removed from the ruins. I was examining her body and putting her possessions into numbered bags when I was informed that Secretary of the Army Togo West was visiting the site and wanted to say hello. While speaking with Secretary West, and without thinking too much about it, I asked him if he would like to pay his respects to her. He concurred, and I left him with the body for a minute. Privately, I wondered if I had screwed up by putting him in an awkward position—he was on an official visit, after all, and seeing a young woman's cadaver albeit in uniform can be a jolting experience. But he paid his respects, and he was sincere about it. Later that evening, I got a call from the Joint Chiefs of Staff office and was told he had been deeply moved.

I'm often asked the same question by people: "What do you

feel when you're searching the rubble for the dead or searching a body for personal effects?" The fact is, I don't have a lot of time on the job for philosophical reflections on the fleeting nature of life. You have specific tasks to carry out, and often you are operating in mentally and physically demanding or dangerous conditions, conditions which require focus, or mistakes are made. You can ask yourself those questions afterward, if you want. I don't for many reasons. One, I am never really between jobs long enough to have that kind of time. Two, I don't see a value in it. I learned early on in life that there is no point, so it becomes wasted emotion, a negative emotion. I am not trying to be cold or insensitive, but I can't bring them back, erase their pain, or make their death meaningful. Sometimes life sucks, and you pick yourself up and go forward. I wish I could do any of that: imagine how great it would be to take such pain away. At some point I will pause for a second and say a few words to myself about the hope that the deceased have found peace, a peace that likely eluded them on earth. That is not a feeling, more a wish to a higher power or spirit, a "God's Speed" sort of message to the souls of the dead. My fear, of course, is that one day all of those negative emotions—fear, sorrow, and pain—will break through or erupt in an overwhelming way.

I am always mindful of the story of Iris Chang who wrote the epic *Rape of Nanking*, a book on the World War II atrocities committed in China by Japan. Sadly, she committed suicide, and many believe it was due in part to the disturbing research she had done while writing her book, including speaking with survivors and going through historical archives. For those unfamiliar with the subject, the brutality rivals that of the death camps in Europe. So for me, the mission is to focus on the living, to help them, the ones I can help, and to pass on the things I cannot change.

If I am feeling down, or it is rough day I prefer to go biking, or rowing out on the water. I am a naturally active person and that tends to be my way of dealing with what I have gone through. Exercise and endorphins are my happy pills, a great way of soothing the mind. But that's just me. I am also asked what I find when looking for the personal effects in a person's pocket. That's simple. Just go through your own pockets, and you'll see. Because most people never know when tragedy might strike.

For me, seeing death isn't always the hardest part. It should be, but it's often not. It is the bureaucracy and response of governments. During this operation, I seemed to get a lot of calls from DC. As I mentioned earlier, the jurisdiction of the response was under the control of the federal government, but very dependent on the state authorities. While we would assist with the recoveries of the bodies, it was the job of State Medical Examiner Dr. Fred Jordan to manage the identifications. One day, I was told the Oklahoma National Guard Adjutant General was sending a team to speak with me regarding the operations. Two brigadier generals and several colonels, all significantly higher ranks than mine, came to speak with me. They took me to a hospital facility for a look around and said that Governor Frank Keating was considering removing Dr. Jordan's control of the operation and handing it over to the National Guard. To which I responded, "Who would run it?" They said, "You would." I explained that I was there in a support role and that any such discussions should really involve the medical examiner, because he would have to issue the death certificates. While there were things I might have done differently, given the circumstances I think Dr. Jordan the medical examiner was doing a good job and should not have to be worrying about politics. But then again mass fatalities are political.

It was in the Murrah building that I received what I still

consider one of the weirdest and yet most typically "political" requests of my career. The sixth floor had been home to a US Marine Corps Recruiting office. Like all the other offices, it had been ripped wide open and exposed to the warm spring skies. But the body of a Marine recruiter had been trapped there, in his dress blues, wedged under an immovable chunk of concrete. There was no easy way to remove the body, especially with men working through the debris many floors below, to the teams working to recover the deceased, and occasional pool media footage. Still, I was surprised when I was asked if I could get up there and cut the body in two and remove the visible part. The reason given was that it would be done out of respect for any family members who might be able to see it. "No," I responded flatly. "We don't cut up US service members or any human remains, unless it is absolutely the only way to recover them, and frankly I can't recall having to do that." I respectfully declined to carry out the task assigned to my unit: instead, we sent a team up there to cover the body until it could be removed with dignity.

Because beyond ensuring that a body has a name, dignity is one of the only things you can actually offer the dead. Everything else has already been taken away from them. What you are trying to do is work as quickly and safely as possible so you can get the body home to the family, so they can begin to make the transition from their old reality to a new one. Sure, it's sad, but your sadness isn't going to change anything. You're sad that people died who shouldn't have died: they didn't do anything wrong, and even when you do something wrong, you don't typically deserve to die for it. But it is what it is—you either do it or you don't do it.

I hate bringing people out in body bags: they sag in the middle and make a person look like so much lost luggage, rather than a person who until a few hours or days before had their own life, family, hopes, and dreams. Whenever possible, I bring people out on a gurney, and always feet first—as you walked in life, so should you be able to travel in death. Whenever my team would bring a body out, everyone would stop whatever they were doing on the pile for a minute or two and pay their silent respects.

Typically, the time when the job takes its toll is when something about the dead person relates directly to an aspect of your own life—the hardened police officer who has seen it all suddenly breaks down when he sees the body of a child the same age as his own kid, or a firefighter sees an elderly person who resembles his lost mother. Because the young and the old are the hardest to recover, because they are the ones society has vowed to protect. We care for the young in the understanding that one day, when we are old and frail, they will care for us. And their deaths always come across as an extremely poignant failure.

As well as the federal offices and agencies, the Murrah building had featured a children's day-care center where workers could leave their kids while they went off to their jobs. At his trial, McVeigh claimed not to have known it was there, although he had scouted the site prior to the attack. Nineteen children were killed by his truck bomb, which went off close to the rooms where they were playing.

One evening, we had recovered the last child who had been killed in the bombing. She was recovered from the Social Security offices, and we had recovered her mom earlier that day. We usually worked with local authorities, to support them. Everyone has their limits, and they had hit their exhaustion point, as had my soldiers. So, I said I would stay and take care of this child.

It was getting dark. The Murrah building and our working

area were lit with temporary lights, the kind that always seem to emit a yellow glow along with the background hum of the generators, the ever-present tinnitus of war zones and disaster areas. Then there was background noise of jackhammers, the constant beeping of trucks and equipment backing up or moving on. As I worked in this "normal" sound, Theresa, my wife at the time, phoned from Virginia. Sitting in our house, probably in our daughter's bedroom, she said my own daughter, who was around three at the time, was about to go to bed and wanted to speak to me.

I couldn't. I told Theresa that I was busy and couldn't speak with my daughter at that time. Then I went back to examining the body of a girl not far from my daughter's age who was lying cold on the table in front of me, in what remained of a church next to the shattered Murrah building. She should have been home with her parents, but of course her mother had already been on our table and now the medical examiner would soon be telling her grandparents that her body had been recovered.

In my opinion, there isn't much of a "why" behind whatever kept my daughter safe that week while bringing another little girl—equally worthy—to her sudden and violent end. More than anything about my job, I think the capriciousness of disaster is what scares people. Unexpected death can and usually does come when you haven't had a chance to tie up all of your loose ends. That leaves so many of the living wrestling with deep regrets, knowing all the things they feel they could or should have said to someone but now will never have the chance. If someone you love is very old or sick or in a hospice, you have time to make amends, to change things. But when someone is taken abruptly, those things can never be changed. I have long been estranged from my own father, for almost thirty-five years. For me he is not a great person nor was he a good parent. Yet, nineteen years ago I tried to connect with him. When I called him, he would tell me about the things we could do. Got my hopes up. But he never called me. I always had to call him. After making calls and none from him I got the message. Sometimes, I am bit slow and I should have known before I tried that it wouldn't be different, but I am also the eternal optimist—I would rather try and be wrong than not try. Now, I have no desire to ever speak to him again. Yet I find a lot of people still hope for that conversation. I don't, but yet when he is gone, the chance will also disappear forever.

We have no way of knowing what the last thoughts of people caught in a disaster might have been, but when I handle their bodies, I can only hope that they found peace and will not be haunted by all the things left unsaid or undone in their brutally interrupted lives. Sadly, for many, I am not sure that is the reality.

2. Luck and Time

This isn't my first weird job. I've had others before, like when I was in college and I worked for the California Department of Justice's Bureau of Narcotic Enforcement to help pay my tuition. We went out and raided large-scale illegal marijuana growers and other illegal drug operations. It was a great job for me, a twenty-two-year-old college student, but it wasn't a job that you wanted to advertise or talk about. For one thing, most college-age people hate the police in general, and narcotics officers even more. For another, certain people were unhappy with the loss of their multimillion-dollar crop and wanted to find you and kill you. So when people would ask me what I did, I would just say I had a temp job in the forest service or was just spending time in the backcountry and try to change the subject. Hopefully that would explain the unkempt look and why I had a forest-green US government–plated truck parked at home.

Life was much easier then. Of course, I had the booby traps, guns, and dogs. But I didn't have to deal with the memories I have now.

I hope you never have to see the things that I've seen or do the things that I've done. I have been involved in the response to so many of the world's worst events. I'm not even counting the homicides and suicides I responded to as a deputy sheriff before I got involved in mortuary affairs.

In my lifetime, I have been to two events that have taken in a matter of minutes, anywhere from 225,000 to 250,000 human beings each. Think about that for a minute: How do you even begin to plan, process, or respond to that? That is what I do—what I have done for the most part since I was twenty-one. I am now fifty-five. That's thirty-four years of death.

On the bright side—and, strange as it may seem, I believe there usually is a bright side—I have gotten to see the world, work with some outstanding people, and I hope, helped countless bereaved relatives lay their dead to rest. I have developed a perspective on life that I think very few people have. I am generally pretty happy and living a fulfilling life, on a strange and fascinating journey, one whose endpoint I know will come but whose timing I frankly don't care about, because experience tells me it's something I have almost zero control over.

After I tell people what I do for a living, I often get shocked follow-up questions: How come you haven't gone crazy after all the horror you have seen? Why aren't you depressed? And what the hell are you doing on a plane when you've spent so many weeks and months sifting through burned and fragmented aircraft ruins looking for human remains?

Well, here's the thing: after all that I've seen and done, the sheer scale of death and destruction that I have experienced, I just don't sweat the stuff I can't control anymore—there is no point. And that tends to allow me to stay pretty calm when others are losing their heads. I'm by no means a fatalist: as you'll see, there are many things you can do to blunt the edges of disaster. It's just the sense of perspective you get when you've been on an epic journey through life's dark side.

Primo Levi, the Italian chemist and writer who survived

Auschwitz, may have taken his own life at the end, ultimately unable to process the horrors he had witnessed in the German death camps. On the other hand, he may simply have fallen by accident from his third-floor landing. No one knows for sure. He did write a sentence, though, that I have always clung to: "The aims of life are the best defense against death."

Such is the randomness of death, and the reason why it is so often portrayed as an elusive character in mythology and literature. It is highly unpredictable and has its own inexplicable ways. My first job in college was working for the campus police department. One day we had a 911 call. The caller was, as it turned out, a woman I knew; I was in the Reserve Officer Training Corps (ROTC) with her boyfriend. She had repeatedly called 911 to say she had taken pills and turned on the gas stove in her apartment. This was back in 1985; the 911 system was still very new, and it did not always show the caller's address.

After this young woman called a few times, hung up, and called back, our dispatchers finally got her to give them her address (in fact, the rather gruff dispatcher told her if she didn't give him her address that he was going to stop answering her calls), which was then broadcast over the radio, and we all responded. Once I heard the address, I knew the location and was first to arrive.

After going through the front door, I was overwhelmed by the smell of gas. To this day, I am not sure why the apartment did not blow sky high. She was lying face down in front of the oven. I turned the gas off, dragged her out of the apartment, and radioed for help—you don't want to be using electrical equipment in a room full of gas. Fire and medical first responders rushed to the scene, and we were able to save her.

I was twenty at the time. I never knew what became of her, but later learned that my friend, her boyfriend at the time, had died as a fireman during underwater dive training. I hope he is at peace now.

A short time later, while I was exercising at the gym, someone there working out keeled over with what I presumed was a heart attack. I performed CPR and mouth-to-mouth until the EMTs got there, but he didn't make it.

A healthy young woman tries to kill herself and fails, while a guy wanting to keep in shape drops dead in the process: Death is its own timekeeper. When your time is up, it's just up. But sometimes, I have found people try and accelerate that clock. I don't think you outrun it, but you can speed it up. Sometimes, I think we feel lucky, as if we've cheated death. But maybe it is no more than it was not our time. I have stayed in two hotels in Iraq that were bombed, but I missed both bombings. Was it luck or just not my time?

That doesn't mean you should be cavalier or careless or stupid: I also see signs of that all the time. It just means you don't worry about the things you can't control and prepare for the things you might be able to control.

There are some obvious and not-so-obvious practical things you can do to increase your chances of surviving disasters. One of the better-known little things I like to remind people about is this: Sit close to the emergency exit on a plane. It doesn't just give you extra legroom during your flight; it also means you'll be first out the door in the event of an emergency during takeoff or landing. For high-speed crashes, forget it: just make sure you have made your will and told relatives what you want done with your body, since it'll save them having to make difficult decisions under massive emotional stress should the worst happen.

I also strongly recommend you heed the instructions on the safety sheet and never inflate your life jacket before you attempt to exit a plane that has landed on water. I have seen crash sites with corpses floating inside the cabin because their inflated life vests had trapped them inside the plane, while their fellow passengers survived.

Ask me about any theoretical catastrophe, and I'll tell you half a dozen little things you can do to incrementally improve your chances of survival. Some part of survival begins with luck, but the real key is giving yourself *time* to get lucky. Preparedness is the opportunity for luck to occur. Take for example a family who, while sailing across the Pacific, has their sailboat sunk by a breaching whale. That is just bad luck. They make it to a life raft, and thirty or so days later a passing freighter sees them and picks them up. That's good luck. What is not luck is that they were prepared to survive for long enough to give luck time for a rescue. They kept calm and focused: in other words, they created an opportunity for luck.

You can always tell when you enter a Mormon household: The Church of Jesus Christ of Latter-day Saints has a doctrine of urging its members to stockpile food and water supplies in case of adversity. Mormons slowly building up a store of non-perishable food and water that isn't just meant to be locked in a cupboard and forgotten about. They use up tins that are about to expire and replace them, so that they don't waste money. In fact, the same doctrine urges members to put a little money aside each week as a bulwark against adversity. It is a useful doctrine to build resilience in a world that may not be as secure as we might like to think. It buys you a few precious days in which to react to the hardships that life throws at you, rather than just panicking and waiting to be rescued.

Look at the meltdown at the Japanese nuclear reactor at Fukushima during the 2011 earthquake and tsunami. As many as 1,400 people died, yet only 1 person actually died as a result of radiation exposure.

So what killed all the others? They died from being *evacuated*, even though there was no pressing need for them to flee. Tens of thousands of elderly, frail, and ill people were rushed from the area surrounding the plant because the *fear* of nuclear radiation—perhaps more justifiable in Japan than other countries, given its painful World War II history—was far greater than the actual measurable radiation threat. In fact, it turned out that the radiation levels in the areas they were evacuated from were barely higher than normal. Many of those people were older, in precarious health. Once uprooted from their communities with no ready access to the doctors and services they were accustomed to, they simply gave up on life.

If I could distill this into a formula for weathering disaster, it would be this: prepare, pay attention, then act, or react, as the situation demands. In burning buildings, people run past a perfectly serviceable exit because they are looking for the door they came in through. In an earthquake, you might be running for the stairs and pass a heavy-duty table that would save your life if you just took a second to consider your best options. People drive past signs warning them of dangerous floodwaters on the road and think instead, "Oh, a little bit of flat water can't be dangerous."

Those elements are key but ultimately have to be combined with another that was drilled into me both at Sheriff's Academy and in the Army, and that is the will to survive. The ability to keep going even when things look bleak, when you feel beaten, and to fight off the sense of loss and despair. Whatever the reason. The will to survive might just get you through a disaster that claims scores of other lives.

3. What Kind of a Person?

The bullfrogs were croaking in the growing dusk, their yellow eyes occasionally flaring in the headlights of the pickup truck that had parked on the riverfront among the California pines. It was a pretty, bucolic scene and probably why the young couple had chosen to stop there earlier that evening. Now, though, the young man was alone inside the vehicle, a cooling corpse.

He had been shot earlier that evening. His girlfriend claimed, somewhat implausibly, that while they were parked by the riverside, she heard what sounded like a backfire, the vehicle suddenly lurched forward, and the man slumped over the steering wheel with a gunshot wound to the left side of his head. I was a twenty-two-year-old sheriff's reserve deputy, working patrol. At the time, we were having some difficulty with her story and she had been taken in for questioning. The coroner didn't want to process the incident until the next morning, which meant the potential crime scene had to be protected. So, my partner and I sat there hours, watching the car battery die and the headlights fade to darkness.

My goal after high school was to attend college, earn my commission as US Army officer and go on active duty. I had gone to Admiral Farragut Academy, a Naval Honor School for my last two years of high school. It was a great school, with awesome people, resulting in lifelong friends all around the world, who at times I unexpectedly bump into. It was also famous for being the only school to have graduated two men who later walked on the moon. I started there at sixteen and it was great introduction to learning self-discipline and how many comfort items you can really do without. I had wanted to be in the military. No real family history there, it just seemed like a career that I wanted to do. When thinking about college, I had first considered the military academies, my first choice being the US Coast Guard Academy. However, my grades were nowhere good enough for that. I did receive six nominations to the four academies that require them—West Point, Annapolis, Air Force, and United States Merchant Marine, but I would have struggled to make it and in the end chose to go the civilian route. I picked California State University, at Fresno (CSUF); it had a new Army ROTC program and was not far from most of my family. I entered as a Criminology/Law Enforcement major. One of the graduation requirements was practical experience. So, I went through the Sheriff's Academy. But I could not be a sworn peace officer in California until my twenty-first birthday. I am still amazed today at the difference in training, screening, and oversight of different law enforcement agencies. Even back then, California required several hundred hours for the academy, the county put all deputies through multiple psychological screening programs, and then there was the training program once you were hired. Every time I look at a case of bad officers, I can see a pattern of bad screening, poor training, and little or no oversight. Because of the military high school, I only required two years of ROTC, and was commissioned as an Army officer at twenty. But I could not go on active duty until I graduated. Shortly after

I was commissioned, while still having two years left to complete school, I was sworn in as a reserve deputy sheriff.

At the same time, I was in ROTC, I also joined the California National Guard. "Besides ROTC and the National Guard, I also worked to pay for school. I started with the California State University Fresno Police Department as a parking enforcement officer. One night on duty at the university, I was writing tickets when a guy pulled a gun on me. His car was parked in a fire zone outside the Theater Arts Department. I was young and stupid, and I let him walk right up behind me—this was before I attended the Sheriff's Academy. As I turned around, he pulled a gun out of his waistband, cocked it, pointed it at my stomach, and said, "That is my car, and I don't want a ticket." I told him it was too late; I had already written the ticket. We stared at each other for a moment. Then he said the gun was a stage prop and walked away. I didn't panic, just called it in to let the campus officers know that there was a guy walking around with a fake gun. He was arrested a few minutes later. The sworn officers reacted more quickly than I did. A judge gave him probation and he was suspended from school. He was lucky: one of our campus police officers in a previous job had been involved in the shooting of a young man who brandished a fake weapon.

I remember thinking as I was looking at his pistol that it was the end of the month and we got paid once a month, and now this twit was going to kill me just before payday. That was when I realized that you don't control as much as you think. When stuff happens, you don't dwell on it, you get on with the job. I also learned that stupidity really bothered me. Injustice bothered me. But not so much dying if I couldn't control it.

Like most people in late-twentieth-century America, I hadn't seen a lot of death before I joined law enforcement. Besides being seconded to the California Department of Justice, I also spent one summer on our Boating Enforcement Unit. Fresno County has several lakes and rivers to patrol. The water can be fun, but it can also be dangerous especially when drinking. On the Fourth of July weekend in 1988, a total of six people were reported as missing, presumed drowned on our waterways. There are models we use to try to predict when a person's body might float to the surface based on their size, body composition, water temperature, and currents. We had searched and recovered some of the people. On one lake in particular there was still one of them missing. Several days later, on a Monday, the watch commander called me at home early. A body had floated to the surface and we needed to recover it. As it sometime happens, we also found the body of another person. A person who had not actually been reported missing. After finishing up and transferring the deceased to the coroner, my partner and I went back to headquarters to complete the re-covery report. While doing that, the desk sergeant called to say there was a group of people at the reception wanting to report a person who had gone missing over the weekend while at the lake. I went upstairs to talk to them. They showed me a picture of their friend and described his clothes. They had no idea I just recovered his body. I told them that sadly, their friend was deceased, and I had just recovered his body. That was something they were not prepared for. They had assumed he had wandered away from their party and was perhaps lost or just missing. Maybe they suspected, but their reaction told me this was not the news they expected.

I had recovered several dead bodies and had been to fatal accidents and homicides, so human remains didn't faze me. I will always remember having to tell a mother and father whose son had been in a motorcycle accident that they needed to come into the hospital in the middle of the night to say goodbye be-cause he was not going to make it. I couldn't have been much older than their son.

It took a long time for me to get used to the fact that I was not much older than some of the people whose families I had to confront. I would go to calls dealing with out-of-control juveniles, and when the parents answered the door, they were always taken back by the fact that I was probably only four or five years older than the kids they were having trouble with. It also meant that a lot of people I knew in college spent their weekends getting drunk, while I spent my weekends arresting people who had too much to drink. While some people I knew stupidly drove their cars while drunk, I was telling other kids' parents their kids were not coming home because they had been killed by drunk drivers. So, life was different for me.

AS FOR MY OWN parents, I didn't have what most might call a normal childhood. My father—and I hate using that term, because a father is someone beyond a sperm donor—was a builder in California. He and my mom had problems, lots of them. One day when I was a kid, I came home from playing in the street and there he was, loading up his little MG and telling me and my two sisters he was moving out. Then he was gone. I was six or seven at the time. Over time, he dated some women we met, some who liked kids and some who didn't. That, combined with the problems he and my mom were having, meant my siblings and I were secondary concerns. He was the kind of person who'd say, "I'm going to come pick you up now," and eight hours later he still wasn't there.

Then there was Christmas 1977. On the last day of school before the holiday, our mother told my sisters and me that we were going to be seeing our father and his brother, my uncle, on TV. I was twelve. They had been arrested by the fairly new

DEA, along with California Department of Justice and local law enforcement, for conspiracy, gun charges, and for the manufacture and sale of methamphetamines. Though fairly common today, meth was not so widespread in 1977. Nor was it as easy to make. It also didn't help that my uncle owned a mountain lion and a pair of ocelots. Turns out my uncle had set up a rather complex lab in his garage, which my father would take me and my sisters to go visit. I knew something was different; I was just not old enough to know exactly what. But I still remember the local newspaper's front-page headline: "Lion, Dogs, Men, Drugs, Cash Are Seized in Laboratory Raid." One of several headlines that would appear over time.

My uncle was eventually sentenced to serve time at Lompoc Federal Prison, where after Watergate, Nixon's chief of staff H. R. Haldeman was also doing time working in the prison sewage treatment center. My father was either not charged or acquitted. We never spoke about it. Sometime ago, my cousin sent me a clipping from the paper saying my uncle was arrested on extensive state warrants. Given his criminal affiliations with certain groups, I would expect that meant hard time at one of California's tougher prisons. Just recently, my sister told me the coroner had called my father and told him that my uncle had died. She said he wanted nothing to do with him.

My uncle was incredibly smart; he worked on early computers, had good jobs. I guess he just got bored. It is weird to think that ten years later I would work for some of the same agencies that had arrested my father and uncle, and arrested people for some of the same crimes. But none of them had a mountain lion. All this history with my father and uncle led to some interesting background checks both for the sheriff's department and the Army.

Then there was my mom. I don't think she ever got over the

divorce and would today, I think, be diagnosed with some mental health problems, but not then. So, we moved a lot. It was hard on my sisters, and many nights ended with a screaming match between them. After one of the moves, my older sister went to live with my dad. A few years later in 1979, I made the decision in the middle of another move to see if I could live with my father. Quite a change in lifestyle. It also meant leaving my younger sister alone with my mom, something that was very hard for her, and one of the few regrets I have in life. I could have run wild: he and I built a mother-in-law-apartment in the backyard of his house for my older sister and me to live in. I went days without seeing him, and I could drink and do drugs, as long as they weren't his, and have as many people over as I wanted—all at fourteen. Luckily, that was not for me, it is a lifestyle I never got into. For the first two years of high school, on the rare occasions that we actually saw each other, we did not get along. Then I went away to military school, at my own request, and never came back except for holiday leave or summer breaks. I have not lived at home since I was sixteen. After my freshman year at university, and after I had signed my Army contract (for ROTC and National Guard), to which his reply was "that's nice," I wished him a good life and told him I would have one. I have barely seen or talked to him since, except as previously mentioned when I tried to establish some contact in 2001 or when my sister was sick.

I know my father and uncle had a hard time as kids, they were taken away from their mother and put in the custody of their father—something that was really unusual at the time. They were shuttled around from relative to relative, in what I am guessing were not the best conditions. I also knew his stepmother was not very nice to them. Which is why his behavior was all the harder for me to understand. When my daughter was born, I could not wait to be part of her life, share her success, and help her when she would need it. My own father has a grandchild he has never seen; missed seeing me being sworn in as a law enforcement officer, a commissioned military officer; missed both of my weddings; and has really only ever seen me on TV, in magazine articles, or in interviews.

I am sure part of the problem was that I liked boys as much as girls. My thought was, why settle for one or the other. Despite living in California, our family did not discuss such things and my preferences were certainly not in keeping with their idea of what a man should be. Attraction is hard to hide, so even if it is not discussed it is present and visible. When you are desperate for your absentee father to love you and want you, you don't tell him that you're bisexual or gay. It was also the '80s and it wasn't something you'd openly discuss with your colleagues in the police or the Army. Between that and not openly talking about being in law enforcement, I probably got quite adept at compartmentalizing the different strands of my life, something that has helped keep me sane in the work I now do. Being different also never really worried me, because there was nothing I could do about it. That acceptance probably helped me with my jobs in the Army and as a deputy sheriff, as much as it does today in my work today.

In college, I met and fell in love with a woman who would become my wife. After being married for twenty-one years, we divorced. Then one day, by luck, I met a wonderful man who I fell in love with and married. He has helped me, deployed with me, and looked into my world, not because he chose to, but because he chose me.

In 1986, when I was commissioned, the Army selected me for active duty, with an initial assignment in Field Artillery and follow-on in Quartermaster. My first assignment was Fort Sill for the Field Artillery Officer Basic Course. After that I attended the Pershing Officer Course (missiles). No one wanted to go into missiles, it was a zero-defect area, where absolutely no mistakes were tolerated, and often a career killer. In the military, zero defects simply means mistakes are not tolerated. None at all. When mistakes happened, people are replaced or careers ended soon after. We used to joke that the commanding general always had a spare captain and lieutenant with him to replace people on the spot. Interestingly enough, all of us who did go were like me, with only an initial assignment in Field Artillery. Pershing missiles were the Army's only strategic missiles. Though we didn't know it at the time, the intermediate range missiles deployed in Germany were about to tip the balance of power and help end the Cold War. The decaying Soviet regime could not come up with a suitably sophisticated defense against the US mobile nuclear batteries. Besides the training unit at Fort Sill, the three units with missiles were all in Germany, part of the US Army 56th Field Artillery Command. So I ended up in Germany as a fire control officer, responsible for targeting and launching three missiles each with a highly accurate variable war head ranging from five to eighty kilotons. By comparison the bomb dropped on Hiroshima was sixteen kilotons.

We would rotate every three months each as a fixed Quick Reaction Alert (QRA) team; field QRA; training; and maintenance. We had a camouflaged launch control center mounted on the back of trucks and trailers. On fixed sites, or QRA, coded messages came over secure communications systems. These messages start as an "emergency action message," and once you received one, you would hit the klaxon, which is a horn. The klaxon signals a potential launch, so the ground crews can get the missiles ready while I would start to decode the message. The guys outside hustled, taking down camouflage netting and making final preparations. The message might be a launch order, a warning, or a whole bunch of different things. Then you'd open a safe with sealed plastic cards known as "cookies" inside. These were authorizations for whatever action you were being ordered to take: you'd open the cookie and check that the numbers matched the message. You then selected which targets to strike from several available ones, and compute launch and flight times to make sure you would hit your targets within a specified period or choose another target.

After all the preparations were made, the platoon sergeant was required to come to the door of the control center and would ask me a series of questions: "Sir, do you have a valid message?" "Yes, I have a valid message." "Are you under duress?" "No, I'm not under duress." He would then go ahead and remove the huge ball-locking pin from the boom on which the missile was positioned—if the missiles were launched with the pin in place, they would strike the launcher and likely explode. The sergeant would do so and show me the pin and told me, "You are in control of the missile." At that point, if required I could turn the key, forever changing the world.

We had a lot of alerts, and sometimes you'd never know if they were part of a drill or the real thing. Fortunately, I was never ordered to turn the key. Of course no one in that position would want to, but I would have with a valid order. If I were in the same position now—with a president like Donald Trump, I am not sure I would have. Those were horrible weapons—I guess all weapons are. But they brought the Soviets to the bargaining table: it's better to have one horrible weapon that gets rid of a dozen other horrible weapons, and we were going nowhere with the growing arsenal of nuclear weapons. It had to stop at some point—even with all the fail-safes there are mistakes, and the ramifications of mistakes with those weapons were unthinkable.

Luckily, the missiles worked as a deterrent, and by the early 1990s, they had helped bring the Cold War to an end. The Pershing missiles were eliminated as part of the SALT II treaty and destroyed. I was transferred to another Special Weapons unit in Germany, but this time working with the German Army. From there, I was off to Quartermaster School and the Mortuary Affairs course, what would become the main focus of my Army career and life. Helping the living by taking care of the dead. The Mortuary Affairs course was only a two-week course, but it would lead to a lifetime in the field. Funnily enough, others may have known that at the time, but I did not. When I returned to Fort Lee to start work at the Mortuary Affairs Center, one of the many gifted civilian employees told me that she knew when I had taken the course a year earlier, I would be back to run it one day. Guess I made an impression.

4. This Is Haiti

first went to Haiti on September 24, 1994, when I was still a captain in the Army. Grieving Haitian mothers would throw their dead babies over the razor-wire fence of our makeshift base because they didn't have the money to buy their infants a burial plot. They wanted us, the US Army, which had just launched a military intervention on their island, to bury the tiny bodies. Life was cheap; death was expensive, at least by local standards; and the bereaved mothers could not afford a funeral. When I was driving one day between bases, I saw a garbage truck run over a guy in the street. The truck didn't stop. The driver kept going while a crowd chased him. The police didn't stop the truck, and beyond the crowd chasing the driver no one seemed to care. Life had little value.

The United States, after years of an influx of Haitian refugees, had decided to act. In 1991, military dictator General Raoul Cédras refused to allow the newly elected president, former priest Jean-Bertrand Aristide to take office. Haiti had suffered great violence and terror under various leaders. President Bill Clinton ordered the 82nd Airborne Division and the 10th Mountain Division to muster at airbases in preparation for a full assault. President Clinton also sent former President

Jimmy Carter at the head of a peace delegation that included General Colin Powell, who had served as chairman of the joint chiefs of staff, to Port-au-Prince to try to persuade Cédras to leave peacefully for a third-party country. It was a risky move as Cédras could have taken the negotiators hostage. But faced with what would have been the largest airborne invasion since Operation Market Garden in World War II, the battle made famous by the movie *A Bridge Too Far*, Cédras agreed to step down. The assault divisions were turned around in the air and a full-scale invasion force was scaled down to a peacekeeping mission. Cédras had officially quit but was nominally still in charge until a new transition government could be set up.

The country was still lawless and broke, and it was easy to spot the people who had held power under Cédras: they were fat while everyone else was skinny, simply because they had always had enough to eat while the others did not. As part of the plan to ensure a smooth transition from one Haitian government to the next—something completely overlooked in later Iraq invasions—General Hugh Shelton, the US commander, made the conscious decision to keep the Haitian military and police forces intact for the time and under Haitian control, albeit under the ultimate control and watchful eye of the US military. Inevitably there was Haitian-on-Haitian violence, as well as clashes between US troops and Haitian factions that were hostile to the US mission. These generally did not end well for the Haitian soldiers involved.

In fact, as soon as I stepped off the chartered civilian 747 that had brought me to the airfield in Port-au-Prince, I was met by a major holding my name on a sign. He told me ten Haitian soldiers had been shot dead in clashes with US troops in the north of the country, near Cap-Haitien, and we would be heading up there immediately by helicopter. When I asked the major what they wanted me to do, he said he had no idea. All he knew was that his job was to take me there.

I was the only member of the Mortuary Affairs unit in country at that point: my job was to advise the Division and Corp commanders. Both had wanted me assigned to staff, but since there was only one of me, I suggested I could support both equally well. I was not yet the commander of the 54th, but still assigned to the schoolhouse (Mortuary Affairs Center) and had been deployed at the last moment. I got on the helicopter and flew to the Marine base at Cap-Haitien, where I was taken to the city morgue. The local police chief showed me one of the ten dead soldiers, the only one still there. He told me there was no power for refrigeration, and with decomposition setting in quickly with the tropical heat, he had ordered them to be buried and had already buried the other nine. I wholly concurred with his reasoning and returned to Port-au-Prince to brief the chain of command.

Within the next day or two I was told to develop a plan to go and recover the bodies and transport them back to Port-au-Prince for a joint investigation. In the meantime, anger was bubbling up in the capital, partly because some old regime Cédras loyalists were still holding on to their positions in the security forces. These protests sometimes exploded into violent clashes with Haitian police, who had long been used to deploying brute forces against any hint of opposition. These clashes occasionally resulted in fatalities that we would have to take care of. One Haitian man who had been injured by a hand grenade blast in a demonstration was transferred to the US Navy's hospital ship the USNS *Comfort*. Unfortunately, he succumbed to his injuries. Normally, we would have simply transferred him back to the Haitian authorities, but with Cédras on the way out—and a lot of crooked judges planning to flee the country with him—there was no one to hand the body over to. After a few days of looking for someone in authority, a judge was found who reluctantly agreed to take charge of the remains. He could not come to our base, and we could not go to his office. The famous catch-22.

Finally, the handover was scheduled to take place in Cité Soleil, one of Port-au-Prince's poorest and most crime-ridden slums, located next to the airport. We arrived and waited by the side of the road. We were a curious sight: two Humvees with American soldiers was still something new. After a few minutes the judge and Haitian police arrived in two pickups, sirens blaring and lights on. I think about eight police officers in all. So much for a quiet handover. He told me that he needed to examine the body, and that he planned to do that right there and then, by the roadside in the slum. I told him that was not a manner in which we would treat human remains and that he would need to accept the body in a dignified manner; whatever exam was needed could be conducted at his office or wherever they did them, but not on the side of the road in Cité Soleil. He then gave me a "take-it-or-leave-it" shrug. I reminded him that two US Army Humvees, one with an M60 machine gun trumped his two truckloads of policemen, and the US Army was now here.

As for the bodies of the ten Haitian soldiers, I put together a team of Mortuary Affairs soldiers who had just arrived in country, and who were backed up by a Special Forces team, to go to Cap-Haitien and disinter the deceased and bring them back. That sounds easy but it's not. There are a small number of jobs in the Army that are specialized and limited, not understood by the mainstream military. Mortuary affairs was one of those jobs, and on top of that, a job many people did not understand and were afraid of. So it's unique. It can also be more difficult because details involving the deceased are often restricted or classified. People are told to support you, but they don't know why.

That was the case here. I flew ahead of the team to Cap-Haitien, which was under the control of the US Marines. They were supposed to support us but knew nothing of the mission. I went to see the Marine Expeditionary Force (MEF) commander and explained what details I could. He told me he did not agree with the mission and would not support it. As an Army captain, I told him the US ambassador and commanding general had not asked my opinion on whether the operations should be done but had only asked how it could be done and then been told to do it and why it should be done. What the MEF commander was unaware of was the fact a joint investigation was part of the agreement for Cédras to leave. I explained that to him, and he went off and came back a few minutes later to tell me he had been ordered to provide me with his own vehicle and support.

It was a delicate mission in very trying circumstances. Graves and coffins are expensive in Haiti, so the gravedigger had simply opened up some older plots in the town cemetery and placed the bodies under other coffins. We went in wearing full helmet and body armor. It was hot, sweaty work digging up the graves under the blazing Caribbean sun. Because of the ad hoc nature of our whole mission, no one had a chance to explain or prepare the local population, or the families, on why we needed to take the bodies. It was a valid mission, just no one told the locals why. Needless to say, they were not happy. As we worked, a crowd gathered at the cemetery gates where we had parked our trucks. I had a Marine security detail and Special Forces team with me, and I tried to explain to the crowd that the bodies were being taken to Port-au-Prince for the Haitian government. This did not help matters since the government was disliked, and the families wanted the bodies to remain there. They started shouting and tried to rush the trucks into which we were loading the bodies. Unfortunately, we had to use pepper spray to stop the crowd. We finally managed to complete the recovery and load into the trucks (in transport containers) the deceased and then scrambled back to the helicopters for the return to Port-au-Prince. That was an extraordinarily painful experience, and I made it my mission to never have to use the police or any force on grieving relatives. It was a salutary lesson in the need for clear communications and enlisting the support of the next of kin. But this was Haiti. A country and problems I would face again, almost sixteen years later. And this time it would be much, much worse.

The death toll in the Caribbean nation following an epic 7.1 magnitude earthquake in January 2010 was staggering. The quake lasted thirty-five seconds—a long time for such a powerful shock—and around 225,000 people were killed in less time than it takes to make your morning coffee. No one will ever know for sure how many died: the infrastructure of the tiny nation—the poorest in the Western Hemisphere—was obliterated, its buildings flattened, its already weak institutions paralyzed. Many of the dead were buried in the ruins of their own homes; lacking any heavy equipment to remove them, relatives poured gasoline on the trapped bodies and cremated them where they lay. Others laid wildflowers on the spot where friends and relatives were entombed. In parts of the capital, aid and recovery efforts were delayed because stacked bodies blocked the narrow roads that had been cleared, creating traffic jams for aid workers trying to navigate the ruins.

The Haitian government's own efforts at taking care of the dead were horrible. Their philosophy was essentially that money spent taking care of the dead was a waste of money that should be spent on the living, although that causes a whole host of problems for everyone. Trucks roamed the rubble picking up tens of thousands of remains, which were then taken to mass graves outside the city and dumped without ceremony, bulldozed into deep trenches.

It was a medieval solution to a biblical-scale problem unchanged since plague carts roamed the ghost towns of fourteenth-century Europe, their drivers crying, "Bring out your dead!"

Death may be the great equalizer, but to paraphrase George Orwell, some deaths are more equal than others. That was certainly the case in Haiti, a place where inequality had always been rife: even before the quake, Haitian school kids who lived in homes without electricity could be seen sitting outside the plush restaurants where Western aid workers dined, not to beg for money but to do their homework in the light that spilled out onto the street.

And in 2010, as tens of thousands of dead Haitians were being bulldozed into massive burial pits, the United Nations contacted me to bring back the bodies of its own international staff who had perished in the quake: 102 UN workers from thirty different countries were killed, the single largest loss of life the world organization had ever suffered. Most of them had been part of the UN nation-building mission, working on reforms to the notoriously corrupt police, advising courts, or participating in the UN peacekeeping mission that was launched in 2004, when President Aristide had been toppled by yet another coup. Some of the UN workers had brought their families to live with them while they carried out their tasks. And that is how I came across five-year-old Kofie-Jade.

KOFIE-JADE WAS A LITTLE girl with a pigtail in her hair. She was mummified by the time we got to her: the pummeled concrete of her pancaked apartment building had dried out her body. We found her under the doorframe, fleeing from the bathtub for the bathroom door when the earthquake hit and the building started collapsing.

In one of those many sad twists of fate, her father—a French-Haitian aid worker—had recently brought the family over from New Zealand, where the girls had been living with their mother while he was deployed in Burundi. He had thought Haiti would be a safer place for them all to be reunited.

At first glance, the six-story building perched on a hill in the upscale neighborhood of Pétion-Ville appeared to have been spared the worst of the devastation. Only a closer look revealed that in fact the apartment block now appeared to have five floors instead of six, its beams blowing out under pressure. The floor above Kofie-Jade's apartment had pancaked down onto the floor below.

Her mother, Emily, who had been out during the quake, rushed back to the hotel to find her family decimated. By some miracle Alyahna, her baby daughter, had survived with just a broken leg. In the immediate aftermath of the collapse, rescue workers managed to pull out the bodies of the father, Emmanuel, and the three-year-old sister, Zenzie. Only Kofie-Jade remained missing, unreachable inside the wreckage.

Looking at the building, I knew it would be extremely difficult and dangerous to find a way in. We would need to dig and drill our way through from the floor above to get into the crushed space where we thought Kofie-Jade's body lay, and that meant we'd have to build a wooden shell inside the highly unstable space to work in. I spray-painted orange markers on the building to see how much it shifted over the next couple of days while we searched other collapsed UN facilities to retrieve bodies that presented less risk. We had a long list of people and the places where they most likely would have been, and one by one we tracked them all down, except for a missing African man whose body we never could find. I suspect he was mistaken for a Haitian and disappeared into the huge burial pits on the northern edge of town. Titanyen had long been used as a grave for the many unclaimed and penniless dead from the capital's hospitals, and the pits were a medieval horror. I went to see them one day, to get a feel for the place where our missing man might have vanished. The area is rugged and treeless and had been used in the wake of the earthquake to dump the rubble from the destroyed buildings as well as human remains. Oftentimes, human remains were tossed into the tangle of rebar and clots of concrete. Crushed masonry was dumped in the deep, long pits that could each be filled with hundreds of corpses before being bulldozed over with dirt, like a landfill. There was no attempt to identify the dead because there was simply no infrastructure in Haiti that could have dealt with that number of fatalities, even before the devastating earthquake.

But I wasn't there to mourn the unidentified dead. My job was to find identifiable people and return them home to their loved ones. The Haitians, while not being afforded any dignity or respect, were at least home; the foreigners were not. We set up our base in the grounds of the Hotel Montana next door to the Karibe Hotel, where Kofie-Jade was entombed. We brought in recovery equipment from the neighboring Dominican Republic, including a large amount of timber to build what was in effect a secure wooden tunnel that would lead us through the rubble of the building: Haiti, a lush tropical forest when Christopher Columbus first set foot here in 1492, is now almost treeless, stripped bare by desperate people and zero municipal planning.

It took us two days to burrow into the heart of the building, shoring up the rooms we worked in with timber frames, grinders, and a jackhammer. The work was sweltering and exhausting, with sparks flying as we cut through twisted rebar like deadwood. We had plumb lines all around to register any shift in the masonry, as well as a safety officer with a horn to warn our team to flee if the building started crumbling on top of us. There were several small aftershocks as we worked, but nothing that stopped us. Debilitating temperatures brought the real risk of heat stroke: a huge pile of plastic water bottles rose up outside the building as we sweated through our clothes.

On the second day, we finally broke through the floor of the apartment above Kofie-Jade's. The first thing we saw was a child's foot. That's when we knew we were in the right place. We spent hours clearing the surrounding concrete and debris. Two people held a rope with a metal ring to steady the jackhammer so we could use it horizontally, before we could finally, gently, extract the small body. It was an emotionally charged moment, and the whole team wanted to help carry her tiny body out on a stretcher. I called our representative at the UN so they could call Emily, then back in New Zealand, to let her know we had gotten Kofie-Jade and her daughter would soon start her journey home.

Because of geography and probably luck, the hotel next door had survived more or less unscathed, and some of the guests were playing tennis as we came out. Perhaps it was just people trying to retrieve some semblance of normality, a release of stress after the horrors they had witnessed. Maybe they just really loved tennis. But some of them had known the little girl before the quake, when she had played with her sisters around the pool and tennis courts. I went ahead and informed them that we were bringing out the child's body and they stopped playing and silently looked on, rackets in hands, as our small procession passed by. I was moved by that moment, sad that the little girl was no more, but proud that through our efforts she would at last be reunited with her grieving mother and laid to rest with her family. Kofie-Jade was going home.

All in all, the operation to retrieve that one body took my team of about twenty people two days, at the risk of all our lives.

The difference between Kofie-Jade and the quarter million or so people thrown into mass graves, or cremated in the ruins of their destroyed homes? Simply put, the determination of a government or other authorities to bring their people home, and the ability to pay for such a labor-intensive operation. Many armies have a similar ideology; their soldiers are willing to risk their own lives to retrieve the bodies of fallen comrades because no one gets left behind, even the dead. Those who put themselves in harm's way need to know that if they pay the ultimate price, their mortal remains will be treated with the respect they deserve. And their families need to know they have their loved ones home again.

The work we performed in Haiti represented the core undertaking of disaster management, but also its limitations. Our mission is to recover the remains of the dead, despite the dangers and hardships to ourselves, and return the bodies to their loved ones for a dignified burial. Then the transition, the crossing of the bridge can begin. However, that work is expensive, requiring modern infrastructure and a lot of manual labor. If a disaster-stricken developing country cannot invest in this way, the results may be shockingly primitive to us.

Unfortunately for Haiti, the suffering did not end with the earthquake. In the months following the destruction, an outbreak of cholera ripped through the shattered country, killing another ten thousand people. The strain of the disease, which had not been seen in Haiti for a century, was traced to a UN camp where peacekeeping troops from Nepal were stationed. With Haiti's hospitals and water-treatment facilities destroyed, the deadly disease tore through a weakened population, adding yet another layer to the apocalypse. Never underestimate the power of nature or believe it can't get worse. Nature is powerful, and it can and often does get worse.

Kofie-Jade's mother found her own way after the nightmare. Reunited with her surviving baby, Alyahna, she went on to set up a foundation to build schools in Haiti and help the country's struggling children. A number of survivors did similar charity work for the country, trying to conjure some purpose and meaning out of a seemingly senseless tragedy. Emily's foundation is called Kenbe La, which in Haitian Creole means "Never give up," and it is dedicated to the memory of her daughters and husband.

I often remind clients, there are many things in life you can rarely control, but you can always control how you respond. Emily is an awesome example of this when she said "I have pledged to Emmanuel, Kofie-Jade, Zenzie, and Alyahna to rise like a phoenix from the ashes."

For the hundreds of thousands of Haitians who never got to say goodbye to their loved ones, or who have to walk the dusty human landfills of Titanyen in the hope that their relatives might be buried somewhere under the rubble, the process of healing will take much, much longer. For many without an answer or a body, the living get stuck at the start of the bridge, waiting in vain for those who can never return, but not knowing it.

5. What's in a Name?

On April 15, 1912, RMS *Titanic* sank. Many know the story—it was the most famous maritime disaster in history. What most people don't know, however, is that it wasn't until 2008 almost a century later, that a young boy—whose body was recovered from the *Titanic*—would be identified and his headstone given a name. His name was Sidney Leslie Goodwin.

How could it take so long to identify a victim of such a high-profile disaster? And what does it say about how we find meaning in death that we could not rest until the toddler's correct identity was established? Because for many, this is the first step to rebuilding something meaningful from a catastrophe: taking stock of exactly what has been lost and assessing what is left.

More than 1,500 people were still aboard the *Titanic* when it slipped beneath the surface of the ocean. Nearby shipping raced to pick up the 705 survivors who had made it to the lifeboats prior to the ship slipping beneath the waves. It wasn't until five days after the sinking that a cable repair ship, the CS *Mackay-Bennett*, arrived at the scene. It had been hastily refitted in Nova Scotia for the task of recovering bodies. In place of its cables and winches, the *Mackay-Bennett* now carried a priest, embalming supplies to handle seventy cadavers, one hundred coffins, and one hundred tons of ice in which to preserve recovered human remains.

Those supplies proved woefully inadequate. Over 1,500 people perished in the calamity, and the *Mackay-Bennett* was quickly overwhelmed. Having taken on hundreds of bodies, the ship's captain made the decision to store only the remains of first- and second-class passengers for burial at home, and to bury the "steerage" passengers at sea. Of the 306 bodies recovered by the Mackay-Bennett, 106 were returned to the Atlantic. Burial at sea is a perfectly honorable disposition. Personally, I want my ashes to be scattered at sea when I die. But respecting the dead is all about having a choice: respecting the wishes of the dead or their families. The poor on the *Titanic* were not offered any choice, just like the tens of thousands of dead put into mass graves in Haiti.

Among the bodies pulled from the cold waters was that of a fair-haired, two-year-old boy. He was unidentified, and buried under a headstone paid for by distraught rescue workers at a cemetery in Newfoundland. The legend on the stone read simply: "Our babe." While working the Swissair Flight 111 disaster, I visited the Fairview Lawn Cemetery in Halifax and saw many of the graves, including these.

There the toddler rested for almost ninety years, until the newly developed art of DNA testing allowed researchers to use genetic material to identify still unknown victims of the disaster. Several graves were reopened, although decomposition and water seepage meant that two of them now contained only mud. "Our babe" had been reduced by time to a fragment of arm bone and three milk teeth. He was initially identified as Gösta Leonard Pålsson of Sweden, who witnesses had last seen being swept overboard as the liner slid beneath the waves. His mother's body was recovered with the tickets for each of her four children in her pocket. However, the identification process was still relatively new. After tracking down the descendants of the Pålssons, it was proven that the boy had not, in fact, been Gösta. The DNA then indicated he might be a thirteen-month-old Finnish boy named Eino Viljami Panula.

This identification process went on for several years. In fact, on August 6, 2008, relatives of the Goodwin family, who were following the attempts to identify the unknown child and believed one of them was Sidney, gathered at Fairview to hold a memorial service for him, and for all the children who perished on the *Titanic*.

There the story could have ended, but for a pair of leather shoes. When the bodies were brought ashore in 1912, police officers were assigned to guard them. The constables were ordered to burn the victims' clothes prior to burial, to prevent them being stolen by morbid souvenir hunters. But one of the officers could not bring himself to destroy the infant's tiny shoes, and he kept them in his desk for years. Those shoes eventually wound up in a museum, donated by the sergeant's grandson. It was several years after the DNA tests had been carried out before some observant soul noticed that the shoes were actually far too big for a thirteen-month-old child. More DNA tests were ordered, and descendants of families of toddlers who were not recovered provided DNA samples, as the scientific method was rapidly improving, yielding ever more reliable results. Much like today, DNA is part of the identification solutions, but rarely stands alone. So Sidney Leslie Goodwin was identified, perhaps the last one of the disaster. His family could now place a name on his tombstone.

BODIES ARE POWERFUL TOTEMS, and we nurture a deep fear of them falling into the wrong hands, of being desecrated or disrespected. The tombs or houses of the dead can become even more potent: the most famous place in India, the Taj Mahal, is a mausoleum built by a ruler to his lost love. Not coincidentally, one of the seven wonders of the ancient world was also a tomb, the Mausoleum of Halicarnassus in present-day Turkey, likewise a monument to a broken heart, built by Queen Artemisia for her deceased husband, King Mausolus, as well as a symbol of vast wealth.

When in the summer of 1934 John Dillinger, the legendary Depression-era bank robber, was shot dead outside a Chicago movie theater by FBI agents, passersby dipped their handkerchiefs in his blood as a macabre memento. Just a couple of months earlier, his contemporaries Bonnie and Clyde fared even worse: after they were shot dead by lawmen in rural Texas, one witness tried to hack off Clyde Barrow's ear as a souvenir. Others cut off pieces of Bonnie Parker's bloodstained dress and hurried away with the trophies, which were no doubt handed down through the generations to incredulous children and grandchildren.

In death, the criminal heroes of folklore inspire such behavior. Likewise, entire cathedrals have been built around the kneecap or finger of many a martyred Catholic saint, preserved as sacred artifacts and revered by generations of worshippers. Death has always added an aura of mystery to a lost life; the body fascinates even as it repels. Even Neanderthals have been found to have decorated the graves of their lost ones with shells and flowers, the ancient pollen surviving until archaeologists could exhume and identify them.

That was probably why the US government directed that the body of Osama bin Laden be buried at sea, in the Indian Ocean, after killing the Al Qaeda leader in his Pakistan hideout. It was feared that any grave would quickly become a shrine, a focal point for radicals and fanatics. I personally disagreed, although no one consulted me. I think the bodies of the dead—even those who have committed terrible crimes—should be treated in accordance with the traditions and culture they lived by. That was a belief underscored by Albert Pierrepoint, England's last hangman who died in 1992 after executing as many as six hundred people. At the end of World War II, and for several years after, he was sent to Germany to hang two hundred Nazi war criminals—sometimes as many as ten a day—but he always insisted on treating the dead with the utmost respect, because the punishment had already been carried out on the living. The dead are no longer a threat. As I said earlier, burial at sea is perfectly respectable, but it is not a Muslim ritual. Bin Laden could have had a proper Muslim burial in an unmarked grave at a secret location.

Some nations have not always recovered their dead. Let me ask you, for example, when the first body of a British soldier killed overseas was repatriated to Great Britain? Given the British Empire's endless foreign adventures, you might say it was sometime in the nineteenth century, when commercial embalming first took off. You'd be wrong: leaving aside World I, when the body of an unidentified soldier was recovered from the mud of Flanders and then buried in a marble tomb, The Tomb of the Unknown Warrior, at Westminster Abbey, it was shortly after the Falklands-Malvinas War in 1982, when the bodies of 64 deceased British soldiers were brought home this only after a very public outcry from family members. Before that, generations of British squaddies, colonial troops, and their officers had been interred in graves close to where they fell in battle, from Yemen to Canada to Singapore. The reason was twofold: for centuries, moving deceased was an expensive and unsanitary business, but there was a deeper, more elemental reason—since the dawn of time, bodies have been used to mark property and territory. In the ruins of Catalhoyuk, one of the world's earliest settlements located in what is now Turkey, archaeologists have found bodies buried *inside* houses, either under the floors or in raised clay platforms that their descendants used as beds, in what may have been the ultimate marker of ancestral ownership. Similarly, the war graves of the British dead seeded distant lands for Queen and Empire. Even Saddam Hussein recognized the universal taboo of the dead, so that when British troops invaded the Iraqi port of Basra in the spring of 2003, they found well-preserved marble plaques marking the resting place of thousands of their forebears who had landed on those same shores in 1915, during the First World War campaign against the Ottoman Empire.

As the World War I poet Rupert Brooke wrote in his poem "The Soldier":

> If I should die, think only this of me: That there's
>   some corner of a foreign field
> That is for ever England.

Brooke would know—he is buried on the Greek island of Skyros, after dying of sepsis, the result of an infected mosquito bite on a troop ship bound for Gallipoli. Thousands of his comrades who made it to Gallipoli and fell in the subsequent slaughter there are buried in the Lone Pine Cemetery in Turkey, close to that long-ago battlefield. Inscribed in stone are the extraordinary words of Turkey's post–World War I leader Kemal Ataturk, expressing a universal respect for the enemy's dead:

> Those heroes that shed their blood and lost their lives . . .
> You are now lying in the soil of a friendly country. There-
> fore, rest in peace. There is no difference between the
> Johnnies and the Mehmets to us where they lie side by

side here in this country of ours. You, the mothers who sent their sons from faraway countries, wipe away your tears; your sons are now lying in our bosom and are in peace. After having lost their lives on this land they have become our sons as well.

While there is some controversy about whether those words were actually said by Ataturk, the sentiment shown in the care of the resting place and the treatment of the deceased is sincere and with meaning. Arlington National Cemetery, across the Potomac from Washington, was once the country estate of General Robert E. Lee, the commander of the Confederate states' forces. The property was expropriated during the Civil War and thousands of the Union's dead were buried there, in what many at the time saw as fitting payback for the commander who had rebelled against his own government—a man who lacked the moral courage to stand for what was right—and in doing so contributed to countless dead who now occupied his family estate.

Grief—the pain of not knowing what happened to our loved ones and ancestors—can echo down through generations. It can topple governments and it can start wars. It is one of the most powerful emotions on earth, yet few people talk about it openly or know how to deal with it. Throughout history, it was the purview of priests and holy men, but in an age where faith has taken a back seat to science, no one has really stepped forward to fill that vacant space. Modern death is predicated on people slowly slipping away in private, out of sight, saying their goodbyes in the hushed confines of a hospice. But when people die spectacularly, in public and in large numbers, no one quite knows how to pick up the pieces, both metaphorically and literally. That is where I step in.

6. Lost and Found

People understood the work I did as a law enforcement officer or as part of the military. However, most don't understand why a private company exists to do this work. That has to do with two things. The first is the fact that governments have geographical boundaries, and unless they are providing mutual aid, they tend to stay within those boundaries. Fortunately, most geographic locations don't see mass fatalities after mass fatalities. They might suffer a plane crash one year, and then none for another thirty years. Clearly, that is a good thing. Secondly, as I have tried to portray so far, responding to multiple unexpected deaths is complex. Success in managing these events comes from experience, and experience comes from exposure. In the twenty years after leaving government service, I have responded to a lot more things as part of a private company than I did for the government. Managing the response involves so many different sorts of personnel. There are the first responders, medical (if someone was first injured or thought to be alive), coroners/medical examiners (coroners and medical examiners are not the same; they are very different jobs), funeral directors, lab technicians, identification specialists, grief counselors, social workers, lawyers and others who deal with documentation, and finally, the

many courts for probate. This does not even include the nice-
ties, such as dealing with the property of the deceased recovered
from the scene or elsewhere. In short, a whole lot of people are
required, each in charge of a specific area, yet with no one in
charge overall. At the center of this, a family, who may or may
not be clearly identified and working together, who then must
navigate this system, usually while in shock and grief stricken.
Managing that takes a lot of resources and government staff for
the day-to-day routine, and a little extra. Most do it very well,
manned by competent and compassionate people.

However, many government agencies are not prepared for
the numerous tasks that are involved in the types of events I respond to. So that is why private companies (transport and natural resource, for example) and governments, who might suffer
a mass fatality, ask us to be ready to assist them. We provide
experience because we respond globally to multiple events, so
nothing is ever really new; and we are neutral and have surge
resources. Frankly, if I could, I would close the company. I would
be happy to never get another phone call or respond to another
loss of life. But if I do that, who will respond? The company I
joined in 1998 and now own, Kenyon International Emergency
Services, started out in the business of cleaning up after disasters in 1906, six years before the *Titanic* steamed out of South-
ampton on its ill-fated maiden voyage.

In June 1906, Harold and Herbert Kenyon, sons of the
founder of an English funeral parlor, deployed from London, to
help identify and then repatriate the deceased who were from
overseas. In total twenty-eight people were killed when a steam
train speeding through Salisbury railway station in southwestern
England ran off the rails and crashed. It was carrying wealthy
New Yorkers who were headed for Plymouth to board some
forerunner of the *Titanic*. The train hit a curve at high speed

and flipped off the tracks. (As someone who deals in transport safety, it is worth noting here that steam engines in those days didn't have speedometers. There was also intense competition to show who had the fastest locomotives, and races from London to the coast were a common way of drumming up publicity.) The brothers mostly used jewelry—watches, rings, necklaces, and brooches—to identify the dead because back in those days people did not carry all the identifying documents we now take for granted, like credit cards and drivers licenses. With that commission, the small firm became the first disaster mortician company in the world.

By the 1920s, Kenyon was dealing with its first plane crashes. Although the first plane crash (we did not respond to this one) occurred in 1908, a twenty-six-year-old US Army lieutenant became the first person ever to die in an aviation accident. Thomas Selfridge was in a gossamer-light aircraft built and piloted by one of the founding fathers of modern flight, Orville Wright. Wright was demonstrating to the Army Signal Corps the technological advantages of his Wright Military Flyer—a contraption of wooden struts and canvas sheets, very similar to the Wright Flyer that made the first ever powered flight at Kittyhawk in 1903. Wright took Selfridge up with him for a spin above the fields of Virginia. But the combined weight of the two men, plus a split propeller that cut a guide wire, proved too much for the craft, which crashed into the ground from a height of 150 feet. Selfridge's head smashed into a wooden strut—he might have survived if he had been wearing a helmet—while the aviator suffered a broken leg and ribs, which left him in the hospital for weeks.

Aviation disasters certainly make up a large part of the history, and I would struggle to think of a year in which I have not attended at least one, sadly there is often more than one. In storage we hold records for hundreds of incidents. Every once in a while, I will have to pull a file to answer a question from a family member, sometimes about events that happened before I was born.

In 2004, we repatriated the bodies of 21 undocumented Chinese laborers who had been illegally working as cockle-pickers, collecting clamlike mollusks on the muddy flats of Morecambe Bay, Lancashire, when they were caught off-guard by a fast-rising tide. They had been smuggled into Britain by Chinese triad gangs, spoke little English, and knew nothing of the local geography. One managed to call the police on a mobile phone and get out the words "sinking water" before drowning.

In 1987, Kenyon was called in to handle the mortal remains of 193 people who drowned when the cross-channel ferry the MS *Herald of Free Enterprise* capsized as it left the Belgian port of Zeebrugge, its crew having neglected to close the loading doors to the car decks. A year later, in 1988, we helped gather the remains from the bombing of Pan Am Flight 103 over Lockerbie, which killed all 259 people on board and 11 people on the ground when parts of the plane rained down on the small Scottish village. The Lockerbie disaster is the very definition of what is called a "mass fatality event," when the number, or condition, of fatalities exceeds the response capabilities of local jurisdiction. Our role is to augment the local authorities, to provide not only surge capacity, but also experience gained from being at different events. Experience that only comes from exposure to the myriad events we see or things we deal with, even simple acts like cleaning clothes. For example, when a terrorist's bomb kills a crowd of people, the police will eventually have to hand the clothes of the victims back to their grieving families. But you can't hand them back covered in blood, obviously, so the police, who do not have washing machines, hand them over to us to launder and catalog, once they have finished with any forensic examinations they needed to carry out. The clothes are generally frozen when they are delivered to us, since that is the best condition for preserving any forensic evidence.

Not everyone wants to receive freshly laundered clothes as their last memento, though. We always ask people how they would like their personal effects returned. A mother of a teenage boy who has washed her son's shirts herself for the past sixteen years may very well want to be the person who cleans his shirt that one last time. You can never make assumptions about what might be "normal." Everyone is different.

OVER THE DECADES, KENYON'S cavernous warehouses in Houston and London have become the ultimate lost and found offices. We have had boxes and boxes of lost glasses, stopped watches, unmatched shoes, torn books, and cracked tablets: whatever people were carrying when they met their untimely end, whatever survived the disaster that killed them. Sometimes we have things from survivors, but sadly that is very rare. We often keep these for years, and they are cataloged for the family members to pore over, seeking something their loved one might have had on their last day on earth. Mementos matter: they are something physical that ties you to the person you will never see again. They matter even more when the physical remains of your loved one may still be missing, or unidentifiable, or have been recovered in a condition that you just cannot equate with the person you once knew.

Some people are so traumatized by their loss that they ponder over these mementos for years, the way a kid might obsess over a catalog of toys his parents cannot afford to buy him. It is an attempt to reconnect with a lost loved one, but also to come to terms with the fact that they are gone. Like the cat in Schrödinger's box, the loved one is somehow already dead yet still alive in the contents of these cardboard containers.

We go to great lengths to ensure that every item in our custody is identifiable, if humanly possible. We retrieve photos from smashed cameras, lift phone numbers from cell phones, scroll through playlists on music players. I've even taken car keys to dealerships to try to trace a vehicle identification number. (Even if they can only give me the country where a vehicle was sold, that can dramatically narrow the field of victims in a plane crash where dozens of nationalities were involved.)

In some countries, we are obliged by law to catalog every last item we find. That can mean we have to even list empty bleach bottles we find washed up on the beach along with people's personal possessions. It is usually obvious they are just flotsam, but we have to list them; then we put them on a secondary site online, but we only direct relatives there if they want to see every item from a crash.

The catalogs that list recovered possessions can be several inches thick, depending on the size of the disaster. Sometimes they can look like something out of a museum or even from the fashion industry.

For example, when a suicide bomber blew himself up at an Ariana Grande concert in Manchester in May 2017, the nuts and bolts packed into the bomber's explosive device killed twenty-two people, many of them young girls who had gone with their moms to see their favorite singer on her Dangerous Woman tour. The youngest victim was an eight-year-old girl. Half of the dead were aged under twenty. They had been dressed to the nines for the show, and the page of the catalog displaying their stylish shoes and boots, clearly their prized possessions, looked like something out of an *InStyle* catalog. The rips in their jeans may have been a fashion statement, but most were from shrapnel. In fact, we found shards of metal still in the clothes we were given. And the long, vertical tears on many of the jeans showed where desperate ambulance workers had cut through the cloth to access the shattered young limbs.

———

ALL THESE LOST POSSESSIONS that we gather and catalog can play a vital role in helping people come to terms with their loss, to cross the bridge. The human mind naturally resists the idea of sudden and devastating loss. It always grasps for some last hope, some doubt that will allow the bereaved to deny, at least for a while, the terrible pain of grief. Without a body or a definitive sign that someone has died, there is always that vague hope. I do a lot of family briefings and often have to explain the identification process and why operations have gone from search and rescue to search and recovery. Because of this at times I am accused of taking away hope. I don't ever want to do that if the facts, or more often the case, the absence of facts support having hope, then I take pains to remind the authorities about the examples like the Chilean miners who survived deep underground for months or the famous Andes crash in 1972, when a Uruguayan Air Force plane carrying a rugby team crashed, and the authorities had given them up for dead. Yet seventy-two days after the crash two survivors walked out of the mountains, resulting in the rescue of sixteen people *sixty-six days* after they had been given up for dead. But when the facts—things like human remains, wreckage, and recovered personal effects are found, the chances of a survivor being found weeks after that are not favorable. Having a positively identified body is the irrefutable fact of the loss. That takes time. We can't account for every person, not for a lack of trying, but it is just not always possible because of the circumstances of the loss, limitations of DNA, or fragmentation.

That was the case with a young man who called his mother just as he was boarding his plane a few years back. He was an airline employee and had been able to get a seat. After the phone call, his mom went home from work, not feeling good, and lay down on the sofa with a headache. Hours later she woke up, turned on the television, and saw the flight her son was on had crashed into the Pacific Ocean, with no survivors. Recovery began at once, but because of the nature of the crash, many of the deceased were fragmented, and DNA analysis would take months to complete. Even before the final results came back, and when they did we did not have any remains for four of the passengers and crew, including her son, she thought maybe her son had survived. Maybe he made it to a nearby island. She asked if the Coast Guard could check. All the records were checked, and he had indeed boarded the flight, but as sometimes happens with these events, we just are not good enough or lucky enough to account for all missing people. Her son just happened to be one of those.

Fishermen and law enforcement had gathered belongings that had washed up on the shore: we were helping identify them and return them to waiting families. We received some of the son's belongings, including two waterlogged passports and a suitcase that appeared to belong to him. But there was something odd about the case—it contained a pack of orange plastic hair curlers, the kind my mother used to wear back in the '70s. I just assumed the search teams had found them and stuffed them in the case, then forgotten about them. I've seen far stranger things than that.

I called the mother and asked if she'd like them delivered or sent. She preferred for someone to bring them in person, so I volunteered.

When I arrived at her house—I think it was a year after the crash, these processes can take a long time—her son's truck was still parked on the driveway, and his room might have been exactly as he'd left it.

I asked her if she wanted us to leave the boxes with everything or to lay the items out and go through them with her and her husband. She wanted us to lay them out. We asked her to leave the room and come back when everything was laid out. My coworker and I put a white cloth on her dining room table and laid out her son's recovered belongings. We then covered them with another cloth so she wouldn't be overwhelmed when she walked back in. Sadly, we are well versed in such solemn rituals.

When we pulled back the cloth the first two items were his passports. She took them, held them in her hands; she put her head in her hands and rocked back and forth. I then showed her the curlers, and noting that her son had short hair, I said that they may have been put in the suitcase by responders while picking things up. It was the curlers, though, that did it for her; they were the items that helped her understand her son was not coming home. They had belonged to her own mother, and she kept them in the suitcase that her son had borrowed for his trip. He knew how important they were to his grandmother and would never have taken them out of the suitcase where they belonged, she told me. She said, "So what you're telling me, Robert, is that my son is not coming home."

"No," I told her, "he is not coming home. He died in the plane crash, and he will not come home, and I am sorry for that."

—➤

THIS ATTENTION TO DETAIL, the process of caring for living or concern for passenger personal effects by some US air carriers was
not something that was considered important until the 1990s.
Not so in many other parts of the world. Up until then the response to a loss of an aircraft focused on the investigation, that
was what was important, not the people directly involved or
their families. Taking care of them was left up to insurers, and it
was typically not a great process for the families. In fact, I would
say that US airlines in particular did almost nothing to help
grieving relatives find their loved ones' remains or help them
come to terms with their loss. Quite the opposite: they made
it almost impossible for families to make decisions or have any
input into the process. Incredibly, the airlines and their insurers
felt they were best placed to make decisions for the families.
However, a series of particularly grizzly crashes, to which the
airlines responded with shocking negligence, brought relatives
of the dead together. At first, the general aim was one of mutual
comfort and solace, but out of their shared experience rose a defined protest for better treatment. They forced Congress to act.

The push for new regulations came after USAir Flight 427
plunged into a ravine near Pittsburgh in September 1994, nar-
rowly missing a crowded shopping mall and killing all 132
people on board. Local and state emergency workers, most of
whom had never dealt with an air crash before, rushed to the
scene, hoping they were looking for survivors but quickly realized they would only be retrieving body parts. Many were
left deeply traumatized by what they experienced: there was so
much blood spattered across the crash site that doctors ordered
all the first responders to get hepatitis vaccines after the first

night of searching. A doctor who was leaving a local hospital when he heard of the crash on the radio sped to help out. "It was the most horrible scene I've ever seen in my life," he told a reporter at the site. "You can't describe it. The pieces . . . the pieces were unidentifiable. It's just indescribable."

The crash investigation became the longest in US aviation history up to that point. It was four and a half years before the National Transportation Safety Board (NTSB) pinpointed a faulty rudder as the probable cause of the disaster. The length of the investigation only added to the anguish of the grieving families, who came together in the absence of family assistance centers in those days. Relatives had to wait up to seven hours to hear confirmation that their loved ones had even been aboard the plane, while ticketing agents were press-ganged into acting as crisis counselors, a job they were completely unprepared to handle.

To make matters worse, the airline failed to let the families know when it went ahead and buried thirty-eight caskets of human remains in a local cemetery: the relatives only found out when they went to a memorial service organized by USAir to bury unidentified body fragments, and saw there were only two coffins for more than 130 bodies. The airline said it had been advised by local funeral directors that a display of so many coffins would only upset the families. Instead, relatives felt that they had been deceived. They were furious, a rage exacerbated by the fact that many items belonging to the deceased had been tossed into dumpsters in the unheated hangar where crash investigators were piecing the plane together for forensic examination. Months later, when the families got permission to go through the dumpsters, the contents had been frozen together into a giant muddy ice cube.

Then, just two months later, on November 11, 1994, an

American Eagle turboprop crashed nose-first into a field in Indiana, killing sixty-eight people. Again the retrieval of human remains, and communications by the airline were a disaster. The airline handed out sixty-eight coffins, each containing some human remains, to each of the families; but the vast majority of the body parts were simply buried at night in seventeen coffins without informing the relatives. Most of the personal effects were destroyed rather than being returned to the families. Months after the crash, mourning relatives visited the field where the plane had crashed and were able to pick human bones out of the dirt.

Pretty soon, the self-created family support groups from both disasters got together and spotted the striking similarities in the way the airlines had handled the tragedies. More families affected by other crashes joined their ranks: they became impassioned activists, determined that relatives in future should not suffer the way they had through incompetence and negligence. They formed their own nonprofit, the National Air Disaster Alliance, to push for change. They began to show up at the normally dry hearings of the NTSB (where a plane crash was traditionally referred to simply as "the occurrence") with photos of the dead, which they placed hauntingly on empty chairs or attached to their own clothing. The final straw came with the loss of TWA Flight 800 on July 17, 1996. Families were caught in the middle of a fight between the FBI and NTSB over who had jurisdiction of the crash. Each agency was giving conflicting press conferences. (TWA was one of the first crashes I worked on when I joined Kenyon in 1998.) By October 1996, the pressure had grown so intense that President Bill Clinton, at the urging and hard work of Jim Hall who was chairman of the NTSB, signed into law the Aviation Disaster Family Assistance Act, which set out all the duties and responsibilities of the NTSB and airlines toward the affected families. Within the NTSB—which until then had only dealt with crash investigations—a special Transportation Disaster Assistance Division was set up to coordinate between the airlines and the federal, state, and local agencies, to help to ensure the needs of shocked grieving families were met. If there has been a law that was earned, then this was it. Today similar laws have been passed in a handful of other countries, but for the most part many non–US carriers had already started to make the families the focus of their response.

IF YOU THINK I am hard on US air carriers, I am, but I am even more so on their insurers and lawyers. I hold the airlines responsible when they don't take charge of the response. Accidents occur, and people understand that. Humans make mistakes. The response should not be an accident too; it should be planned and resourced. You cannot control the event, but you can control the response. The best you can do is zero—you can't un-injure a person or bring back the dead. The only thing you can do is not make it worse. Unfortunately, some airlines turn control of the response over to insurers and lawyers, who just don't get it. While there are many good ones, the few bad ones really have an impact. They seem to lack empathy or any understanding of what families or even the airline employees have gone through. I think it is mainly because many of them choose to not go on the scene and instead delegate tasks or work only with lawyers representing families months after the loss.

I was in London one day after the Grenfell Tower fire, meeting with an aviation insurance lawyer. She asked what the number of deceased was in the awful apartment tower fire that had just taken place. I explained that the coroner had raised the total number of deceased by one to include an infant that was stillborn because of the injuries the mother suffered in the fire. I added that it was certainly a hard time for the family. She responded by saying they could probably solve that by having another baby. I was floored. I just looked away in disgust. How do you argue with that total lack of understanding or empathy?

One of my biggest issues is that it will take some time for insurance settlements and payments to occur, and in some cases, that is a big fight for the family. While I accept it is possible that some people may use a loss to improve their positions, I have rarely seen it. I have never met anyone who would not give up everything they have ever owned to get their loved ones back. This process creates hardships for families. Bills don't stop because a person has died in an aircraft crash. It can take time to identify the proper family members, and the goal of most air carriers is to do this within fourteen days, and then issue assistance payments. That has become the norm, but it wasn't easy to achieve. It was a battle with some insurers. Perversely, it is quite the opposite for an airline to settle the claim for the loss of their owned aircraft. If you asked me what American Airlines's most profitable day was, I'd guess it was May 25, 1979, when AA Flight 191 from Chicago to Los Angeles crashed shortly after takeoff, killing 273 people. That plane was insured for $26 million. Unlike a car that you might buy for $20,000 and insure for $5,000, a plane will remain insured at the price the company paid for it throughout its life. In 1972, American had bought the DC-10 for $26 million: by the time of the crash, most DC-10s were being scrapped and the plane's value written down to $10 million. In keeping with the policy, since the plane was not salvageable, the airline was reimbursed the $26 million. While bereaved families could spend years litigating to get $100,000 in compensation for the death of a loved one, within a few days American Airlines knew a check for $26 million was in the mail. The profit sat as a line item on their 1979 10-K. A 10-K is an annual report required by the US Securities and Exchange Commission giving a summary of a company's financial position.

Today, if airlines fail to meet the strict criteria set out by law, they face stiff fines, sanctions, or even jail time for corporate executives. For example, in 2014, Asiana Airlines was fined half a million dollars for failing to rapidly establish a toll-free number for worried relatives to call after one of its planes clipped a seawall while landing in San Francisco the year before, killing three people and injuring dozens more. Ironically, they had listed Kenyon as part of their response plan, even though they had canceled their contract with us years before, either believing an accident would not happen, or that they had the resources to manage. Here is the thing, I don't think anyone in Asiana woke up that day and said, "Here is my chance to make it worse." They did make it worse, but they did so because they probably never believed an accident would happen to them—or thought that if it did, managing the response would be the responsibility of the government or someone else. Then when the accident did happen, they did not have the experience or resources to either deal with the problems that were theirs to manage or to meet the needs of the families who had trusted them.

7. Picking Up the Pieces

The young man on the phone—whom I had met in the days following the tragic loss of Alaska Airlines Flight 261—was of mixed heritage, an American whose family originally came from Asia. He was only in his early twenties. He was having to grapple with a tragedy that someone so young shouldn't have to face: his parents had both been killed in the plane crash, during the flight from Puerto Vallarta, Mexico, to Seattle with a stop-over in San Francisco.

This plane crashed after the failure of the horizontal stabilizer. The pilots tried to gain control by inverting the aircraft—literally flying upside down, a moment captured to great effect in *Flight*, the 2012 Denzel Washington movie. However, once the worn-down jackscrew—which controlled the movement of the horizontal stabilizer—was stripped, the highly experienced pilots lost all control of the aircraft which crashed into the sea. There was nothing anyone could do to land that plane.

The more pressing issue for the stunned young man now was what to do with his parents' mortal remains? Eighty-three passengers—quite a few of them employees of the airline who had been taking advantage of the post-Christmas lull to grab a quick winter break in the Mexico sunshine—and five crew had died when the plane plunged into the Pacific, just off the coast from Los Angeles.

The young man's relatives wanted the remains to be interred back in the old country, but he and his brother, as well as other members of the family living in the United States, wanted them buried in their adopted homeland. So he was conflicted and seeking advice. Should he bury them in their country of birth, or in their adopted homeland of the United States?

"You can do both," I told the young man. As a result of the high-speed impact, many of the deceased were fragmented. There was no wrong answer here. In my opinion, it didn't matter to his parents: they were dead. It mattered to the living, and the living had to make the decision. So in the end, the remains went to both places.

During my career, I have been asked so many of the same questions, over and over. The questions are surprisingly simple. The answers are straightforward, too. They are just not easy. That is why, whenever I am asked certain questions, I always ask the person, "Do you understand the question you are asking me? Because once I give you the answer, you will never be able to not know it."

I often have to explain difficult matters to people who are in deep shock. For example, I once worked with a woman whose husband had died in a plane crash in the Middle East. She was in a state of emotional paralysis, so some of the people tasked with guiding her through this terrible moment in her life thought she was cold and didn't care. But that wasn't the case at all. No remains of her husband had been recovered, and therefore she was struggling to believe he was actually dead. But he was dead. This is a fairly common response: if there is no body, there is no death.

The local authorities said the only remains they had in the

morgue were various "unassociated fragments," and that was that. An assembly of body parts that were not attached to each other, in other words. Without a grave to visit or even a concrete answer as to her husband's death, this woman couldn't process the fact that he was gone, just like that. So, I went with one of my colleagues, Allan D. Wood—we called him Woody for short and he was one of the finest funeral directors I have ever known—to the morgue to look at the remains ourselves. This meant going through the "unassociated fragments," running my gloved hands over the body parts. We got lucky: when everything was untangled, it was a single body, all parts joined together by skin or sinew, with specific identifying features. By tracing the connective tissues and laying him out, we were able to establish that in fact all the limbs were actually still attached—just barely—to the body and were not just a pile of random parts. It didn't resemble her husband in any way she would have recognized, but it was him. Mission accomplished.

That night, Woody and I drove her to the airport; after ensuring her husband's casket was loaded on board, we went back to the terminal and guided her to her seat.

It was then that she started to cry. She was taking her husband home.

MASS FATALITIES ARE MESSY, and I do not mean just physically. The chaos of human affairs can frequently be suppressed in life, at least for a while, but rarely in death. All the problems we have in life, the secrets we keep, don't go away in death. They are just transferred to someone else. When a plane crashes or a bomb goes off, all those suppressed problems can spill out like a suitcase bursting open.

I have also seen people simply unable, or at times unwilling, to make decisions about disposition of their loved one's body. Their answer is to not recover it, which doesn't work in plane crashes or other mass fatalities because during recovery we don't know who is who. It also creates legal challenges. Because once the body is identified the coroners and medical examiners have to turn it over to the families. In one case a family told us, "Our dad died when the plane crashed. We don't want to know if he is identified or what happens to him; in our thoughts he is in the ocean where he died." So in this case, we had them complete the required legal documents, and if he was recovered we would have buried him in an unmarked grave, keeping a record of exactly where it was in case they ever changed their minds.

A lot of our work has been with plane crashes, from aircraft that go down on takeoff to crashes in remote mountain ranges. Or the wreckage might be deep under water, as was the case with the Alaska Airlines flight. In that case, recovery is largely a question of Coast Guard, Navy, fishing, or specialist vessels working to recover the deceased, the wreckage, and personal effects. In the case of Alaska Airlines Flight 261, which crashed into the Pacific off California's coast on January 31, 2000, other pilots in the air witnessed the doomed flight fall from the sky and reported the location of impact. The air traffic controllers responsible for Los Angeles International Airport (LAX) had also been talking to the pilots even as he struggled with his plane: they had offered him clearance to land at the airport but, judging by the final loop of the cockpit voice recorder, he knew his flight wasn't likely to end well and chose to stay away from populated areas. A true hero. He stayed over the ocean where he circled and tried to solve the problems they were having with the aircraft. By the time he inverted his plane in a desperate bid to retain control, his passengers would no doubt have guessed they weren't making it home. The captain had told passengers they were trying for LAX and thought they would be landing soon, and up until the last few seconds, I am sure he thought he could. However, with the plane being inverted and the sudden dives, I am sure he would have sent some people into prayer and others into shock.

At 4:20 p.m., the cockpit voice recorder picked up the captain saying, "Here we go."

Then the recording cuts off. The plane had crashed. Within minutes, notification of the crash was broadcast on emergency channel 16, a channel almost all boaters monitor. The area was quickly filled with boat captains headed to the scene of the crash, hopefully scanning for survivors but quickly realizing that what they would be pulling out would be debris, bodies, and personal possessions.

In sea crashes, some of the heavier wreckage—such as the landing gear—sinks fast but the smaller, light pieces can float for much longer and spread over a large area. When a plane crashes at high speed into the sea, the impact is pretty much the same as if it had crashed into the ground: it disintegrates. At sea, however, there are few distinguishing features, and the pieces are often very small, so time is of the essence. Luckily, the seas off Los Angeles are crisscrossed by shrimp and squid boats, which carry a lot of lights for night fishing. They quickly started hauling debris out of the sea: the tides would wash more up on the beaches of Ventura County in the coming days.

My company was not originally contracted to deal with human remains, only personal effects. But because I had also previously taught the California Office of Emergency Services Mass Fatality Class for several years and written the only book at the time on responding to mass fatalities, my friend at OES, the law enforcement chief, had asked me to meet first with the Ventura County Medical Examiner. So I did. Dr. Ron O'Halloran was the medical examiner—a great guy and, I think, a good ME. He had never dealt with a disaster on such a huge scale before and he told me that if the airline just gave him the passenger manifest, he would issue death certificates for everyone on board. Clearly, there had been no survivors. I think he thought that would be easiest on the families. We sat on the dock and chatted, as we chatted. As we chatted, though, I told him that I knew that what he was saying made perfect sense, but that if he went ahead and did that, he would look like he didn't care even if, talking to him, I could tell he did care. I also told him, "You won't last the night." It was a simple piece of advice, and he was quick to accept it. So the operation began.

The head of Alaska Airlines, John Kelly, was scheduled to hold a briefing with the shocked families, and I was due to stand next to him and address the process for personal effects. Just before he took his place on the podium, he said, "If I get questions about the human remains, I'll hand those over to you." I said, "Sure, I don't mind. But just so you know, Alaska has asked us only to deal with the personal effects." Sometimes the complex contracts that airlines negotiate mean that various tasks get parceled out to separate companies or agencies. It seems like a cost-saving measure in normal times, but in an emergency, it doesn't not make a whole lot of sense. In fact, we no longer accept those terms. That was certainly how it seemed to Kelly in that stressful moment. He said, "Well you are now," meaning you are in charge of the deceased now.

One of the first questions came from the brother of one of the deceased passengers, who was also an employee of the airline. He was furious that his brother's identity had already been leaked to the press, before he had even had a chance to inform all the members of his extended family. Some relatives had discovered their loss from the news, and he was understandably upset. We had not even taken possession of the personal effects at that point. I told him we would look into what had happened and get back to him. It turned out that one of the fishermen who had gone out looking for debris had taken a local news photographer with him. They had found the dead man's passports and the photographer snapped a picture of them and published it.

Notification can get very, very messy in the aftermath of plane crashes. And messy is painful for those who are grieving. The ex-wife of a man who had died on the flight had no idea that he had taken their children, together with his new spouse, to Mexico on a holiday. By law, she should have been notified and in some places the airline is supposed to check that the children had permission from custodial parents before boarding them. But how do they know? They see a family headed out on holiday and did not feel the need to verify that the children were leaving the country without the mother's knowledge. The mother had no reason to be worried about reports of a downed passenger jet. Probably the first she would have heard would have been friends calling her to express their condolences. She would have likely asked "For what . . . ?"

IN ANOTHER CASE WE had two releases and repatriations delayed because of false paternity suits. A lawyer had convinced two women to come forward and claim that two men on the flight had fathered children. One of the men was gay and had a long-term partner. Because same-sex marriage was not recognized at that time, a child, if it was his, would have become their legal next of kin. DNA testing proved they were not the fathers. It was a scam. But it caused delays and was horrible for the families involved. Sadly, this happens every few crashes, when someone thinks they have stumbled upon a quick get-rich idea. They check the papers for single victims, thinking they are easy targets and often people without wills.

I always tell people that there are four key documents in life. Your birth certificate, which gives you an identity and nationality. Your passport, which allows you to travel and enter back into your own country. Your death certificate, which allows your family to settle your estate and shows that you lived. Finally, your marriage certificate, which in many ways is the most important one, because beyond the commitment to another person; in a much more practical sense, it is your way of telling a court whom you entrust to make decisions of vital importance if you fall ill, are incapacitated, or die. It is the positive declaration of whom you consider your family.

The lack of a marriage certificate, or the inability to have one because of discriminatory laws, is a big problem in our business. I can't tell you the number of times long-term partners have been blocked from decisions around the disposition of the deceased, or from collecting their personal effects because they were not the legal next of kin. In most jurisdictions—not just in the United States—the absence of a marriage certificate means the legal next of kin are parents or biological children if they exist, and if they are underage, the other parent of the child who is often the guardian regardless of the length or status of the relationship the person had with the deceased. So, you could have cohabited with your beloved partner for twenty years and have all your rights to claim their body and personal belongings instantly erased by an estranged mother or father, who may have never approved of their child's relationship in the first place.

THE RECOVERY AND IDENTIFICATION of the dead can be a long drawn-out process. That slowness impedes the recovery of the living. It is not just the lingering uncertainty and possible denial that the worst has happened, but also the fact that people often feel obliged to put their lives on hold indefinitely while they wait for us to come back with mortal remains.

The father of a British nurse was killed in 2010 when an Afriqiyah Airlines flight from South Africa crashed on its approach to landing in the Libyan capital Tripoli. One hundred and thirteen people died in the crash, most of them Dutch nationals returning home after their holidays and expecting to change planes in Tripoli. We had informed the British lady that it would likely take a few weeks for a positive ID on her father. It wasn't going to take a year and half but about three or four weeks. She stayed at the Family Assistance Center in Tripoli and was welcome to stay as long as she wanted. When we are operating the Family Assistance Centers, I often walk around and check on things. One day while doing this she stopped me and wanted to talk. She was conflicted; she was a grown woman and had her own life back in the United Kingdom— work commitments, bills to pay, pets to care for, but as the oldest daughter her family expected her to stay until her father's remains were released. Otherwise they would see her as a bad daughter. "What do I do?" she asked me. A question I have been asked before. "Here's the thing," I said. "We're going to be here, and we're not going to leave until all the IDs are made. We will look after your father as if he was our father, we'll call you every day. If you feel you need to go home, do that. Explain to your family that you can't be in the morgue, explain to them that you are just sitting in a hotel room waiting. Because they don't understand. As soon as we think we're getting an ID we'll fly you back here." And that's the trust you have to build, because you are asking people to trust a system, after another system has so tragically failed.

My work in law enforcement, the military, and Kenyon has exposed me to different kinds of people and situations; it has been a good teacher at reading people and sometimes figuring out the real problem, not just the one expressed. A woman remains in my memory from 2016. She lost her parents-in-law when a flight from Paris crashed into the Mediterranean Sea off the coast of Egypt. No Mayday call was issued before the jet vanished from the radar, although the plane's digital data-link system did send a signal that a smoke alarm had gone off in one of the toilets. The Egyptian Navy and Air Force started searching an area of more than five thousand square miles for debris. On the second day they had located floating wreckage, luggage, and human remains. But it was a week before signals from the missing plane's emergency locator transmitter were detected, narrowing the search down to an area of just three square miles.

The sea was around two miles deep at the site of the crash, and almost a month passed before a special recovery ship capable of retrieving the sunken flight recorder arrived from the Irish Sea, where it had been deployed. Almost another two months went by before it returned to port and transferred the recovered remains to Egyptian forensic experts in Cairo. That is a long time for relatives to be waiting for a result.

During the initial briefs, I was explaining to the families the process of recovery and that we expected it would take several months. During the briefing, this woman was quite direct with her questions and insistent on going to the crash site. I told her that was not within the power of the airline and access was being denied by the military who were in control of the site. After several exchanges, she said, "Look, thank you for briefing, but I don't believe you. I want to go out to the crash site. I need to see for myself. I have seen a picture of what I think is her purse, so you must let me see it." I explained that this was out of our control, and why I did not think the authorities would agree to it. But we would ask again, and we did. And again, access was denied. During the breaks, I walked up to her, and said that I knew she didn't believe me, and that I was sorry, but these were the only answers I had for her. She stood silent for a moment and then she started telling me how she had booked the flight and had driven her in-laws to the airport for their ill-fated flight. I listened and then I said that if she was blaming herself, I understood, but she had nothing to be blamed for. She had chosen a well-regulated airline, with a good safety record, on a regularly scheduled flight from a major airport. Why the plane crashed we don't know, but no one had any way of knowing it would. Sometimes it happens. So she did nothing wrong. I don't know if that helped, but people sometimes need to hear that it wasn't their fault.

Mass fatalities are hard because the period from the initial notification until a positive identification is made can take months, in some case years, and in some cases not at all. During this period, there is uncertainty and without a body people are hesitant to take personal action—like cleaning out a loved one's closet: What if the authorities are wrong and my loved one comes back—they will think I gave up on them? Nor can they often take legal action like removing a deceased from their bank accounts. In a "routine" death, the system forces you to make decisions, such as funeral arrangements, getting documents in order, all things that for most people are part of the transition from what was normal to what will be normal. They are active steps in confronting the reality of a loss. It is quite the opposite for many in a mass fatality; you are told your loved is gone, but you can do almost nothing to act on that information and start to process the loss. It is a horrible place to be in without support or with no understanding of what to expect and how to navigate it.

8. Sunken Treasure

Modern aircraft carry a lot more than just people. They also carry vast money transfers from bank vaults, gold from national reserves, priceless antiquities, and expensive race cars. State Department officials have sometimes taken me to one side and quietly asked me to retrieve diplomatic pouches full of sensitive cables. In one case, I was tasked with discreetly finding the next season's playbooks for the Oklahoma State Cowboys' basketball team when a private plane crashed in a snowstorm with two OSU players and a number of senior coaches aboard. Beyond the sentimental items, there is also often property or belongings that are important for other reasons.

That was the case when Swissair Flight 111 plunged into the Atlantic nine miles off the coast of Nova Scotia, Canada, on September 2, 1998. The scheduled flight from New York to Geneva was a regular "Who's Who" of senior United Nations officials, minor royalty including a Saudi prince and a relative of the last Shah of Iran, academics, show business celebrities, and the son of boxing legend Jake LaMotta. In fact, the flight was known as the "UN shuttle." The crash also decimated global AIDs research—a conference on the disease had just taken place in New York and several of the world's leading scientists were headed back home to Europe.

As a regular flight from the world's business capital to the world's banking capital, it also carried a spectacular cargo in its hold: more than ten pounds in weight of diamonds and other precious stones that would be worth around half a billion dollars at today's market value; a Picasso self-portrait, *Le Peintre*, valued at $1.5 million; and fifty kilos in paper money—amounting to tens of millions of dollars—bound for the deposit vaults of Swiss banks.

Hundreds of years ago, if a Spanish galleon laden with gold sunk to the bottom of the sea with its crew and cargo, there was very little the Spanish crown, or the grieving relatives of the sailors, could do about it. The gold and the human remains would have to wait hundreds of years in their watery graves for any chance of salvage. (However, in the eighteenth century, the Spanish fleet did keep crews of African and Indian divers on standby in their gold ports around the Caribbean. The boats were ready to set off whenever one of the treasure galleons bound for Spain went down, many of them off the coast of Florida.)

But three centuries later, technology is such that investigators were able to retrieve 98 percent of Flight 111 and its sixteen tons of cargo. During a five-year investigation that cost almost $60 million a large section of the fuselage was reconstructed in a warehouse in Halifax to study what exactly went wrong. A suction pump was used to scour the ocean floor of Peggy's Cove, dredging up around a million items of debris and rock, which was then sifted thoroughly. But of the diamonds, which had been enclosed in a metal tube for safekeeping, there was not a trace, raising a key question in the minds of investigators: Had the precious stones ever even been on board the doomed flight? And if so, what might that say about the cause of the mystery crash?

Facing a bill of $300 million in insurance payouts, Lloyd's

not surprisingly wanted to ascertain exactly what had happened to the precious stones it had underwritten, including one that was featured in an exhibition in New York's American Museum of Natural History, "The Nature of Diamonds," that had closed just days before the plane left JFK.

One of the first things airlines or shipping companies do upon learning of the loss of a vessel is to claim the wreck, thereby legally announcing that they have salvage rights. Otherwise, under maritime law, whoever gets to the wreck first can claim the wreck and its cargo. In the past, that law was exploited by so-called wreckers, eighteenth- and nineteenth-century gangs who would use lanterns to lure ships into shallow waters or onto rocks where they would break up, allowing them to claim the salvage on their cargos. Ironically that was also quite an industry in Key West, where we now call home. Government-owned vessels are automatically declared "war graves" even if they go down in peacetime. That means they cannot be salvaged, but civilian vessels are still fair game to salvage companies, and the case of Swissair 111 was particularly urgent. The Royal Canadian Mounted Police maintained a mile-wide exclusion zone around the crash site for more than a year as investigators scoured the area, but the search for the missing diamonds became an increasingly sensitive point for the families, to the point where they rallied together and managed to legally block the salvage operation. Lloyd's would just have to absorb the shocking loss.

So what did happen to the diamonds, and how do you balance the competing demands of investigators, insurance companies, and grieving families?

The captain of the Swissair plane was Urs Zimmerman, an experienced fifty-year-old former Swiss fighter pilot who radioed air traffic control shortly after takeoff to report a problem with smoke in the cabin. It was just after 8:00 p.m. on this red-eye and the crew were into the meal service to the business-class passengers. The captain issued a "Pan Pan Pan," an alert of less urgency than "Mayday." He asked permission to land at Halifax in Nova Scotia. Canadian airports have been famous for handling transatlantic diversions, such as Gander in Newfoundland. Gander was to become famous a few years later when thirty-eight international flights to the United States were grounded there in the days after 9/11, stranding some 7,000 people who spent more than a day marooned in their planes before being taken in by the townsfolk. Sadly, it was also the site of Canada's worst air disaster as well as worst for the US military, when on December 12, 1985, Arrow Air Flight 1285, a DC 8 charter flight carrying 248 US soldiers, on their way back from peacekeeping duties and 8 crew members crashed shortly after a short stop in Gander. Two major changes were made following this accident. One, the soldiers were carrying their personal files, including medical records, with them, which made identification a difficult task, and as a result of that crash, soldiers' records were no longer hand-carried with unit movements. Second, because of problems with the investigation, the Canadian Aviation Safety board was disbanded and replaced with the Transportation Safety Board (TSB). The same TSB investigating the loss of Swissair Flight 111.

Unable to locate the smoke, but believing it was an anomaly from the air-conditioning system the pilots knew they needed to land and have the problem fixed. Sounds simple, but it is really not. This is one of the biggest challenges pilots face in an emergency, and it is not something automation can solve. Because the pilots have to make a determination on the level of threat or danger to the aircraft and then decide the risk level for an emergency landing. Sometimes problems are very obvious, and landing becomes the immediate priority and the risk of not being completely ready to land are outweighed by the need to get on the ground. On the other hand, where there is a problem, but pilots perceive they have more time, time is taken to get better prepared and minimize the risk of hurried landing. In the case of SR111, as mentioned, the light smoke was originally thought to be from the air-conditioning system anomaly and while important to get the plane down, the pilots likely felt they had time to dump fuel and be better prepared. In other words, it was safer to take a little more time. Which is how they were trained.

Once the pilots were given permission to divert to Halifax, they have several things to do. First, they have to continue flying the aircraft. Secondly, they have to deal with the problem—in this case the smoke. Thirdly, they need to familiarize themselves with the new landing airport. If it is one they have been to before, then it is easier. Regardless, they have to review approaches and inputs needed to aircraft flight systems. Finally, they have to determine the readiness of the aircraft to land. If the cabin crew was in the middle of service, how long do they need to stow everything away safely? They have to calculate the weight of the aircraft. Weight can be an issue; planes take off heavier than they land. An overweight landing can create its own problems.

Unfortunately, and probably impossible to know in flight, until it was too late, was that it was not smoke from an air-conditioning anomaly, but from a fire in the newly installed entertainment system wiring, that was spreading in the area above them. As the fire burned and gained more air, the smoke increased and systems failed, ten minutes after declaring the "Pan Pan Pan," the pilots declared an emergency, and seven minutes later the plane impacted the waters near Peggy's Cove, about thirty miles south of Halifax. The aircraft shattered into thousands of pieces. Only one body, of a man seated by bulkhead was found intact.

The initial search was launched by fishing vessels, known in Canada as the Canadian Coast Guard Auxiliary; the country's huge coastline can't possibly be fully patrolled, and seafaring people tend to be self-sufficient and look after their own. Luckily, the area is a rich fishing ground, so a flotilla of trawlers responded to the call, though recovery of body parts is a psychologically challenging task—one of the searchers was so traumatized by what he saw that he later sued the Canadian government for exposing him to such horror, although a judge eventually dismissed the case. The first news the head of Swissair heard about the loss of one of his aircraft was the wake-up call he received from a reporter who phoned him in the middle of the night, Swiss time, asking for a comment. That is not unusual and something I often use as an example of the need for rapid communications in emergency situations. I also use this case as an example of the great job done by an airline, which focused on addressing the consequences of the loss and responding to the crisis.

The Canadian Navy has a large base in Halifax, some fifty miles up the coast from Peggy's Cove, so the recovered debris and body parts were gathered there. Kenyon was retained to handle the repatriation of the deceased and the return of the personal effects.

Over time it would be apparent that in addition to the recovery of the deceased and the wreckage, the recovery of the cargo would be just as important to some. However, as is sometimes the case, not all the wreckage, the deceased, or the cargo is found. That fueled conspiracy theories, some of which persist to this day. Lloyd's insurance did in fact pay out the staggering sum of $300 million to cover the loss of the diamonds, which had been stored in a strongbox together with ten pounds of other jewels. All those millions of dollars in currency had gone missing, too. The Picasso had not been specially packaged by the owners and was doubtless destroyed on impact. We believe a piece of the frame ended up in our warehouse and was examined by insurance adjusters on a few occasions.

A special ship in effect fitted with a "giant vacuum," was brought in to scour the seabed, fifty meters down. It recovered millions of pieces of fuselage, wiring, human remains, and destroyed possessions, which were all sent to the sifting center in Halifax. In all, more than 18,000 kilos of cargo were recovered.

Needless to say, all this was devastatingly painful for the grieving families, who were far more concerned about retrieving some keepsake of their vanished relatives than an insurance company's search for missing diamonds.

Kenyon set up an office in Halifax. The Royal Canadian Mounted Police were supporting the TSB as they finished the inventory of personal effects. They were then transferred to us in Houston. Because this investigation was so complex and intricate, at times some of those items were returned for further examination by the TSB. They would call and ask us to send back clothing or possessions that might hold some clue as to where and how the fire had broken out. For example, we would receive clothing from the Canadian police and take it to Houston to be stored and cataloged. Cataloging was how families claimed items that we could not link to a specific person. The personal effects catalog for the first recovery operation—in the end there were two—consisted of four catalogs each several inches thick. If we had established who the clothing belonged to, that could help investigators narrow down the person's location on the aircraft and might shed some light on the spread of the fire.

I would love nothing more than to say that we are always successful in working with families. But that would be a lie; sometimes there is nothing we can do and what we do is seen as wrong. I hate that but I am powerless to change it. In the Swissair loss there was one such person. She had lost her husband.

The father of her child. She would look through our catalog, claim items, which we would send to her as requested. She would then tell us they were wrong, and we would go back through our system to make sure we had sent the correct item, and we had. This went on for some time. I even invited her down to Houston to go through all the personal effects directly, my way of saying to her, "Look, what exactly can I do for you?" She declined and went back to making the same sorts of requests. When it was time for the one-year memorial she did not attend. She started a safety organization, and I hope it has worked out for her and her family.

Sometimes things go badly, because we cannot give people what they want, when they want. But usually in the end they work out. We always remember it was never about us, and always about the survivors, and the families of the deceased. At the one-year memorial of Swissair Flight 111, we were asked to bring jewelry items for families to look through and see if they could identify things, to make it easier for them to claim them. I did not agree with it for several reasons.

The personal effects process, while straightforward, is one that touches on many human emotions—fear of what some might discover about a person or their family, hope for the return of something special that was feared lost, a reminder of happier days or articles that "paint" a picture of someone's life. They are not just things to be picked up and sent back. Some don't want them back.

First, we must recover them, and that can be simple, or can involve a lot of equipment. It is often very detailed and painstaking work going through debris and wreckage to find that ring, a piece of a watch, sim card, or bracelet buried beneath rubble. Then we have to take everything to one of our facilities or set up a temporary one. Everything is then inventoried for chain of custody, and in some cases if wet—think of water putting out fires—weighed wet, then weighed dry. This is because sometimes the total weight of items matters for investigations. We then try to arrest any further damage, by freeze-drying, or air-drying, and separating items stuck together. During an inventory we look for things to help us identify who the owner of that property was. Some things are very easy; they have a name on them. Others are not, but through a lot of hard work we can find out who it belongs to. For example, we recover a lot of photos, printed copies, film, tape, disc, and memory cards. We look at the images we find and compare them to photographs families have given us, or for pictures of events they have told us their loved ones were attending—such as a wedding or holiday—so we do everything possible to get those recovered images to the families. Even after lying on the ocean floor for months, we have been able to recover and return photos. We look for anything that is unique and record it. Some contain multiple names; other things have no identifying features. Every item is then photographed, usually a closeup for detail, and then a shot of the whole. This information has to be quality checked. We then end up with a list of belongings that we can associate with an individual.

While we are doing this process, we or the authorities are in contact with the survivors, or because most events are mass fatalities, among the families of the deceased we are trying first to establish who the legal next of kin is or more specifically the person eligible to receive effects. Most times identifying the legal next of kin is straightforward, but in about 10 to 15 percent of the time it is not and working those cases is very difficult. If we know who the next of kin is, we explain that we will end up with two distinct phases. The first phase is known as "associated," meaning that we can conclusively link something to an individual. The second is the "unassociated," meaning something we can't link to any person that we believe is missing or involved. So we ask the survivors of the families if they would like to be involved in this process. Some say no, some say yes to both, some say they only want to be involved in the "associated" phase. For us, it is about giving as many choices as possible. For those that choose to be involved, we send them an inventory of what we believe is associated to their loved ones and description of the damage. We ask them to tell us what they would like returned, what level of cleaning or restoration they prefer, and how they would like it returned—mailed or hand-delivered.

While that phase is underway, we create catalogs of the unassociated items. On the same day, we send everyone the catalog or a link to it—online is what most now prefer—but in some places especially where government controls internet access, there is a mistrust and we send a print version instead. Then we give people a set period of time, usually forty-five days, or for large events, ninety days, to go through the catalog and place a claim for those items they believe belonged to their loved one. Sometimes, people will call us right away and say they have identified a watch or something that they are certain is their loved one's. If we can't trace a serial number or find another identifying feature, we have to tell them that we still must hold on to the item until the end of the period to give all families equal chances. Then, if only one person has claimed an item, we go back through and ask them what level of cleaning or restoration they want, and how they would like the item returned. For some, the waiting is very difficult, but there is nothing we can do. We will, if asked, call them every day to tell them that there are no other claims as yet. If there are multiple claims for the same items, before making any decisions, we go back to all families involved and explain the multiple claims issue and work to resolve it. Usually they are easy to resolve, such as a person claiming something they recognize as belonging to their daughter-in-law, while at the same time, the daughter-in-law's own family is also looking at the catalog and see the item and claim it. Some are not easy, though. Think about the number of things you buy that are special to you, like jewelry, watches, or rings; all things that have significant value but are produced and sold in multiple quantities worldwide.

After explaining this process to our clients, they asked us to bring the unassociated jewelry to Halifax for the one-year memorial so that families could get a better look at it, even though they would not be able to take anything they recognized home. The memorial was being done in the middle of the claim period—the 90 days in which families can claim items. Nothing is released during that period, so as to give all families a fair chance to get their loved ones' property back. Also, not all families were going to the memorial, and some that were would not want to see all the jewelry at that time. For some, that would be like showing them a memory of their loved ones and then taking it away. We had a woman who was now a widow, who was sure she had found pieces of her husband's most prized possession, a gold Tissot watch. The part we had was a bezel and part of the band. She would not accept that she could not take the watch. I just listened to her. When I had a chance to speak, I simply told her: "I understand that you are sure this watch is your husband's, you're sitting there looking at it, this piece of it. My challenge is that I have seen several gold Tissot watches, so we know there was more than one. Right now there are family members who haven't come to the memorial and who are at home looking at the pictures. I also know you're worried; you fear it might go to someone else, and I know what I am saying doesn't help. But we have no choice but to be fair to all and to wait for the end of the claim period. If at the end of the claim period, nobody has claimed this watch, then I can easily return it. If someone else also claims it, I'll write and tell you and we will get together and resolve this." This was the conversation that she and I repeated for several days and it never changed. At one point, when she was holding the watch, she said,

"What if I just walk away with it?" I said that would be really un-fair to others and I did not think that she was that type of person. So she handed it back to me, probably one of the hardest things she had done since losing her husband.

I try not to use the word "system" or "legal processes" because this part of the process is an intensely personal and emotional one for people, and *system* and *legal* are bureaucratic words, for bureaucratic processes. Instead, I explain there are other people who deserve the same chances because they have suffered the same losses. Sometimes we need to have multiple conversations like this, and we do. People often come back and thank us; they tell us they don't always remember what we said, but they re-member we listened and when possible, we asked what they wanted; and when we told them something, we gave them the reasons, too. In the end, with no other claims against with what was left of the watch, we packaged it in a jewelry box and re-turned it to her as she requested. Some will say, well why didn't you just give it to her, and that is simply because it does not always work out that way, and then we do more harm.

In the end, the Transportation Safety Board investigators spent years on the reconstruction of the plane, piecing together thousands of fragments of debris on a metal frame in a warehouse before they could pinpoint what had caused the deadly fire. Spec-ulation had been rife that it might have been a bomb planted by terrorists, or that, given the failure to find the missing diamonds, someone might have brought the plane down to disguise the fact that the diamonds had never even made it on board. The final re-port of the investigation—which took four and half years, cost $57 million dollars (Canadian), and was 338 pages long—concluded that the plane's brand-new inflight entertainment system had suf-fered a technical fault and started a fire that burned out key sec-tions of the aircraft's wiring and filled the cockpit with smoke.

9. The Terrorist Attacks

To me, it looked just like any other plane crash—no smoking hole in the ground as many people might expect, nor anything that might even be generally recognizable as the remains of an aircraft, but instead a pulverized and scattered debris field. Scraps of metal, fabric, plane insulation (there are always insulation pieces), some human remains. All of this was consistent with what had been reported: a jet plane had slammed into the ground at enormous speed.

The signs are not always visible as to what caused an aircraft's demise but there are always clues about how it came down. The tiny fragments and deep crater in that field in Shanksville indicated that the plane had hit the ground mostly intact. Larger pieces of debris scattered over a very wide area would indicate a midair breakup or explosion of some kind: even with bombs, sizable parts of the fuselage fall to earth. Remember the almost intact cockpit and nose section of the Pan Am plane that landed on the village of Lockerbie? To pulverize a plane with a bomb, you'd have to line the entire fuselage with explosives, something that would be extremely hard for any terrorist group to do without being detected.

But this was no ordinary plane crash. This was United Flight 93, hijacked by four Al Qaeda terrorists after taking off from

Newark just after eight o'clock on that bright, sunny morning of September 11, 2001, bound for San Francisco. In an act of ultimate courage, the passengers had stormed the cockpit to gain control of the aircraft or at least stop the terrorists from using the plane to hit the US Capitol Building. In a secure bunker beneath the White House, Vice President Dick Cheney had already authorized the military to shoot the plane down before it could reach Washington, DC. During the struggle for control of the aircraft, United Flight 93 nosedived into a field near Shanksville, Pennsylvania. There were no survivors.

From the initial notification that the first plane had hit the World Trade Center in Manhattan, and my scramble to the Pentagon, Shanksville, and New York City, it would be almost a month before I would return home. The morning of 9/11, I was just backing my SUV out of the garage to head into work when my wife ran out to tell me that a private plane had crashed into the World Trade Center. To most people, that first crash just seemed like a freak accident. And since plane crashes are my stock-in-trade, I knew it was not unprecedented for a plane to fly into the side of a symbolic building. In the last days of World War II, a B-25 bomber carrying servicemen to LaGuardia airport had crashed into the Empire State Building while trying to land in heavy clouds. The accident killed three people on board the plane and eleven people inside the building. As I drove to work, the radio was reporting that it was a private plane, but then I started receiving emergency calls from government contacts, officials in FEMA, and the Department of Defense warning me that it was a commercial plane—not an accident—and that there were likely more crashes that would occur.

By the time I'd got to the office, another plane had hit the World Trade Center's second tower, and it was clear life had changed very radically. I was glued to the phone by now, talking to federal emergency officials, state medical examiners, and Kenyon staff who might be able to reach the disaster sites. I was the chief operating officer of Kenyon at the time—the CEO had been in Mexico on a business trip and was now grounded there, so I was in charge. At that time, there were only two fully equipped mobile morgues in the United States: FEMA had one and we owned the other (even today, there are still only three at the national level—FEMA built an extra unit). All flights inside the United States had been grounded, but FEMA offered to send one of the few airplanes still cleared to fly to Houston to pick up my team. Their morgue was headed for New York, where there were initially estimates of ten thousand dead, given the scale and target of the attack. They wanted us to head to DC. But since our business is not rescue or going after survivors and getting two reefer trucks on a plane is difficult, we said we would drive and be there within twenty-four hours. That afternoon we packed our kit and headed out in a convoy. Just before leaving I stopped at the house so I could make sure to see my daughter; I knew it would be some time before I would be home again. I wanted to tell her that things would be okay. Driving through the night with Kenyon's emergency morgue and our black SUVs across the southeastern quarter of the United States, we headed for the Pentagon, a building I had been in many times before and where some of my colleagues now worked.

The drive took more than twenty hours. Sometimes, we would stop for gas and refreshments, and people would just offer to pay our bill (I always politely declined) because they correctly assumed that a small team traveling through the night on otherwise empty roads in black SUVs were only headed to one of three places. It was a small way for shocked people to feel they were contributing somehow, to overcome the sense of helplessness and shock. As we drove, I was constantly on my cell, trying to get ahead of the chaos that I knew was about to engulf a system of governance that had been so brazenly attacked. Luckily, I knew both the Virginia Medical Examiner and the Armed Forces Medical Examiner: the former was Dr. Marcella Fierro, on whom the best-selling crime writer Patricia Cornwell had modeled her most popular character, Dr. Kay Scarpetta. Marcella had assumed that her office would be handling the fatalities from the Pentagon, since the building is located in Virginia. However, because it was federal property, I double-checked with the Armed Forces Medical Examiner, who told me the Department of Defense would be handling it. I realized that the state and federal bureaucracies weren't talking to each other; big bureaucracies rarely do in emergencies.

I called Marcella back and advised her she could stand her people down if she wanted to. That is one of the advantages of being an independent with an extensive contact list. I know all the people involved and am not caught up in the red tape of a government agency. By the time I arrived in DC, our own marching orders had also been changed, and we were asked to quickly move the mobile morgue to Shanksville.

In Shanksville, the Somerset County Coroner Wally Miller was in charge and supported by the US Department of Health and Human Services Disaster Mortuary Operational Response Teams ("DMORT" for short) and supported by our equipment and logistics. DMORT was created in 1995, just after the Oklahoma City bombing. The man behind their creation and the driving force was a New York funeral director Tom Shepardson. We didn't get along when we first met in Oklahoma, but later became very good friends. He would have done, I think, some awesome things for the country, but sadly he passed away in 2003 of a heart attack while shoveling snow. I miss him terribly. DMORT is like Kenyon, and much of their equipment lists and operations flow from what Kenyon established. The investigation was of course managed by the FBI and supported by the NTSB. So as usual a whole lot of acronyms were present! I spent my time making sure people had what they needed and trying to help Wally and the FBI with lessons learned from previous incidents.

I only stayed at Shanksville for a couple of days before being summoned up to New York. The sheer scale of the attack on the United States had by then become evident, and the nation was in shock. I was asked to go to the World Trade Center wreckage, Ground Zero as everyone called it. It was night time when I arrived, and I walked past the eerie evidence of a city that had been taken utterly by surprise—cafes whose tables were still adorned with a half-empty glass of orange juice, food still on plates, jackets hanging on the backs of chairs. As the towers came down, people had literally leapt to their feet and ran for their lives. It was not the first time I would go through a modern-day city that appeared more like a ghost town, and sadly not the last time.

Companies that had been based in the World Trade Center had lost thousands of employees, and they realized they needed to deal with very large numbers of shocked and bereaved relatives.

We had several different jobs that we were trying to do. The largest was setting up a family assistance center for a company that had lost several hundred employees. We also provided call centers and a family assistance team for the New York City Fire Department, which had of course lost scores of its firefighters, including one of its battalion chiefs. I had run into one of the heroic firefighters who perished on 9/11 years before, when he had volunteered to help search the rubble in Oklahoma City. During the course of the response, I spent a lot of time answering questions, talking about processes, and trying to guide actions. Sometimes I would receive calls that told me people I knew from the military or emergency services had been killed.

Many of the large firms were scrambling to set up call centers or had assigned employees to scour hospitals looking for injured or missing coworkers. Because we do this for a living, Kenyon already had call centers with operators who are trained for this type of work in place. In this case the majority of the victims' relatives lived in the same place, New York's tri-state area, so our main job was to get them the relevant information to allow them to begin processing what they had just gone through, and to know what they might be able to expect. We organized briefings: we drafted someone from the city medical examiner's office to explain what condition their loved ones' bodies might be in; and we called upon structural engineers who could explain the physics behind the shocking collapse of the Twin Towers. As out-of-town relatives of victims began to arrive (they either drove to the city or came by air once flights had been resumed), we found them accommodation in hotels and began to loop them into our regular briefings, so that as their shock began to dim they had a fair idea of what was going to hit them next—the long years it would take to recover body fragments, or the idea that they might never receive any part of their loved ones, that they would never know for sure how they had died. With heads of companies, I walked through the process of when to ask for death certificates, when to stop payment of salaries, and what that action means for families, who have no remains and may not be accepting that their loved ones are deceased because there is no physical proof as of yet. This can be a difficult process: logic says there are no more survivors—look at the wreckage—and getting a death certificate means you can process insurance payments. But it is not logical for many of the families, it is emotional, because the death certificate and life insurance payments are someone else saying your loved one is dead, even when you don't yet have a body.

One of the worst hit companies was Cantor Fitzgerald, a

company we did not work with. Cantor Fitzgerald was a financial services firm. The CEO Howard Lutnick lost his own brother and 658 employees. The firm had a policy of hiring relatives of employees, so the loss was even more devastating as families lost multiple members. Their offices had been between the 101st and 105th floors of the North Tower, just above the impact zone of the hijacked plane: no one who was in their offices that day escaped with their life. Lutnick himself only evaded certain death because he had been taking his five-year-old son to his first day of kindergarten when the plane struck. With two-thirds of its workforce deceased and no way of trading, it looked like Cantor would go under. Lutnick had a tough choice to make to save the firm: in a national television broadcast, a sobbing Lutnick said he would suspend the paychecks and health benefits of his deceased employees to avoid the company going under but pledged 25 percent of the company's future profits to victims' families for five years, an amount that would come out at around $100,000 per family. The move stoked up a lot of anger, families were unprepared for this. He missed the point that by doing this, he was in effect saying everyone was deceased and he was moving on. Not all families were at that point. Frankly, the business decisions can still be made, but there was a much better way to do it. One widow, mother-of-three Susan Sliwak, vented her anger to ABC News. "Howard Lutnick is not the man that's going to tell me my husband is dead. That's not how I want to find out, on TV with the rest of the world." I don't think Howard Lutnick wanted to hurt anyone, quite the opposite, and I think he was shocked by the response.

But learning on the job can have devasting results for both the families and the person learning. A lesson that Malaysia Airlines learned, much to the pain of the families after the loss of Flight MH370. The way you do it is to first explain to the families that you are offering the option of the death certificates to those that choose it, but that it does not mean the recovery stops. For some families, in fact most, this is a process they want to start so they can begin their transition. But the choice should be theirs.

Almost a month after I'd left home, I returned to my family in Texas. But not even a week had gone by when, in the middle of the night, I was called because Italy had suffered its deadliest air accident ever. A Scandinavian Airlines plane with 110 people bound for Copenhagen had hit a small private jet in thick fog at an airport in Milan. Again, the initial fear was that this was another terrorist attack, since it happened just days after the US invasion of Afghanistan, and the United States has air bases in Italy. However, it was an accident: the tower had cleared the SAS plane, because the small aircraft's pilots told the tower that they were at the end of the runway—in reality they were in the middle. So, I was off again. The rest of 2001 was spent between Italy, New York, and shorts stops at home.

Because of my extensive travel for work, I tried every year to do a daddy-daughter trip. My wife didn't like to travel, so she did not go with us. I took my daughter on a vacation to Alaska, we went on safari in Africa, and we traveled throughout Europe. But these were not just fun trips. We also visited places like the Apartheid Museum and Nazi concentration camps so she could see the history she had learned about in school. I wanted her to understand how fortunate we are, and that others are not so fortunate, and how such horrors occurred. Most importantly, I wanted her to understand these things will happen again if we allow them to. In April 2002, I took a rare solo break and went trekking in Nepal, to base camp at Mount Everest. The base camp lies at 5,600 meters, or 17,600 feet. It was quite empty in 2002 because of the 2001 murders of the Royal Family and the ongoing civil war. Unfortunately, I got acute mountain sickness just prior to base camp and had to start descending. Since I am never really off the grid, I had a satellite phone with me, and naturally it rang one evening.

Almost three thousand people were killed on 9/11 in New York, and the New York City Office of the Chief Medical Examiner (OCME), Dr. Hirsch had pledged to identify every one that could be identified, no matter the time or cost.

The first challenge to that was how to prepare and then hold the remains in a dignified manner without hindering any current or future DNA identification efforts. The long-term plan was to store them, out of sight of the public but accessible to families, in a memorial that was to be built on the site of the attack, so they needed to be preserved rather than frozen. The medical examiner had asked for a meeting. I promptly changed my flights, and instead of heading home, I went straight to New York City. Traveling light is not something that I can do, and that means I always have a suit and my work things with me, no matter where or what I am doing.

With their experts—and they had some very good people—we developed a plan to preserve the human remains without chemicals, to remove any fluids in which bacteria could thrive, and then vacuum seal the remnants, effectively carrying out a sort of mummification of the remains. We worked in an area that the OCME had named "Memorial Park," an area of refrigerator trucks and a work area that had been assembled in the back lot of the city medical examiner's offices, a faceless beige compound backing onto the East River. Next to the steps leading into each truck were mounted flower arrangements, similar to those in a funeral home, while the Stars and Stripes hung from masts to remind the scientists and technicians that what they were dealing with, day in and day out, were the remains of thousands of murdered Americans. One of those same flags now hangs in our Houston headquarters, a reminder of our work in those fateful days.

We knew that one day, DNA-testing techniques would far outstrip what was possible in 2001, and that there were desperate families who had not yet had any part of their loved ones restored to them. So it was that on an overcast May morning in 2014, more than twelve years after the attacks, the 7,930 remaining human remains we had preserved were transferred in a somber ceremony, in three coffin-size metal cases, to a special repository in the newly built memorial on the granite plaza of the World Trade Center. There, the grieving families have a private "reflection room" to visit, away from the hubbub of what has become a major tourist attraction in the city. This of course has created controversy, for some of the families feel it is not a dignified final resting place. Yet many more support it. Sometimes there are no easy answers. I think that for the OCME they don't consider it final, because they hold hope that one day, they will be able to return more remains and identify all of those that perished. Such is the perseverance and ethos of many in this field. So there the deceased will remain, under the jurisdiction of the city medical examiner's office, until future advances in DNA allow these badly damaged human remains to finally be identified.

THE INVASION OF AFGHANISTAN and the collapse of the Taliban after 9/11 came in swift succession. At the time, it appeared to be a decisive victory, yet twenty years later the war is still being fought. Driven from their safehold after their spectacular attacks on 9/11, Al Qaeda needed to show they were still a potent force. They began scouting for new targets, something easy to attack but that would also cause shockwaves around the world.

In October 2002, they found the perfect "soft target": the tourist paradise of Bali.

Three bombs went off in quick succession one night in Kuta Beach, an area full of bars, clubs, and foreign tourists. One device was inside a suicide bomber's backpack in an Irish pub, another was packed in the trunk of a car parked on the street outside, and a third, smaller device was left outside the US consulate. In all, 202 people were killed. The country that lost the most victims that night was Australia. In fact, this was Australia's 9/11. Bali was such a popular tourist destination for Aussies—beautiful, safe, and with well-connected flights back home—that it was almost considered by Australians to be an extension of their country. The general thinking in those more innocent days was that no one would ever attack Australians; they were seen as neutral, like the Swiss. The bombings came almost as much of a surprise as the attack on the World Trade Center had. Al Qaeda said the slaughter was payback for Australia's support for the invasion of Afghanistan, a military operation that dozens of countries had backed. The strike was also calculated to send shockwaves through the island—a small pocket of Shiva-Buddhism in the vast Islamic nation of Indonesia, home to more Muslims than the entire Middle East. It was also meant as a slap to Indonesia itself, which prided itself on being a peaceful and democratic beacon to the Muslim world.

When the bombs went off, I was at a conference in Hong Kong, so I jumped on a Cathay Pacific flight. It was almost empty except for a group of men who, who from their near identical 5.11 pants and polos, were clearly FBI. Besides me, they were about the only other people on the plane. Going back, the plane would be full, evacuating the wounded as well as the hordes of terrified tourists who were fleeing the island. Bali's hospitals were swamped. They'd never had to cope with carnage on such a scale. There were so many burn victims that some of the wounded had to be kept in hotel swimming pools to cool their charred flesh. The morgues, and really what were just holding areas were full, and bodies were being stored wherever space could be found, wrapped in sheets and often laid out in the open. When refrigerator trucks were eventually brought in, they were so overcrowded that workers had to squeeze body parts inside as bagged limbs fell out of the back. It was a gruesome scene.

Worse, there was no unified effort: instead every country involved wanted to take care of their own, but that is impossible when you don't know who is who. As a result, forensics experts from two dozen countries were gathering bone or tissue samples from the same body parts. That meant a lot of tissue was being taken and needlessly tested, a waste of resources and an affront to grieving families. A lot of them wanted to take a sample from the femur of the dead. As I noted to a colleague at the time, that meant that today you could be six foot tall, but by tomorrow you're five foot nine, and by Friday you're four feet tall. It is precisely that kind of chaotic stampede I try to avert whenever I am enlisted to help out in such cases. Ironically, because of the physics of suicide bombings, the bomber himself is usually the easiest person to identify: the force of the blast tends to fragment the bomber's body but keep his head intact.

Kenyon was asked to repatriate the bodies after the Australian Federal Police had carried out the forensic identification themselves. We always make sure we understand the local customs and religious beliefs surrounding the handling of bodies. These are important things to know: the religion and culture of the deceased; the families (which may be different); and the location in which the death occurred. The least important is your own religion and culture. But because of inexperience or stress it is often what people fall back on when making decisions or plans. Which causes problems. Not intentional, but problematic.

In Bali, we worked for the Australians, while other countries did things their own ways. One day, I was approached by a consular officer from another embassy; they were managing their own repatriations. He said he could not find any trucks or drivers to move the bodies of the deceased, and he assumed it must be because we were monopolizing the trucks and drivers. I told him we had hired only a few and there were many more. I then asked him if had brought a monk or more properly called sanyasi or sadhu with him when he was trying to hire the drivers and trucks. He told me in a rather proper way that his citizens were not Buddhist or Hindus. I explained that he was in Bali, a place were the dead can have great power over the living, and that to talk of death and to transport bodies without the proper respect or prayers being offered was to invite the souls of the dead to remain in the area (or, in this case, the truck) to disturb the living. I suggested that if he were to work within the culture norms of the area, he might have better luck. Which of course he did. This is a problem I encounter far more often than I should. I don't understand why, but people always assume their culture or religion is the only one that matters.

The Australian police decided to take the personal effects of its citizens back to Australia to do their own forensic testing: this was, after all, a crime scene on a massive scale. After they were finished, we then took custody of the personal effects. We would take the personal effects to the United States to process them. Once complete the personal effects would be returned to Australia for the police to return them to families. In fact, I brought the personal effects with me on a commercial flight back to the United States. When going through security to transfer them to the Houston-bound flight, a TSA agent wanted to test for explosives; without any sarcasm, I tried to explain that the clearly marked, labeled evidence bags would certainly test positive for residue since they were the belongings of people killed in a bomb blast. One supervisor later and I was on my way. It would take several years to bring the killers to justice—the mastermind of the attack was killed in a shootout with police in Jakarta in 2010—but Bali was to set a pattern in the terrorist attacks that would, over the years, take the Kenyon team around the world.

———

BEFORE DAWN ON A January day in 2013, as Algerian and international workers were getting ready for a day running the huge natural gas plant in In Amenas, on the edge of the Sahara in Algeria, dozens of pickup trucks full of gunmen drove up, firing off bursts from their AK-47s to announce their arrival. Without any resistance, the fighters from an Al Qaeda–linked group took more than eight hundred workers hostage. They immediately started separating the foreigners from the Algerians: Arabic-speakers were ordered to recite Muslim prayers to prove their faith. The foreigners, including many European and Filipino workers, were bound, gagged, and some of them strapped with explosives. Some were then tied to the metal pipes of the gas plant, which the terrorists aimed to turn into a huge bomb. The attack was designed to interrupt European fuel supplies and sow terror across the region, but the Algerian terrorist who led the group, Mokhtar Belmokhtar, also wanted to use the hostages as leverage to slow a French military advance against Al Qaeda and other religious extremists in neighboring Mali.

The managers had been quick to react, though, and as soon as the gunmen started shooting, they rushed to shut down the plant. The terrorists did not understand enough about engineering to get it up and running again in order to blow it to pieces. The Algerian army quickly surrounded the site, and unfortunately, they were in no mood to take prisoners—they wanted a show of force to deter any future terrorists from trying the same thing. Their country had been ripped apart by religious extremists (including Mokhtar Belmokhtar) in the 1990s and here in In Amenas, they were determined to crush them no matter what it took, even if it meant hostages had to die, too.

The carnage was swift and by the time it was over, forty foreign hostages and twenty-nine terrorists were dead. The terrorists shot some of the hostages, blowing up others: some managed to escape by hiding under their beds, later sneaking out during the chaos, fleeing into the desert as the gunmen searched the plant room by room. Meanwhile the army's attack helicopters targeted anything that moved, even pickups that were carrying both terrorists and hostages.

Kenyon was hired to coordinate the list of missing persons and manage the repatriation of the deceased. I flew to Algiers and worked with a small team in the morgue, really just a room where the bodies were brought in for washing the deceased prior to burial at the main cemetery in Algiers. Perhaps, unsurprisingly, the scene was chaotic. There were police teams from many different countries, some working together, others on their own. For many it was the first time they had seen something like this.

In one case I watched as a police officer escorted a deeply traumatized survivor (who had also been a hostage) through the carnage of the Algiers morgue and asked him to make a visual identification of a body. This is something you just don't do for several reasons, the main one being visual IDs are notoriously unreliable: if a body is sufficiently intact for you to believe someone might be able to identify it, it is certainly intact enough for other forms of ID to be performed on it. Secondly, this poor soul had just been through the most terrifying ordeal you could imagine. Reliving it in the morgue was not going to help him.

On top of that, I received a call from a British coroner who told me that she would not accept that form of ID, and that I of all people should know that. I explained that we were not making the IDs, and it was actually a police officer from her country. She told me to tell him to stop that. I did have a conversation with the officer and suggested that he should consider the established forensic methods. He had not done this before and was under intense pressure to get the bodies back. They followed my suggestion, and all the bodies were forensically identified.

IN TUNISIA, IN 2015, there was another attack. It was considerably lower-tech than Bali or In Amenas, but it was still deadly. A lone gunman had concealed an AK-47 inside a beach umbrella at the Mediterranean resort of Sousse and with four magazines, he walked down the beach shooting foreign tourists dead. Then he went into a hotel and shot as many people as he could find. The gunman fled the scene and ran into a police unit that shot him dead. By the time he was done, thirty-eight people—thirty of them British holidaymakers—were dead. Our task was to set up family assistance centers, identify and recover personal effects, and assist in the repatriation of the bodies. In this case many of the families we helped were themselves survivors of the attack.

The Tunisian police had collected all the personal items from the beach after the shooting ended. The local police considered all these things, phones, and tablets, for example, to be personal effects, and they handed them over to us for return to the families. But the British counter-terrorism police, who had flown out to take the lead in the investigation, considered them to be crime-scene evidence. This is because any one of the holidaymakers could have filmed people rehearsing for the attack, in the days before it occurred and not realized it. They also might have taken images of the attack before they abandoned their phones and ran or were killed. But the Tunisians would not give them to the police, only to us. This is one of the challenges with governments: they can work well together for many things, but when it comes to the deceased it enters a whole new realm. We then liaised with the families and explained to them what the British police wanted and they were okay with that. Again, it is about choices.

NOT ALL OUR OPERATIONS in response to terror attacks have been in far-flung places: fanatics are capable of striking anywhere. The attacks cause a brief ripple of panic and grief, but their frequency has by now rendered them almost mundane, one more item in the endless news cycle of our modern lives. Since 2017, we have been activated for two deadly attacks on London Bridge, whose crowds and central location—both in the city and the national psyche—seem to draw extremists. The first involved three men who plowed their car into the crowds crossing the bridge and then leapt out and started stabbing people as they ran across the bridge. The second, in 2019, involved a former Al Qaeda supporter who had been jailed seven years earlier for plotting a terror attack. He was attending a gathering on prisoner rehabilitation when he began to stab the very people who were trying to help him reenter society, killing two of them. Before police shot him dead, he was memorably chased off by a man wielding a narwhal tusk that he had grabbed off a wall at Fishmonger's Hall, where the rehabilitation talk had been taking place. We did not handle the narwhal tusk, as it was not the property of one of the deceased.

10. Death and Truth

I describe the response to a mass fatality as like working within a situation that is triangular, and I need to maintain a perfect triangle in which all of the angles are equal. By that, I mean there are always three things you have to keep in mind and keep balanced. One angle is the deceased. They have a right to dignity, respect, and an identity. The second angle is the living, the survivors, the families, and the communities, like a school that loses a group of students or village that loses many residents. The third angle is the investigation. In criminal cases, survivors and families will want someone held accountable. In an accident, they will want to know change will be made to prevent the same accident from occurring again. At times these three needs will have competing interests and balance can be difficult. Take the bombing of Pan Am Flight 103, over Scotland. The families wanted the deceased recovered as quickly as possible, but if you rush in to do that and don't have an organized method, it is likely that evidence such as the small piece of microchip that eventually led investigators to Libya's involvement in the attack—and to the subsequent prosecution and conviction of two people—would have been overlooked. Because of things like this, explaining processes and answering questions is hugely important. Information often needs context and in a mass fatality that context can be difficult to convey.

I approach the information I pass on to relatives, and to the general public, with extreme caution. *How* they will interpret the information they have received? I am not trying to conceal anything, the truth always comes out, but instead making sure the context is there. For example, if you ask me, "Was my loved one alive when the plane hit the water?" I would have to clarify what exactly is meant by "alive." If you mean physically alive, as in breathing, depending on the autopsy results, they might have been. But if you mean "conscious," or aware of what was going on, then that is often a different thing. The G-forces in a crashing plane, or the lack of oxygen, can frequently mean that even though a person was still alive they were unconscious, and thus unaware. Being clear is important, and documenting the response is especially vital in the criminal or terror cases. Some people live on sowing disinformation and sparking fights that affect others' morale and unity. They want us to doubt ourselves. Because I have been in involved in some very high-profile events, I often end up seeing the conspiracy theories and at times the pain they cause.

Even as I was scanning the debris of United Flight 93 at Shanksville, people flocked to internet chat rooms—still a relative novelty in 2001, and one whose power was vastly underestimated—to report that the plane had been shot down, and that there was something the government wasn't telling us. People looked at the footage of the wreck and couldn't identify what they assumed a crashed plane should look like—even though to someone like me, the crater denoting high-speed impact was perfectly normal. They figured it must have been blown up by the government for some nefarious reason. Soon that morphed into the enduring 9/11 conspiracy theories that claimed President George W. Bush and Vice President Dick Cheney had conspired to blow up three thousand Americans so that President Bush could get revenge on Saddam Hussein for allegedly plotting to kill his dad. The internet has fueled these theories to a degree that has probably never been seen before in history, but quite often these conspiracies latched on to some element of actual fact, misconstrued or deliberately twisted, and built entire alternative realities out of them.

I had witnessed this phenomenon before. When I was the commander of the 54th QM Company Mortuary Affairs, I responded to the loss of USAF Flight CT 43, the flight that was carrying Ron Brown, President Bill Clinton's commerce secretary, on a trade mission to help rebuild the shattered economy of the postwar Balkans. Shortly, before the crash, I had just rotated out of Bosnia, having been there since December the year before, returning to Fort Lee in Virginia. I had left a team and an officer in charge in Bosnia, so that I could return to command my unit, which was still at Fort Lee. The Army immediately sent me back because of the crash. My job and that of the soldiers assigned to me was to recover and to prepare the bodies so the USAF could fly them to the Port Mortuary in Dover, Delaware, where the Armed Forces Medical Examiner would complete the identifications and release the deceased to their next of kin.

The plane had attempted to land and appeared to be going around when it struck a mountain just beyond the runway in Dubrovnik in Croatia. It is a notoriously difficult airport to land at, and even more so in bad weather. In some crashes the deceased can be mostly intact: it just depends on the dynamic of the crash, speed, altitude, etc. This recovery was bit easier than many, although politically sensitive. We were based in and operating the response from the Dubrovnik airport in Croatia, but the crash actually had wreckage and deceased in both Croatia and across the border in Bosnia Herzegovina. Normally, those countries would have complete and total jurisdiction. However, there was the Dayton Accord, but it had not addressed the possibility of a nonhostile aircraft accident. Of course, both countries, and others were just months out of very bloody regional war. So the United States was taking charge. Initially, the Croatian authorities were holding the position that the deceased would not leave until their two nationals had been identified, a problem that was being addressed in Washington and Zagreb. However, we got lucky, and using the records the Croatians had for their nationals, we were able to identify on site their two nationals and release them, and the other thirty-three deceased were prepared for movement home.

To ensure privacy and keeping with US Military Mortuary Doctrine, the transfer cases holding the deceased have no names on the outside, and to ensure equal treatment, myself and my senior NCO kept the only list with the tentative ID. That way as each transfer case was brought off the aircraft at Dover, they were equal, and no one could level a charge of favoritism against the White House, something I had discussed with the Pentagon during many calls. However, just before loading the transfer cases into the aircraft, the aircraft commander, a colonel, asked me which case contained Secretary Brown. I told him that was not something I would answer. He reminded me of his rank and my rank, his being much more senior, of course. I simply told him that he could take the matter up with the Pentagon, as that is who I had been communicating with. He left, without retuning my salute. Oh well.

Shortly after returning to the States, I was asked to come up to the Pentagon and deliver a briefing, and then lessons learned. One of the pathologists had noted what he considered a possible gunshot wound to the secretary's head, but it had not been fully investigated. It was an error by the Armed Forces Medical

Examiner, who was trying to get the deceased released, but not a cover-up. There was no gunshot wound. A furor erupted. Senior politicians including Maxine Waters, at the time the head of the Black Congressional Caucus, demanded further investigations (Ron Brown was himself African American), which all came up with the same answer. An accident. The pilots should never have tried to land there, and whether there was pressure or not by the delegation, a similar scenario has played out on many losses, involving senior people and pilots trying to land when they should divert. Yet entire books have been written about the "cover-up," and to this day doubts persist—which is why people like me have to ensure that our words and the context they are spoken or written in is perfectly clear.

Which is not to say the conspiracy theory was completely far-fetched. The most effective ones have some resonance with the truth, and if you study aviation history, there are several examples of murders on planes, as outlandish as that sounds.

In 1987, David Burke, a California ticketing agent for Pacific Southwest Airlines was sacked for filching $69 in onboard drinks receipts. In revenge, he decided to kill the manager who had fired him. The manager commuted daily on a company flight from his home in Los Angeles to San Francisco. Using his security badge to smuggle a pistol on board, Burke boarded the plane and even wrote a note on his sick bag, "Hi Ray. I think it's sort of ironical that we end up like this. I asked for some leniency for my family. Remember? Well, I got none and you'll get none." He then shot his former boss twice twice: the pilots heard the shots, but when the air stewardess entered the cockpit and the captain asked, "What's the problem?" Burke also shot her dead from behind, entered the cockpit, and announced, "I'm the problem." He then killed both pilots and the plane crashed into a rocky hillside above Cayucos, San Luis Obispo. None of the forty-three people aboard the morning commuter flight survived.

Even that strange tragedy has its own eerie precedent. In 1964, a debt-ridden and depressed former member of the Philippines Olympic sailing team, Francisco Gonzales, working in a warehouse in San Francisco, decided the best way to kill himself would be to board a Pacific Air Lines Flight 773 from Reno, Nevada, to San Francisco, with a concealed .357 Magnum, which he would use to kill both pilots. And he did. The plane crashed with all forty-four passengers and crew on board. The last words on the cockpit voice recorder were those of one of the pilots saying: "I've been shot! We've been shot! Oh, my God, help!"

Conspiracy theories have always ridden the slipstream of disaster: the difference is that in the days since 9/11, the internet has allowed them to reach audiences that conspiracy theorists of the yesteryear could only dream of. The attraction of a conspiracy theory is that it affords some sense of insider knowledge, of control, to a person who may otherwise feel overwhelmed in a fast-changing world where the old rules have been swept aside, a world where new threats seem to appear every week. Of course, they have also been wholeheartedly weaponized by terrorist groups, hostile governments, and our own politicians to leverage an electoral or geopolitical edge, and the decline of the old gatekeepers in the media—whose revenues have been destroyed by free online advertising—has merely facilitated this.

So it was that when I was recovering bodies in New Orleans during Hurricane Katrina, where the government's response had been so horribly bungled and more than one thousand people died, the conspiracy theories were already flying. Some residents claimed the levees had been deliberately blown up to drive the African-American population out of the city, while Kenyon was bizarrely accused of complicity in hiding bodies killed by what one very persistent conspiracy theorist called the "Katrina virus," which, as far as I could tell from the deranged letters threatening lawsuits that he sent us, seemed to be something designed to wipe out humanity by 2050, for reasons that remain obscure to me to this day.

Conversely, these days, when the world is afflicted by a very real virus, COVID-19, there are plenty of rumors swirling the globe that it is caused by 5G cell phone towers, or that any proposed vaccinations will be used by Bill Gates to implant microchips to track people's movements.

We live in what is often described as a "post-truth world," where people trust a stranger on Twitter over what they see on the news; where the grief-stricken parents of first-graders shot dead in their own schoolroom are "crisis actors" paid by the deep state to allow the government to take away people's guns. In my experience, however, many of these new conspiracy theories are just old ideas with a new spin and a new media platform.

After all, my very first experience with a mass killing was the Oklahoma City bombing. The Murrah building was destroyed by Timothy McVeigh, an army veteran inspired by the white supremacist novel, *The Turner Diaries*, in which a white man uses a home-made bomb to blow up FBI headquarters. McViegh carried out the attack in retaliation for federal government raids on the Branch Davidian cult headquarters in Waco, Texas, in 1993, and the shooting of Randy Weaver's son, dog and wife, during an attempt to arrest Weaver at Ruby Ridge in Idaho the year before that. Sadly, a Deputy US Marshall William Degan was also killed. In fact the Murrah building was bombed on the two-year anniversary of the horrible end of the Waco raid. Those deaths, where law enforcement operations that went tragically wrong, inflamed the passions of so-called sovereign citizens, paranoid Americans who believe the federal government is essentially tyrannical. These people and their beliefs were largely over-shadowed by global terrorism and the war on terror, but they never went away. They are back and growing in numbers, and their conspiracy theories occasionally merge with other irrational ideas about how the world works. Given the ever-growing frenzy of online hatred, the fever-pitch of conspiracy theorizing, and the success of extremists at weaponizing credulity, it seems not unlikely that one day I will again be pulling dead Americans out of federal buildings or responding to other terrorist attacks. They won't be new, just different location and different time.

11. Preparing for the Next (But Not the Last) Disaster

There are many ways the soon-to-be dead can say their last goodbyes in the modern world.

People caught in the World Trade Center phoned relatives with messages of love and forgiveness, or pleas for help; the doomed passengers of United 93 texted their last words out to the world; the phones on the bodies of teenagers killed in a fire at a Brazilian night club in 2013 still lit up with missed calls from desperate and distraught parents as they were pulled out of the wreckage by firefighters. An Afghan man who leapt to his death rather than face the flames of Grenfell Tower in London in 2017 managed to phone his brother before he jumped and left a heart-rending message: "Goodbye, we are leaving this world now," he said. "I hope I haven't disappointed you. Goodbye to all."

The message I saw in New Orleans in 2005 was low-tech: a letter handwritten by an older couple to their daughter after Hurricane Katrina had pounded the Gulf Coast and a storm surge had caused the city's levees to break. The house was in a poor district, the Ninth Ward, its front wall covered with the scrawl of graffiti left behind by the various search teams who had been looking for survivors.

On the table was the letter, placed in what the elderly couple had assumed would be the safest place for its survival, when they realized their own was increasingly unlikely. Maybe they could have been saved, but the search and rescue operation in New Orleans was such a huge disaster in itself that in all likelihood, they probably never had a chance.

The couple may have already been in poor health when the waters started to rise. It was sweltering hot and the air-conditioning and all the other electronics had gone in the storm: they had no way of communicating with the outside world, and they could not go out into the flood—a murky, foul-smelling mix of river water, sewage, gasoline, and whatever else had leaked into it, not to mention the snakes and gators. The rescue workers called it "toxic gumbo." Even if you could swim, you wouldn't want to chance it in that. They had limited supplies of bottled drinking water. With no TV, phone, or radio they would have had no way of knowing if help was ever coming. Minutes would have felt like hours. They may have had a flashlight or a candle, but the darkness would have still been overwhelming. As the waters steadily rose, over the porch, up the steps to the first floor, they were pushed upstairs. Perhaps they sat through the dark of the first night telling each other, "Tomorrow help will come," but then the next day came and went and no one showed up to rescue them. They would have thought about going to the attic, as many did, but realized they had no tool that would cut through the roof if the waters didn't stop rising, and they would be trapped.

Feeling their hope fade, they wrote their final letter. I was searching the house for any human remains when I picked it up and don't recall the exact wording, but it was, in essence, simple and heartfelt. We found their bodies in the muck that had filled their house, turning a family home into a swamp.

———

ONE OF THE THINGS I tell people is, don't prepare for the last disaster that just occurred. But that was exactly what happened in the streets of New Orleans, choked not only with toxic floodwaters but also with those who saved countless lives: National Guardsmen from Texas, park rangers from Wisconsin, fire-fighting teams from New York City, any number of private security contractors, and the Cajun Navy, volunteers from the surrounding areas. Four years after 9/11, America was still totally geared up for a massive foreign terrorist attack, and the heavily armed forces in New Orleans were better prepared to face Al Qaeda fighters than help the hopeless survivors of the city's Ninth Ward. Police cars and Humvees glided past dead bodies in the streets, not knowing who to report to and lacking the equipment to act themselves. One poor woman was "buried" on the sidewalk outside some restaurants in the French Quarter, covered in a tarp held down with rocks and a scrap of board scrawled with the helpless message, "Here lies Vera, god save us all."

If truth is the first victim of war, then efficient organization is the first casualty of any natural disaster. While bodies were lying in the streets of New Orleans, and exhausted evacuees straggled through the streets of Baton Rouge carrying whatever they had salvaged on their backs, the biggest concern seemed to be security of government responders, as if this was a war zone, not a natural disaster zone. Armed guards were busy guarding the multitude of operations centers. Don't get me wrong, security is important, but the level should match the threat. Security should also be trained how to assist. I saw a couple, asking one of the many security contractors at an operations center how to get help, where they could find shelter: the security guard just barked at them like an automaton: "This is a secure area; you have to move on." On the positive side, each and every time I went in or left one of the operation centers, you can bet my personal computer was verified to ensure I was not stealing a government computer when I left the building.

The rescue and recovery operation fell under the jurisdiction of the Department of Homeland Security, an organization that had been hastily formed by the Bush administration in the days after 9/11. It was stitched together in response to the 9/11 attacks out of twenty-five government agencies from the Nuclear Incident Response Team to the Animal and Plant Health Inspection Service. Into this unwieldy mix was tossed FEMA, which had become a world-class response organization under President Clinton, led by experienced disaster managers. The Federal Emergency Management Agency was tapped to take the lead on flooded New Orleans. From the get-go, it was a terrible organizational match: FEMA is a disaster *response* agency that fell under a disaster *prevention* agency when it became part of Homeland Security in 2003, so most of its resources had been diverted to warding off the next man-made terrorist attack. The last thing that America was ready for was a natural disaster.

At the time, the federal government owned just one portable morgue, which was still in New York City after 9/11. That's why FEMA, whose role is to coordinate national assets, contacted us. I told them I could truck in our mobile morgue unit and a support team. FEMA told us that DMORT would be doing the forensic work, so I sent a small support team with the truck to deliver the morgue to Baton Rouge, an hour's drive north of New Orleans, and about a four-hour drive from us in Houston.

At that point, no one knew how many people had died when the levees broke, but FEMA had already ordered 25,000 body bags, so the scale was clearly going to be big.

What I was not prepared for was the fact that no one seemed to be coordinating the recovery of the dead, and everyone was waiting for someone else to do so. I watched for a week as the morgue and my team were moved from base to base, ending up farther away than if we had stayed in Houston, and never once setting up or doing any work. I had seen the stories of the bodies not being recovered but thought those were one-offs. Seven days after the hurricane hit, I went there myself and asked for a meeting, and told FEMA I was pulling my people back to Houston, adding that they could easily redeploy if needed.

In that meeting—packed with people from FEMA, the military, the public health service, the Louisiana National Guard, state police, and Department of Health—we spent hours discussing how to search homes, offices, and hospitals. There were thousands of places that could hold bodies, most of them private residences. The US Army said they would search by knocking on the door and asking if anyone needed help. Of course, the dead don't typically respond. When asked if they would go into homes to recover bodies, the state was told no: under Title 10 of United States Code, active-duty military can't do that. The DMORT teams, being federal, were also told they were not allowed to do that. Seven days went by as the state waited for the federal government to respond—in keeping with what emergency planners had been teaching—as their own resources were exhausted from rescue and lifesaving, not to mention from the incredible damage suffered by many people to their own property and the risk to their own families. To further complicate matters in Louisiana, which used to be French territory, their legal system is based on the Napoleonic Code, not English

Common Law like the rest of the United States. In short, this meant each parish would need to issue their own death certificates, so the location of recovery mattered. While the storm and flooding did not respect legal boundaries, the process for recovery, identification, and release of the dead had to follow them.

And searches were not going to be easy. Houses were filled with mud that could easily conceal a body. The remains might be in an attic with a barricaded door as the house owner fled the ever-rising waters. Even finding the right house can be difficult as some were moved off their foundations and pushed all over by the floodwaters. The decision was made that a full-scale search would be unlikely for now, and we would start with building a database of people reported missing, and of people reporting sightings of bodies.

At that point in the meeting, the lead person from the Public Health Service asked if we would do recoveries. "Yes," I said, knowing exactly what the next question was going to be.

And that was: "Well, how many can you do in a day?" she said. That is always a really bad question, because the limiting factor is really how many can you find in a day for us to recover? So I responded as many as they could find or send us to. "Five hundred?" she asked. I responded, "Yes." "Can you do five thousand? "Yes," I repeated. "If you can get me five thousand bodies, I'll recover five thousand bodies." Because I knew they couldn't. At this point a couple of my coworkers, guys there who worked for me, looked like they were going to have a heart attack. I explained there were a number of ways we could do this: if there was a neighborhood that was full of bodies, I'd send in a refrigerator truck and collect the bodies there. If there were fewer bodies scattered through a larger area, I'd deploy teams in trucks to bring them back to a central collection point. So they asked when we could begin, and we told them it would take a few days to bring in the numbers of people we need and set up the logistics. They agreed.

At that point, Dr. Lou Cataldie from the Louisiana Department of Health and an outstanding person, I might add, lost it. He yelled at me, "Who the hell are you, and why has no one mentioned you before?" I explained who we were, and that the federal government had brought us in. I had made a courtesy call to his office, but given the general breakdown in communications, it was clear he never got the message. He told me that with or without help he was going to start recovering bodies today, as they had waited too long.

"Fine," I said, "Get a vehicle and we will go with you." So I and a few of our team suited up in PPE—personal protective equipment—loaded up into military trucks and drove off with Dr. Cataldie through the receding floodwaters to one of the downtown hospitals to start our work.

Hurricane Katrina had turned New Orleans into a modern ghost city, its dying nervous system throwing up strange incongruities as we drove through. Downed trees blocked the city's roads, and on the six-lane I-10, cars stood abandoned on the grassy verge: not beaten-up old cars, but pristine new ones, ditched wherever their owners ran out of fuel. For a hundred miles around the stricken city, petrol pumps had either run dry or been commandeered by the police. The lifeblood of the region had been drained.

The huge central artery of Airline Drive had become a deep and tranquil canal, where rescue airboats, more accustomed to cruising Louisiana's swamps, were gliding off in search of survivors, past the golden domes of a MacDonald's that ducked into the brown waters. Skimming across the flooded streets, the bottom of our shallow-draft vessel would bump over the rooftops of submerged cars. Bloated bodies floated facedown in the fetid water, and abandoned, starving dogs howled from rooftops of half-drowned houses, constantly lifting their feet because the tarmac coverings were so hot. In some of the worst hit areas, entire wooden houses had been lifted from their foundations and floated away, leaving gas main bubbling to the surface, sometimes on fire, a hellish spectacle. In the Ninth Ward, desperate police officers had briefly taken over a looted supermarket and turned it into a makeshift base as their own station was inundated: they had moved semis and bales of recycled cardboard boxes to create a secure perimeter and a used a train of shopping carts—one with an American flag jammed into it—as a makeshift gate.

Fire consumed beautiful old wooden houses in the Garden District, and even if there were firefighters on hand, there was no water pressure in the lines for their hoses. Despite hysterical media reports of gangs going on looting rampages and shooting at rescue helicopters, the vast majority of people we passed were desperate citizens sitting outside their houses with cardboard signs that read: "Hungry. Please Help." The looters that were caught were mostly people who had gotten tired of waiting for help and had helped themselves—many of them ended up in a chain-link prison compound erected in the central bus station that Burl Caine, the governor of the notorious Angola prison in Louisiana, had set up after being drafted to deal with miscreants.

That first day we drove with Dr. Cataldie to one of the main hospitals to start picking up bodies. The hospital had been evacuated but the medical staff had left a rudimentary list of where they had left the bodies of patients who'd died before the Army came to move people out. Dr. Cataldie said a body had been left in the MRI room several floors up. We pried the doors of the hospital open and waded through the ankle-deep water of the lobby. People had clearly been living on the mezzanine: we saw abandoned blankets, human waste, cardboard "HELP US" signs, and empty cans of food. The place was like a hothouse, since the emergency generator had been in the basement and had been swamped by the floods, cutting off the air-conditioning on the very first day. The door to the MRI room was locked so I asked Dr. Cataldie if he wanted me to break in. He nodded, so I started to swing a fire ax at the door—I wasn't leaving the place without a body—when one of our police escorts hollered at me to stop. "Wait a minute," the cop said. "you can't take metal around MRIs." For a second, I stared and then said, "That may be true, but my feeling is that the power is off, so I'm going to risk it." I hacked through the wall to the opening mechanism and released the doors. Inside, we found a woman's body, which we carried out on a backboard. Our work in New Orleans had finally begun and would last for several months. Capping off a year that started with the Boxing Day tsunami, progressed through a very difficult plane crash in Cyprus, and was ending with a hurricane.

I HAVE ALWAYS BEEN a fan of the media, I often seen them as partners in response. When I took my daughter to the Apartheid Museum, in Johannesburg, South Africa, I showed her the pictures made famous by a group of award-winning photographers, called the "Bang Bang Club." These pictures showed the post-apartheid violence that took place leading up the first free elections. I explained how at first the photographers were attacked, and then the African National Congress explained to people that without the pictures, the stories would not get out, that the events "wouldn't happen"—that this was why a free press was vital for accountability and making change. So, I was very disappointed one day, when Dr. Cataldie and I were driving around and saw what we thought was a body and a camera crew filming it. The fact they were filming was upsetting, but it was not what bothered us. As we got closer and the film crew fled, we saw it was a mannequin clearly staged to look like an abandoned corpse. What's even worse is that I later saw that same mannequin in several other pictures. This is why some members of law enforcement see the press as the enemy. What I wanted the media to understand is that every time we chase down a report of a "body" we use up valuable resources. Any resources squandered on fake reports could have been used to collect the actual deceased. As for pictures of the deceased, we are very careful, when the media is with us, not to reveal any identifying information. We don't want a family or a child to ever grow up with the last picture they have of their loved one being a body on the cover of some magazine or news report. Even it is not identifiable to the public, it may be to the family.

Hurricane Katrina was the costliest and deadliest hurricane in US history—so far. It submerged about 80 percent of New Orleans, causing some 1,800 deaths and more than $150 billion in damage. Scouring the city, responding to police reports, we came across bodies in all imaginable places: in a Blockbuster video store, the back seat of a car, a church, in a rehab center, a dentist's surgery, one hanging off a fence, and one even tied by a rope to a tree: most likely the person had died waiting to be rescued and neighbors had hitched the body to a tree to prevent it floating off as the floodwaters rose. Many of the bodies were found in places you'd normally expect to find dead bodies: hospital morgues and funeral homes. Those places had been evacuated like everywhere else before staff could take care of the cadavers that a large city produces even on a normal day. Some of the dead had apparently been very old, frail hospital patients who were euthanized—or murdered, according to a later police prosecution—by doctors who knew they would not survive the trauma of evacuation. A year after the disaster, a doctor and two nurses from Memorial Medical Center were arrested and charged with murder for the alleged homicides, but a grand jury later decided not to convict them for their controversial decisions, a reflection on just how hard decisions can be in the wake of such a breakdown in society.

Charges were brought in another homicide case, though, in which some of our own Kenyon employees were called as witnesses. Our people are forensic anthropologists, ex-police and medical examiners, trained in the handling of dead bodies, and they also know that large-scale disasters and mass fatality events can be golden opportunities for bad people to add more bodies to an already large toll, or to hide bodies. That happened at the Danziger Bridge in New Orleans. As the city was collapsing in the days immediately after the levees broke, a group of off-duty police came across an African-American family and opened fire. Perhaps they were amped up because of endless media reports about gangs of Black youths looting and opening fire on rescuers, allegedly seeking revenge on a police force that was frankly not famous for its racially progressive attitude. Whatever their motives, they killed a seventeen-year-old boy and a forty-year-old mentally disabled man who was found to have been shot in the back. Kenyon was summoned to testify in the trial, since we had handled the bodies that had been left behind in the street. We had flagged the bodies as suspicious, since it is not that hard to tell the difference between someone killed by gunshot wounds and someone who drowned. The police officers initially claimed they had been fired upon, but a witness said they had started shooting on the unarmed group "like a firing squad." After two trials, the officers were convicted and jailed.

IN ALL, WE BROUGHT in over 775 bodies, 22 of them in just one day. Every one of them was a tragedy. Then of course there was St. Rita's nursing home, a neat complex of aluminum-sided buildings that looked like the set for a horror movie by the time we arrived.

The building was still stranded from the road running out of the southeastern suburb of Chalmette by about three hundred feet of water. It was wooded country on the edge of the bayou. Cut off from the outside world, the home had kept its grim secret for more than a week after the hurricane hit. We brought in flat-bottom boats and a motorboat to get across the de facto moat around what had once been a secure housing facility for the frail and elderly.

Inside, you could see the last desperate signs of the struggle by elderly patients and their caregivers as the floodwaters rose by six feet in just half an hour: over the front window, a table had been nailed to a window, and wedged in place by an electric wheelchair. An ax lay on the reception desk, hammers and nails next to hastily boarded doors and windows. Electric wheelchairs locked wheels with trolleys, perhaps from the chaotic last minutes of evacuation or perhaps as some kind of Hail Mary barricade against the floodwaters. Stretchers still stood at the doorway, together with mattresses that had been used in a desperate attempt to float patients out.

The owners of the nursing home had believed they were facing just another tropical storm like others they had ridden out: they stocked up on generators, food and water, and argued, not unreasonably, that a lengthy and strenuous evacuation of frail, bedridden patients, some of whom were in their eighties and nineties, could actually cause deaths.

It was a fatal miscalculation, and they were completely unprepared for the wall of water that swallowed their property.

The twenty-four patients who managed, with the help of nurses and staff, to get onto the roof as the rooms filled with water were eventually rescued by boat; the bedridden and wheelchair-bound drowned, screaming for help.

Our teams tread through almost a foot of thick mud that carpeted everything; clouds of mosquitoes swarmed all over. The fact that this had once been a clean and by all accounts well-managed medical facility made the filth all the more striking. One of the elderly patients was found in the thick mud on the floor, wrapped in a shower curtain. Another elderly lady was found draped across her wheelchair.

We found a number of bodies in other nursing homes and senior living facilities across the city—they were, after all, the most vulnerable citizens of New Orleans. But St. Rita's was by far the most shocking scene and the deaths there resulted in a protracted court battle that the owners ultimately won, arguing that they had been prepared for a hurricane, not for the catastrophic collapse of the city's levees.

Even those who managed to make it out of the drowned city, after days of hunger and thirst in the reeking heat of the Houston Astrodome and New Orleans Convention Center, were not assured of survival. When Army helicopters finally started flying thousands of exhausted survivors to Louis Armstrong airport, medical teams set up triage centers to try to save those who weren't already too far gone after days without medicine for diabetes, high blood pressure, or any of the other chronic health problems the stranded were suffering from.

At the airport on the outskirts of New Orleans, exhausted doctors improvised colostomy bags out of plastic shopping bags and duct tape, using baggage carts to transport those deemed too sick to save to quieter hallways, where volunteers sat with them as they passed away. Many died there in the first few days; thirteen thousand people passed through the airport on the first day alone of the evacuation, dropped off by wave after wave of Army helicopters. For many the terminal was just that—a terminus. An extra morgue unit was set up at the airport to accommodate those who survived the initial disaster but succumbed to the chaos that followed.

WE CARRIED ON WORKING for months after the flooding. As we finished up our work, a new hurricane, Rita, was already bearing down on the Gulf Coast. That year was the most active US hurricane season on record at that point: our journey back to Houston was slow and arduous because as we approached the city, hundreds of thousands of people were fleeing the path of the storm. Not surprisingly, given what had just hit New Orleans, Rita saw the biggest hurricane evacuation ever, with as many as four million people scrambling to get out of the way. Then, a few weeks later, Wilma hit the Caribbean and Florida, and according to flood records, damaging the house my husband and I now own in Key West.

I never found out if the letter that the dying parents wrote ever made it to their daughter: we passed it on to the authorities, but I fear it may have gotten lost in the chaos and the dirty water that filled the city's streets.

12. Known Only to God—And Science

haven't always been in the business of recovering lost bodies and bringing them to light. I used to also hide them.

One of the things that has always bothered me is the high number of unidentified dead in the world, along with the equally high number of missing persons. Part of this problem is lack of training for first-line responders. Bodies and the locations where they are recovered from often contain a lot of information. But just like learning and understanding a foreign language, it requires skill and practice to see and understand that information, the nuances and the subtle things that make a big difference. In many cases it also requires dogged determination to chase down the many potential roads that this information leads to.

When I was in school studying Criminology, we were just starting to learn about the US FBI Behavioral Sciences Unit, a unit that was trying to understand serial killers. Much of their work was from taken from examining the scene and also the deceased, to gain insight into the hows and whys of the killings. I think it is important that there are opportunities for first responders to learn before starting. Unfortunately, those are limited, and because of that we pay the price.

I used to train law enforcement officers in ways to search

for and recover concealed bodies, usually murder victims. The bodies I used were real, supplied by people who had agreed to donate their mortal remains to science. I would hide them the way most killers would—in a shallow grave, and usually buried whole, because it's a lot of work to dismember a cadaver and extremely messy to boot. Murderers, in my experience, don't usually have an inclination toward hard work. But they do have patterns and deliberate, predictable behavior. You just have to look.

Fortunately now, there are body farms, where dozens of bodies at a time are exposed, or left in water, or partially covered, all so that scientists can study the process of decay. Viewed by some as macabre or as even a desecration of the dead, they are incredibly important to forensic research. They have helped forensic experts pinpoint the exact time of death—a key plank in any legal defense or conviction—by studying the release of gases emitted by bacteria feeding on a corpse, or the development stages of blow fly larvae which feed on decomposing flesh. By examining the exact chemicals given off by decaying bodies, they have aided police in the detection of the missing. When I started in this business there was only one: now there are half a dozen or so tucked away in well-protected spots across the world. The hard part is that few law enforcement officers attend them, and while they benefit from the research, I think they would benefit more from taking practical workshops there. Seeing a dead person for the first time, especially one that is decomposed or has suffered some type of trauma is difficult and can be a lot to process. The shock of seeing a body, the smell, and sounds can divert a person's attention, causing them to miss key elements or details of the scene. It is not the norm to see dead bodies in the condition we often do, so people often freeze for a moment, not sure how to react; some get sick and others withdraw. However, repeated exposure reduces that shock. When the first exposure can be done in a controlled environment, people have support, can be somewhat prepared, and therefore better able to manage a scene in the field. I think it is so hard, because we are looking at something we can all relate to and that is another human being, and for many people their first thoughts are that this could be them or someone they know.

Sometimes when a new body farm is opening, I am asked to write a letter attesting to their importance in order to secure backing from local authorities, who may be wary of the unusual nature of these study centers.

They have a fascinating origin. The first one was set up in 1972 after a forensic anthropologist, Dr. Bill Bass, in Tennessee was asked to inspect the grave of a Civil War officer. The police had noticed the tomb appeared to have been disturbed and the body inside looked suspiciously pink-fleshed and intact: they believed that a murderer might have dumped a fresh deceased into a century-old grave. But analysis of the corpse's teeth and clothing revealed that it was in fact Lieutenant Colonel William Shy, who had been incredibly well preserved because of a well-sealed iron casket and skilled embalming. Clearly, more work was needed on the process of postmortem decay, and the first facility dedicated to observing bodies decay in various environments, from open fields and shallow graves to water tanks and car trunks, was set up. As I did my job over the years, I realized how much it was needed. I once spoke with a detective, after a class I had taught, and he wanted to show me some pictures and get my opinion on them. The photos were of a badly damaged body found in the mountains of Northern California, considered to be a victim of bear attack. While I agreed that the remains had been scavenged, my concern was the ligature marks that were evident in the picture indicated human involvement. I have never seen a case of an animal using material to strangle a human.

While I understand the aversion to having real bodies for research and training, it is an important tool both for health care and forensic education. From a physical reaction standpoint, the same neural systems involved in facial recognition are the same neural systems that are involved in processing traumatic memories. This is why we don't support or use visual identifications as a means of forensic identification. It doesn't work, something I have to explain or argue about far too often. So, when people see a body to identify it or to process a scene, it can be traumatic, and trauma has the capacity to disrupt the processing of contextual information. People miss things.

Almost as important as the recovery of the deceased is the gathering of information about how they died. People want to know what happened and they want the truth. When you look at how families, especially over multiple generations, deal with the uncertainty of not knowing specifically what happened to a loved one, it is clear that the journey they take as they cross their own personal bridge is often very different from families who had definitive information about their deceased loved one. In others words, it is much harder for families when they don't have answers or information, when a person just vanishes or no information is provided. Imagine what it is like for a family member to leave for work one day and just not come home? To be told something has happened, but not much else is horrible, and leaves more unknown than known. When this happens, what the mind can conjure for the unknown is often found to be far more worse than what actually happened.

We spent a little bit of time drafting considerations about family involvement and potential outcomes for the government of New Zealand to consider as they were discussing reentry in the Pike River Mine. In November 2010, the Pike River mine suffered a horrific methane gas explosion. Twenty-nine miners were classified as missing and presumed dead, not least because

three other blasts occurred in the weeks after the initial explosion. But no one knows for sure, because no one has actually been
able to access the area of the mine they were working in. Now,
nearly a decade later, a new recovery mission is underway. While
many had said that the miners' bodies might never be recovered,
to the families that was unacceptable. Part of the Labour Party
campaign in 2017, seven years after the disaster, was the prom-
ise to establish the Pike River Recovery Agency, a government-
funded agency that would study if and how the mine could be
reentered. Sadly, though, this will not be like the rescue of thirty-
three Chilean miners trapped by a collapse in the San José Mine
just three months before the Pike River explosion.

What concerned me, however, was the impact it might have
on family members if the recovery team found evidence that any
of the miners survived the initial explosions. What if they found
a camp, like the one those miners in Chile had? What if someone less experienced was in charge of the mission and decided
the knowledge might be too hard for the families to take? In
these kinds of situations, what is found must be presented to the
families with complete honesty. As long as it is information each
family wants, they should be told before the political leaders, the
media, or the world—whether the miners survived the explosion
and died over time or were killed in the initial blasts. That means
having well-trained teams, free of political interference. There is
no hidden message here; I am not implying interference happens in New Zealand. I think they have a very good system and
people. I am simply stating what can and does happen at times
in the world. It is amazing how often families don't get the right
information, because they don't have the opportunity to speak to
the people who are part of the recovery operations.

About two years after making the recoveries in the loss of
CT-43, the crash that killed Secretary of Commerce Ron Brown,

I got a call from the Armed Forces Medical Examiner (AFME). I was no longer at Fort Lee or commander of the 54th at that time: I was at a new Army assignment, this time in California. The AFME had been speaking to the parents of a young woman killed in that crash, and they had thought that, because of the location where her body had been found, she had survived the crash and been crawling to get help and had died under some brush several hundred yards away from the impact point—alone, cold, and in pain. I could understand that; they had not been to the scene. They had carried that painful thought for over two years. One person did survive the crash but succumbed to their injuries shortly afterward in the hospital. I always explain those deaths as people who in died in the crash, just not at the same time as everyone else, because no matter the level of care, some injuries simply can't be survived. Some people take longer than others to succumb.

As part of our recovery operations, we had mapped the recovery location. Distance, elevation, etc. We did not have a seat map, so we did not know the likely positions people would have been in in the aircraft, but we did know the recovery location. As noted earlier, this plane hit a mountain and came to rest in pieces on the mountain and across small valleys or hillocks. The force of the impact dispersed seats and bodies forward of the point of impact, as we would expect. This young woman had been recovered where gravity had taken her mortal remains. I got on the phone with the parents and walked them through the recovery from the notes I had taken and provided to the Army. The parents were lovely people, who like others have been active in associations geared toward not only safety improvements but also ensuring that in the United States the family assistance laws apply to government-owned aircraft. Nonetheless, it was frustrating to think that I could have answered their questions so much sooner and maybe prevented some of that torment.

To find the body of a missing loved one is to find the definitive answer to the most fundamental question in life: "Is the person I loved gone forever?" You may not like the answer, but at least you have it and can begin to process it. But not having a body, and therefore being tormented by that slim hope or doubt, is the most painful thing that can happen.

Beyond the mass fatality events and the people who go missing as individuals, there are the prior conflicts or the war dead. We live in an age of changing and often disruptive technology, and DNA identification is at the forefront of these changes. As we saw with Sidney Leslie Goodwin, forensic science can now reach deep into the past to identify the dead. Wars we hope will no longer produce "unknown soldiers," and even some of the unknown soldiers of the past conflicts were actually not that unknown.

Around 7,700 US troops are still listed as MIA, or Missing in Action, from the Korean War, which began in 1950 and ended three years later. Some of them have recently been brought home, their belated repatriation a side effect of the brief thaw in US–North Korea relations. This is something the Army, as the lead in this area, has been planning and trying to do for many years. Access is the only limiting factor. The Defense Department's $80 million forensic lab in Honolulu, run by the Defense POW/MIA Accounting Agency has familial DNA references for 92 percent of the dead soldiers. The war was recent enough for close family members, mostly children at the time, to still be alive to offer up genetic material. By contrast, only 4 percent of the 72,000 service members still unaccounted from World War II have genetic material waiting to be matched.

As the Second World War was ending, the military spent years consolidating temporary cemeteries into larger ones, and if requested by the families at the time, repatriating the bodies of identified people back to their hometowns. The harder ones were those that could not be identified or had disappeared into concentration camps or were executed while in captivity. Many of those were interred as unknowns.

Today, for recoveries from prior conflicts, research is the first step before any planned recovery mission. Many militaries around the world have large archives of unit diaries, records of battles, and location of losses. Many of these are declassified now, and in addition, those working for the government, families, and military associations can now routinely access that information. And they do. Then it gets tricky.

For many years, especially in the United States, the DOD and specifically the lab in Hawaii operated as unchecked authority with the final say over what prior conflict recoveries are done. No matter the research provided by families, the military operated under the position that the recovery of prior conflict dead was their responsibility. I think I understand that, and more important, the motives behind it. In the military, the idea of not bringing everyone home is an abomination. Drilled into every leader at every level is the accountability for their people. First question I asked my subordinates as commander, and the same one I ask now when I send people out and they return, is: What is the count? Is everyone accounted for? Therefore, some in DOD can see it as a failing, if the family has to make the recovery. For others, though, it is about the bureaucracy and their job is to protect the system, their system. There is also a fear that as more recoveries are made, mistakes will be uncovered, and that is probably the biggest decision driver. What the Department of Defense is missing, and I have seen it before, is that mistakes will be tolerated, and people have even come to expect them. Given the limited technology, the sheer volume of deceased that were recovered and buried at the end of World War II is amazing, but it was not without mistakes. And it is never one mistake, because if one identification is wrong, then it has likely resulted in another wrong identification. What is hard for people is the idea that they are being stonewalled.

For the families, time is running out, and they see themselves as part of the solution. Sadly, the cases in which the families have had success, for the most part have been when they have taken the US government to court. At times I am asked to provide examples of what is possible. For instance, I was recently asked to provide information to the families of seven US service members who were killed during the Japanese invasion of the Philippines in 1941. You might think that, given the high profile of these fighting men—one of them was the first soldier to be awarded the Medal of Honor in World War II, another was the only US general ever executed by the enemy—more would have been done to identify them. But no, the seven men, including one who survived the notorious Bataan Death March only to die in a POW camp, are believed to be buried in the Manila American Cemetery in what used to be Fort McKinley, near Manila, their graves simply marked "Unknown."

The families have spent years researching, talking to survivors of the men's units, poring over military burial records—to be able to identify the graves where they believe their loved ones lie. But the military is currently refusing to disinter them, partly because of its innate bureaucracy, and partly due to the fact that one of them, twenty-three-year-old Lieutenant Alexander "Sandy" Nininger, had previously been exhumed and the test of his remains were inconclusive. However, as we saw in the case of the little boy from the *Titanic,* older DNA testing can yield blurry results on even older bodies, and the accuracy of the techniques is constantly evolving.

Nininger was a hero by any standard you might want to apply. He rushed to the aid of a unit under heavy attack, defending the line with his rifle and grenades against Japanese sniper fire before being killed himself. The Medal of Honor was awarded posthumously. His death is still a painful memory for his surviving nephew, John Patterson, who last saw him when he was about to head off to war in 1942. "He was the hero of my life," Patterson, now an old man, told the press recently. "I was six when he died, and I remember the reaction of my mother to the news that he had been killed. She was just hysterical. Really I don't think she was ever the same because they were very close."

Despite the ethos of "never leave a man behind," a noble sentiment, for some the reality of it is a vast, slow-moving bureaucratic machine, institutionally averse to decisions that might stir controversy or rock the boat. This case is still tied up in the courts.

This is not something particular to just the United States, not even close. When I ask people when they think the last World War II cemetery was opened, they usually hazard a guess of sometime in the 1950s, or maybe the 1970s at the latest. No. The latest mass internment of German war dead was in 2019, when 1,837 more soldiers were laid to rest in the Rossoschka German War Cemetery not far from Volgograd. Another cemetery opened in 2000 is located near the western Russian city of Smolensk, the scene of a major battle during the Nazi invasion of the Soviet Union in 1941. Only half of the 30,000 soldiers buried there so far have been identified. The reason Germany is still burying its dead fighters from the Eastern Front is that they had no access to the area until the fall of the Berlin Wall in 1989. Three years later, the German war graves commission started working with Russia's post-Soviet authorities to locate and identify their dead: since then, they have found a staggering 800,000 bodies. The Dukhovschina cemetery, near Smolensk, will eventually be the final resting place of 70,000

German soldiers, larger than the German war cemeteries in northern France and Belgium.

The main reason Germany is now able to properly bury their dead is because recovering missing human remains has always been as much dependent on political and legal constraints as physical ones. Wartime history can be hard to bear for modern countries and can be positively toxic for politicians to get too close to. For instance, when Japanese prime minister Shinzo Abe visited the Yasukuni Shrine to Japan's war dead in 2013, he walked into a firestorm of criticism because it is seen by China—which lost millions in the war with Japan—as a symbol of Japanese imperial aggression. For the same reason, Japan has only recently started searching the Pacific Islands where it fought the United States for the bodies of its missing soldiers.

Another reason for these recoveries, reburials, and identifications is that scientific progress—what remains might feasibly be identified—has has succeeded in weakening the prior government inclination to simply let bodies "rest in peace," even while relatives are tormented by years of not having a grave to visit.

One of the most striking cases of this was the long, posthumous journey of Air Force First Lieutenant Michael John Blassie. In May 1972 Blassie was a twenty-four-year-old combat pilot, flying his Dragonfly tactical bomber to attack North Vietnamese troops besieging South Vietnamese forces at An Loc, in the south of the war-torn country. During the mission, antiaircraft fire struck his wing and he crashed in an area crawling with enemy soldiers. It was five months before the South Vietnamese retook the area and US Mortuary Affairs could retrieve the body, by then reduced by the tropical heat and environment to just a few bones and scraps of a parachute.

It seemed to be Blassie, but another US aircraft had been downed in the same area, so the remains were shipped back to

Hawaii labeled only "BTB (Believed To Be) Michael Blassie." Their official designation by the US Army's Central Identification Laboratory was simply X-26.

In 1973, as the war was winding down after the Paris Peace Accords, Congress approved funding for a new monument to the men who had fought and died in South Asia. What they needed to complete the memorial, however, was an unknown soldier to place in the tomb on the Washington Mall in the nation's capital, between the memorials to the World War II dead and the fallen of Korea.

Finding a candidate was not such a simple task since forensic methods of identifying human remains had advanced. So it wasn't until May 1984, fourteen years after his death, that they settled on the remains of Lieutenant Blassie as the one who would be carried through the nation's capital on an Army caisson and have a twenty-one gun salute rendered over his coffin. His casket was shipped across the Pacific Ocean to Hawaii in the helicopter hangar of the USS *Brewton*: for the whole of the seven-day voyage, sailors and Marines mounted a death watch over the casket. Wherever you go, most unknown soldiers are always under armed guard, a symbolic compact with men who made the ultimate sacrifice that they will never be alone, nor will their tombs ever be desecrated.

Lieutenant Blassie was now Vietnam's unknown soldier, even though the military sort of knew who he was. As with the little boy in the *Titanic* grave, doubts nevertheless persisted: investigative journalists traced the journey of the remains back to the area around An Loc and alerted the Blassie family to the body's likely true identity. On May 13, 1998, the grave was opened, and the bones removed for mitochondrial DNA testing. Those tests proved once and for all who the fallen soldier really was. Two months later, Lieutenant Blassie's body was interred by his family in his hometown of St. Louis. Vietnam no longer had an unknown US soldier.

From when Britain first designated one of its nine million dead or missing after World War I as "unknown," and laid his remains to rest in Westminster Abbey, until the Falklands-Malvinas War, this soldier remained the only dead British soldier to return home from that "war to end all wars." Soldiers of the United Kingdom were buried close to where they fell, in Belgium, northern France, or in graveyards scattered around the sprawling theaters of various conflicts. But that does not mean they are forgotten or unattended. Even today, a full century after the guns fell silent in World War I, the traffic still stops every night at 8:00 p.m. at the Menin Gate in Ypres, Belgium. Then buglers play the "Last Post"—a ceremony repeated every night since 1928, except during the German occupation in World War II. The Menin Gate contains the names of all British and Commonwealth solders missing in World War I. I have been there several times; it is a touching experience. Every so often you will see a name has been removed, as a soldiers' body is recovered and identified. You will also see many small plastic red poppies, placed by different names, along with handwritten notes to long-lost family members. Over time, the British government has learned that families would prefer a choice whether or not to leave their loved ones in far-off battlefields.

Following World War II, Lorna Wingate, the widow of British Major General Orde Wingate, a colorful character who led the Chindits special forces behind Japanese lines in Burma and who died in a plane crash in India in 1944, petitioned Lord Mountbatten to have his remains disinterred and brought home for a family burial. Despite the two having served and worked together, Lord Mountbatten—the uncle of Queen Elizabeth II who was killed decades later by an IRA bomb planted on his fishing boat—replied that it was the policy of the British government that General Wingate's remains should stay there. Ironically, his remains were moved twice, ending up not at home but in Arlington National Cemetery, in the United States, one of about sixty or so non-Americans to be interred there. He was on a US Army Air Corps plane, with a US crew. Immediately after the crash, the local villagers buried the bodies in a common grave and later reported them as commingled and unrecognizable. In 1947 the British government moved all of the bodies to a common grave at Imphal War Cemetery, a Commonwealth Military Cemetery in India. Then in 1950, while the US military was still working on recovery around the globe, the common grave was disinterred because there were Americans in the crash, and all remains were moved to Arlington.

13. Mass Graves and Conflict Zones

There were hundreds of bodies lined up on racks in the abandoned salt mines just outside Tuzla. Some were in body bags, some just wrapped up in plastic. It was cold, the winter of 1995, and that helped keep the smell of decay to a minimum. Not like Haiti, where you could find the morgue just by closing your eyes and following your nose.

One of the Bosnian policemen who had accompanied me on my trip to the mine pointed at the rows of the dead, arranged on wooden shelves that had been lined up against the hewn walls of the ancient tunnels, many without a name attached to them or anything that might indicate how they had ended up there. At the time I was the commander of the 54th Quartermaster Company (MA) assigned to establish a Mortuary Affairs Collection Point for the US Army in Tuzla, where the US forces were establishing their bases. "When are you going to help us out with this?" the police officer asked. I looked at him and could only shrug. "Sorry, it's not our business," was all I could say.

Tuzla, like much of the region, had taken a beating; people were tired. The peacekeeping missions had largely failed, not because of the peacekeepers but because of the politics, and the dead from bombings, and mass executions—murders really—had started to pile up. This time around, unlike Haiti, the 54th had been sent into the Balkans well ahead of the main units shortly after NATO had agreed to forces on the ground. The Dayton Accords had been signed just before Thanksgiving 1995. My soldiers were told the holidays were canceled and we shipped off at a few hours' notice, first to Germany with all our morgue equipment, then straight to Tuzla, the third largest city in Bosnia, famous for its ancient salt mines and still recovering when we arrived from heavy bombardment by the Serbs. My Mortuary Affairs unit arrived to a base still occupied by Swedish and other Scandinavian troops who had been part of the failed UN peacekeeping mission.

From the start, it was clear that NATO was there to ensure that the deaths stopped—a hugely important and at times a difficult task. Rebuilding the country and creating a lasting peace was going to be someone else's job.

No one in the alliance's command structure had given much—if any—thought to what they should do with the human debris of the worst conflict on European soil since the Second World War. My instructions were simple: identify and repatriate any NATO service members who died carrying out their duties enforcing the Dayton Accords, and do the same for the occasional foreign aid worker who died in a country bereft of any medical official who could legally write up a death certificate or evacuate a body back home. (Even repatriating the bodies of non-NATO personnel often got me grief from my chain of command, such is the rigidity of the military.)

My concern was that lasting peace in the Balkans had always proven elusive. I get it, I was a soldier, and followed the lawful commands of those above me. But it was frustrating to watch. By this time, I had seen death on a random basis, be it an accident, a terror attack, or homicides. But here in the Balkans, death was on an industrial scale, something I had only ever read about, something I could have once caused myself if I had launched my missiles. Like many, I thought this was a thing of the past. But it wasn't, it was 1995 and right here in front of us. Our leaders didn't seem to grasp or want to understand that without dealing with the dead—without helping the bereaved and displaced find answers about their missing loved ones—we were only marking time, delaying the grieving and the ultimate recovery of a country torn to shreds by internecine war. The people who had drafted the peace accords only wanted to look forward, not back and admit to the horrors they had been party to. And one of the key elements of looking back was the care of the dead.

Just as naming and returning the dead to their loved ones is a vital part of healing after a plane crashes or after natural disaster strikes, the same process on a mass scale can help heal a war-torn country, especially one peppered with mass graves full of unanswered questions. Many who have lost their entire family and have no idea where their bodies are, don't want to "forget about it and move on." The US and NATO high command seemed to be largely copying the model of Marshall Tito, the World War II Communist partisan leader who went on to lead Yugoslavia for decades. I found that troubling. His model had been to ignore the past conflicts. He was a great force for unifying the country, but it was only held together by a military force, not a model for long-term success or being the right way. But whenever I brought up the issues of mass graves, nobody wanted to get involved. I pointed out that when there is a body you have an answer to the most fundamental question that anyone can ask after a conflict: Is my loved one dead? How did they die? Where? And with answers, people can start to transition to the recognition that life has changed. Sure, it doesn't work for some, but for many, it does. However, without a body most can't even begin that process, stuck in a violent and painful past, victims of endless rumors and speculation: "Oh, I last saw your son in a camp, so maybe he's still alive."

When I got to Bosnia in 1995, people were still chasing rumors of hidden camps where these missing people were allegedly still being held, alive, because there were so many who had disappeared—forty thousand of them. People asked, where could they all be? They couldn't *all* have been killed . . . could they? People knew it had been a brutal, dehumanizing conflict, but still, the human mind is slow to grasp the scale of such horrors and quick to cling to some desperate hope.

Why we didn't want to get involved, I am not sure. It might have been out of a sense of collective guilt or shame. There are those who say, if it's not your country, then it's not your business. I don't agree. With the great power that many countries hold comes great responsibility. After World War II, many countries had said after the Holocaust, "Never Again." But then we sat by and let it happen, again and again, and this time we didn't even have the tensions of the Cold War to blame. We sat by and watched as 800,000 people were butchered with machetes in Rwanda. We wrung our hands as concentration camps and massacres appeared across the Balkans and President Clinton watched in horror as Somali gunmen pulled the charred corpses of a Black Hawk helicopter crew through the streets of Mogadishu and asked, "How can people do this?" So, we looked away, closing our eyes to the very darkest side of human nature. The decision to bomb Bosnian Serb positions in 1995 and bring an end to the war was a good start, but it came years too late. By then people just didn't want to know about the dead. So we ignored them. Meanwhile, I'd see people we suspected of being wanted war criminals walking around the streets of Bosnia, but we had no mandate at that point to do anything about it. Whenever I raised this point with my superiors, I was told, "Captain, that is not our role."

Tito, made it a country that many saw as a success, a bridge or cross between a communist government, but one with some open market reforms and the western governments, despite the early years of repression and murders of dissidents. Many people will remember the 1984 Winter Olympics in Sarajevo. It sure as hell looked very different when I was there eleven years later. Tito had kept a lid on the seething ethnic and nationalist resentments between Bosnians, Serbs, Croats, and Slovenians; Christians and Muslims; simply by repressing any talk about ethnic identity and, of course, killing those that opposed him. This suppression of old resentments—for example, the Croats had sided with the Nazis in World War II while the Serbs had paid a heavy price for resisting the German invasion—served its purpose while he was alive. However, just about twelve years after his death and the fall of the Berlin Wall, all of those generational hatreds had burst forth in a series of wars across the Balkans, an eerie echo of the conflicts that the century had started with, and which had ultimately triggered World War I. And those old hatreds didn't suddenly go away because there were American and NATO troops on the streets of Tuzla and Sarajevo: don't forget, there had been UN soldiers, a Dutch contingent, protecting the alleged "safe zone" of Srebrenica when General Ratko Mladic's Bosnian Serb forces marched in with no resistance and took away eight thousand Muslim men to be butchered. And no one was being held accountable. Wherever I went in the Balkans in the years after the war ended, all I ever met were victims—everyone told me their side was the innocent and injured party. Everyone had lost someone, but it was always the others who carried out the atrocities in the civil war. The old enmities continued to bubble away, the corpses were slowly pieced together, buried with no names on their gravestones and no real place for the brutalized people of Bosnia to grieve and mourn.

On occasion, I would go and check out some of the mass graves myself, just to get the lay of the land in case the order did ever come for us to do something about it. Driving around the war-ravaged countryside, I noticed how few young or middle-aged men there were: they had either been killed or they had fled. We'd drive through villages that had been completely de-stroyed, or villages that were empty because of the number of the mines still hidden in the ground. Sometimes a town was completely intact except for one or two houses that had been destroyed, and you knew that they had once been occupied by families from the wrong ethnic group. Sometimes we would cross what had until recently been a front line between warring factions and be confronted by a "poor-man's roadblock": a mi-litiaman in mismatched combat fatigues who had put an anti-tank mine in the road would tell us we couldn't cross. I'd have to remind him that I had a radio and could call in significantly more firepower, and there would be no question about who was going to win the argument.

Once in a while I would fly down to Sarajevo to visit the var-ious coalition headquarters offices, one of which was in the same hotel that Archduke Franz Ferdinand of Austria had set out from the morning of his fatal tour of the city on 28 June 1914. Driving around the streets, I'd see trenches, the defensive lines where Bosnian fighters had spent years in the freezing cold, and it reminded me of the World War I battlefields I'd read about. At those times, I'd wonder about how much we had actually learned in the eighty years since Gavrilo Princip shot the archduke. I also realized that the phrases "never again" or "it can't happen here" were more wishful thinking than reality and that if we are not careful, it is really not that hard to descend into chaos and war.

Fortunately, in 1995, there was group determined to resolve the issues of mass death in the Balkans. Dr. William Haglund, an American forensic anthropologist who headed the NGO Physicians for Human Rights, was determined to bring the perpetrators of the Srebrenica massacre to justice. I and many others in my field consider Haglund one of the pioneers of the use of forensic anthropology in death investigations and the prosecution of war crimes. He was incredibly single-minded in his work, even camping out near the mass graves he was working on in order to prevent anyone trying to hide or tamper with the evidence. He and his team at PHR started the slow and painstaking process of excavating and analyzing, years amassing the evidence that finally helped put Bosnian Serb leader Radovan Karadzic and his top general, Ratko Mladic, behind bars for life in The Hague. But the task of identifying a million bones strewn across the Balkans was simply too large a job for any single NGO. And monk-like dedication to the task is not enough in such a politically charged environment, where bitter feuds still linger, and former deadly rivals have to be cajoled into working together. That takes considerable diplomatic and political skill, because if a particular government feels it is being unfairly treated or discriminated against, it can simply shut down an excavation and the investigators are left with nothing. Something more needed to be done.

In 1996, President Bill Clinton—perhaps haunted by the delay in executing what turned out to be a highly successful military intervention in Bosnia—called for the establishment of the International Commission on Missing Persons (ICMP), which would set up several centers across the Balkans to collect and DNA test the hundreds of thousands of bones of unidentified missing people from the four-year war.

Four years after I had been deployed with the US military, I returned to Bosnia with Kenyon to help establish the protocols and processes that the ICMP would need to launch such a mammoth task. We deployed full-time and part-time forensics experts, who went on to train local staff to take over their jobs and do the work themselves after they had left, because ultimately it was a problem the people of the Balkans would have to solve for themselves. Each nation wanted their dead identified by their own people because, ultimately, they didn't trust anyone else.

I went back to the tunnel outside Tuzla that I had visited during my Army deployment. It was still full of bodies, though I could not say for sure they were the same ones I had seen before. And they were not the only ones. All across Bosnia, there were storehouses for unclaimed bodies, often bare concrete buildings with broken windows in which shelves of bodies in plastic body bags, or body parts in cloth sacks, had been stacked. Thousands and thousands of them. The equipment that was being used to examine and identify them was bare basic: I found human skulls on metal tables with little more than a brush to clean them off. We had to build new facilities, equip them to modern standards, and train people in forensic sciences. But one of the key elements of the work was political.

If we dug up a grave in Bosnia, we had to dig up one in Serbia and one in Croatia, because while the Bosnian Serbs were arguably the perpetrators of the worst atrocities, they weren't the only ones to fill mass graves. We had to excavate regardless of ethnicity or nationality, or who might blame whom—that is how the political and legal backing necessary to actually do the legwork of recovering the dead is obtained. And they can only be identified with the support of the local population because you have to reach out to ordinary people to gather antemortem DNA samples in order to actually put names on the deceased. I spent a week traveling around the region, meeting with political community leaders, quietly marveling that everyone claimed to have been simply an innocent victim of someone else's aggression. Each meeting started the same way, a cup of tea and the words, "You must understand, we are the victims here."

The ICMP grew and grew. Today the organization has now identified 70 percent of the missing whose bodies were dumped in mass graves and pits across the Balkans, including 98 percent of the victims from the Srebrenica massacre. The DNA testing techniques it pioneered in Bosnia's death pits made it one of the cutting-edge institutions to identify victims of wars, mass migrations, and natural disasters, and its forensics experts have now been drafted in to work on many of the same disasters that I have, including Hurricane Katrina and, in 2004, the Asian tsunami. The organization has outgrown former Yugoslavia and has a new permanent headquarters in The Hague. The knowledge base of its staff has expanded so much that in recent years, they have been called on to identify the badly burned remains of people who died in California's wildfires and are currently working on the unknown bodies left behind in the wake of the 2015 migrant exodus, when a million people fled the wars and famines in Syria, Libya, and sub-Saharan Africa to try to reach Europe by land or perilous sea crossing, one of the largest mass movements of refugees in history.

While ICMP is one of the largest such groups, there are many others working on cases of the disappeared. They are very active in Latin America. I have worked with some providing training and suggestions. When I retire, I hope to be able to lend some help. One of the most promising and tragic identification projects is the case of the children who went missing during the civil war in El Salvador. Children were taken by the government from their parents; sometimes the parents were killed, sometimes not. The children were then placed out for adoption to other families and often told their parents had died when they in fact had not. Now those children are adults, and the parents are looking for them. A program was started to collect DNA from the parents, and children who believe they may have been kidnapped can submit their DNA. The program started in 1994, and by 1996 it had arranged twenty-nine reunions.

One thing I learned from projects like these is that the right to an identity is a basic human right. What was most disturbing and frustrating about Bosnia's mass graves was that the killers often dismembered the corpses and spread the pieces and personal possessions in different mass graves, both to exacerbate the pain of the bereaved—so it was as though their loved ones had never even existed—but also to try to cover their own tracks.

Saddam Hussein, by contrast, was quite a neat mass murderer: he at least left the bodies of his victims intact, even though there were hundreds of thousands of them. His executions lined them up to make the mass shootings more efficient, but that also made the exhumation simpler after he was eventually toppled. That should have made their recovery less complex than Bosnia. But then as I was soon to discover, Iraq was its own set of complex and maddening problems.

ROUTE TAMPA WAS THE US military's name for the highway that ran south out of Baghdad, a straight shot through the desert past Babylon, on to the port of Basra in the Gulf, and ultimately to Kuwait, the main rear base of the US military alliance.

Route Tampa also led directly through Saddam Hussein's old killing fields, the place where he had tried to hide the bodies— except he hadn't tried very hard, since the Iraqi dictator wanted his people to know precisely what happened if you stood up against him. You ended up being led, bound and blindfolded, into a field and shot in the back of the head on the lip of the shallow grave that would hold your remains. If you were lucky, they wouldn't torture you first. If you were really lucky, none of your family was forced to share the same pit.

In the weeks and months following the fall of his regime in April 2003, thousands of people were marching along Route Tampa and the side roads that wound through the palms tree and rice fields, along sluggish tree-lined rivers that had irrigated crops since the days of Babylon. Many of them were Shia pilgrims, heading south in freedom for the first time in decades to celebrate their festivals in the holy shrine cities of Najaf and Kerbala.

But many were on a different kind of spiritual search. They were looking for the dead and missing who had vanished in these fields over the years. Rumors had abounded for months— unreliable reports published in the first independent newspapers in half a century—of farmers who had spotted army trucks arriving in the night just before the Americans started bombing, prisoners marched off and never seen again, gunfire in the desert areas along the edge of the fields. In the post-invasion chaos, desperate families were heading out, often on foot, in broken-down taxis or minivan buses, to look for their lost ones.

Usually there was no one overseeing these impromptu disinterments of mass graves. No police to oversee the crime scene because the police had been complicit in the crimes and had fled their posts when the first American bombs started falling. The men and women thronging the shallow pits were ordinary people, some of them armed with shovels, some simply digging through the earth with bare hands that were cracked and caked with dust. Their eyes were wild, desperate, and hopeful at the same time: the grief and pain of years of not knowing, the hope that they might finally lay their loved ones to rest in Wadi Salaam, the giant cemetery in Najaf that was reputed to be the largest graveyard in the world, and which would soon be overflowing with the bodies of those killed in the brutal civil war that was still looming in the summer of 2003.

Many carried a family photo showing the missing person, maybe an ID card, but mostly they knew no one would be able to identify their brothers, fathers, sisters, and children from photos anymore. Instead, they held on to a memory of what the missing person had been wearing the day they disappeared—a pair of blue plastic sandals, a striped shirt, a certain style of belt buckle. They knew any rings or jewelry would have been the first things to be stolen as their loved one headed through the gates of Abu Ghraib or into the hands of the local *mukhabarat*, the ubiquitous secret police.

So, they dug into the ground until they hit the first tangled limbs. Usually these were only about a foot or two down—Saddam's executioners made their graves long and straight, but shallow. After all, who would dare to come sniffing around here, knowing the consequences? Every time a body, or a yellowing limb, was pulled out of the reeking ground, an impassioned cry of "Allahu Akbar" went up and people rushed forward to examine it for any identifying signs. Those that could not be identified were carried to the cemetery by local religious charities, usually linked to the political parties that had flooded into the country, mostly from neighboring Iran, after the fall." Those that relatives thought they could claim were taken to Baghdad's central morgue to be issued a death certificate by the overworked forensics staff.

The morgue itself was a target for body hunters. Mothers came in asking for any documentary evidence of missing children, accosting forensic workers who were already knee-high in a new wave of corpses from the violence swirling through the chaotic city. I saw these wretched souls as I traveled around Baghdad in the summer of 2003, although I was not there to help with the excavations or identifications. As in Bosnia, the US military was not helping heal that particular wound, leaving it to fester as the country boiled over into its own civil war. Besides, the US and British military had more pressing issues— Saddam had escaped capture and his followers were organizing a guerrilla resistance movement that was killing coalition soldiers every few days. Huge car bombs were blowing up across the city as Iraq's unguarded borders were allowing thousands of jihadists, Al Qaeda terrorists, and Iranian agents to flood into the country to fight the newly arrived Great Satan.

And one of those bombings is what brought me to Baghdad, an active conflict zone. When I show people our offices, many stop at the collection of flak vests and helmets we have, not realizing that at times we have to go to active combat zones. No one thought terrorists or insurgents would attack the United Nations. To be sure, UN peacekeeping missions had been attacked many times in the past, UN planes had been shot down and the occasional special envoy assassinated, but there were no attacks on the actual organization or people appointed as representatives by the secretary general. After all, the UN was not there to enforce the US occupation, but to help rebuild the shattered country. Like the Australians in Bali, its leader never imagined the organization would be a target. That is why they set up shop in a poorly protected building, the Canal Hotel: their security was lax by comparison with the heavily fortified US headquarters in the all-but-impenetrable Green Zone, and that was done deliberately to set them apart. The accessibility allowed Iraqis to come and seek aid, said the mission's Brazilian head, Sergio Vieira de Mello. Unfortunately, it also allowed a suicide bomber sent by local wannabe Al Qaeda leader, Abu Musab al-Zarqawi, to drive a truck filled with explosives right up to a poorly built cinder-block wall right beneath de Mello's office. The explosion ripped the west side of the building open and left de Mello and more than twenty-two of his staff dead.

Chaos swirled around the status of the UN building in the middle of US-occupied Iraq, just as it had surrounded the federal building in Oklahoma City that had been blown up almost a decade earlier. The hotel was under exclusive UN jurisdiction but in a country with no functioning independent national government, one under military occupation by a foreign power, the United States, no one knew quite what to do in the midst of this growing quagmire.

The office of the UN Secretary General hired us to identify the bodies of de Mello and his staff and make sure they returned home. Our job would be to cut through military red tape and get the deceased home. Easier said than done, though.

For a start, there were no commercial flights in or out of Baghdad—the airport was still closed after the fighting, its tarmac littered with the charred carcasses of ancient Iraq Airways planes. Meanwhile the country's roads were rife with armed bandits and, increasingly, guerrilla cells. I contacted a friend in the RAF and he put us on a British flight out of Brize Norton to Basra, which was under British control, then arranged for us to get on a military C-130 to Baghdad. Even getting out of the airport presented a logistical challenge: our British, RAF plane landed in a zone of the vast complex known as BIAP (Baghdad International Airport), which UN drivers were not allowed to enter. And the UN itself is deeply bureaucratic and territorial.

When the escort eventually found me, the driver told me he was part of UN security, not the secretary general's office, and he would have to call on a satellite phone to get clearance from his superiors, while we waited.

When I finally got to the Canal Hotel, the carnage was obvious. The low-rise concrete building had been ripped to pieces by the truck bomb: despite the increasing number of bombings—the Jordanian embassy had been blown up just a few days before—no one had covered the windows with Mylar, a kind of clear adhesive that prevents glass fragmenting too badly in a blast. The damage to the building from the shattered glass was catastrophic. The walls were covered with blood in places, and the special envoy's office—which had looked onto the dirt track the suicide bomber used—was a jumble of broken office chairs, tables, and collapsed ceiling tiles. The US military had already removed the bodies by the time I arrived, but I searched for any human remains they might have missed. Going through the building, it was clear how woefully unprotected it had been, and I wrote to the secretary general's office with a brief report on my findings. After all, if the thinking was that no one would attack the UN because it was supposed to be a neutral player, they understood very little about the nature of asymmetrical warfare and terrorism. And they seemed to have forgotten the salient fact that around a million Iraqis had died under a decade of UN sanctions that preceded the Anglo-American invasion, so there was little goodwill toward the world body here.

My letter was not needed: the UN left the country after the bombing. They lost twenty-two people, including the UN Special Representative Sergio de Mello—a man sometimes touted as a potential future secretary general of the United Nations—his chief of staff and several other experts in humanitarian affairs. That is the power of mass fatalities: just as the shock at losing a Black Hawk and the subsequent bloody rescue in Mogadishu prompted the US military to leave Somalia in 1993, the attack on the UN headquarters was enough to force them to evacuate from the country for years.

US soldiers who had rushed to the scene had treated the wounded and taken the deceased to the Army's mortuary collection point at Baghdad International Airport. That mortuary collection point is the same facility in Baghdad where all deceased US military were prepared for movement back to the Port Mortuary at Dover Air Force Base. The US Armed Forces Medical Examiner had already sent a team to collect evidence from the deceased and identify them, with the United States claiming jurisdiction. Instead of arguing about it, it made sense to work together as we had done so before, as long as we were involved, although our preference would have been to move them all to Jordan and do the work there. Regardless, to make identifications they needed records from the families. We started the process of collecting identifying documents from the victims' home countries to establish a positive identity, such as dental records or DNA tests from relatives. While we were doing this, the family of one of the deceased, a Muslim woman, asked if her body could be washed at a mosque, in accordance with Islamic traditions. This was not as straightforward as it might sound—Baghdad was in the early stages of what would very shortly become a full-fledged insurrection against the occupation. Every day US troops, aid workers, and foreign diplomats were being targeted by rocket-propelled grenades, roadside bombs, or suicide bombers. Sometimes it was as simple as an Iraqi man in civilian clothes walking up to a US soldier at a busy checkpoint in the street and shooting him at point-blank range. Every day, there was another, more brazen attack.

But our goal is to try and achieve whatever we can to meet

the needs of the families, so we asked the local Iraqi UN staff I was working with to see if there was a mosque that was safe to go to. She was Sunni, so the mosque needed to be a Sunni mosque. Because of the bombing, her body could not be washed, but they would say prayers over the casket. We could take pictures to give to the family. They said they knew a place: it turned out to be in one of the most dangerous parts of the city, where Sunni insurgent groups were already coalescing and carrying out attacks on the US military. But he told us the imam would ensure safe passage and appreciated what we were doing. I and one of our female team members and local Iraqi drivers then took her to the mosque.

Mr. Tun Myat, the UN security coordinator, who had traveled to Baghdad in response to the bombing and had heard about what we were doing, made an unplanned visit to the mosque. He wanted to pay his respects. I understood his desire to be there, but he arrived with a large and well-armed security detail, which was not what the imam had agreed to. I explained that to Mr. Myat, and that official-looking convoys were increasingly the targets of attacks by Iraqi resistance fighters. We finished up quickly and departed, thankfully without incident and having cared for the deceased and the family. As part of the UN internal reviews, he later stepped down from his position.

Another challenge we had was that the US Army had released the bodies of all the Iraqi nationals to the local authorities prior to the arrival of the Armed Forces Medical Examiner. We had asked them not to do this, explaining that these people had died in the UN compound, and that involved certain jurisdictional rights. What we wanted to do was make sure the right bodies went to the right families, and to identify the families, because they were entitled to assistance from the UN. However, there was a reserve colonel—whom I had spent time with while on active duty trying to teach Mortuary Affairs—who thought he knew better and with whom I clashed several times during the recovery. I guess I had not been as good a teacher as I thought.

We had set up our family assistance center in Amman, the capital of neighboring Jordan, since Iraq was way too dangerous and lacked the facilities to embalm the bodies for repatriation. We had reached an agreement with the Armed Forces Medical Examiner on issuing death certificates and what constitutes an identification. UN staff come from all over the world, which means it can be difficult to collect the necessary records, and at that time the UN had no program to collect DNA samples, or fingerprints, or dental records, or even detailed next of kin information. That is something we have recommended for them and any agency or company that deploys people to hazardous locations for long periods of time.

We were having trouble finding records for one woman, that would establish a positive identification. The Armed Forces Medical Examiner did not want to release her, something we understood. However, we also understood that these events are political. In this case the family of the woman had gone to the Jordanian government in protest. They did this at the time when we were sending a military flight with all of the deceased who had already been identified to Jordan, so they could be embalmed and repatriated to their home countries. There were sixteen nationalities involved. While at the airport getting the deceased loaded, a person from the US State Department asked me why we were holding the flight up and had had the Jordanian airspace closed. Since I didn't have the power to do this, I made some calls. It seems that because of the family protest, the king had ordered the airspace closed until the aircraft had her remains on it also. So I talked to the Jordanian officials and asked them if they were comfortable receiving a deceased without a death certificate, and if they would make the identification there. They agreed. I then asked the Armed Forces Medical Examiner: Would they release the deceased to us based on those grounds? We were all fairly certain that we had the correct deceased: there had only been a few women killed, and all the others had been positively identified, so by exclusion this made sense. This of course is much easier when you have a complete list of the missing and those already identified, but because of the earlier release of the Iraqi nationals we were not 100 percent sure. We prepared her body, and she was loaded onto the aircraft. The flight was allowed to take off and, more importantly, land.

It was, however, not to be my last trip to Baghdad. The question of all those neglected mass graves still bothered me, and so when the Coalition Provisional Authority (CPA)— essentially the US occupation government—asked me to study the feasibility of excavating them the following year, I returned and toured some of the sites, including some in the north, the Kurdish semiautonomous region. They wanted to exhume and rebury the bodies of hundreds of people killed during Saddam's chemical gas attacks in the late 1980s. The mustard gas strikes, the most infamous of which landed on the village of Halabja in 1988, earned Saddam's top general the nickname Chemical Ali.

Both the tasks set out by the US-led coalition and by the Kurds were logistically difficult. I explained to the Kurds that one of our concerns was that poison gas would likely have been trapped in the heavy clothing of the people who had been killed, and some test openings to determine would be required to find out if the deceased were still contaminated. I had spent a long time in the Army finalizing the doctrine for dealing with contaminated human remains. It can be done, but it is time consuming and requires a lot of logistical support. Nonetheless, we would raise the issue with the CPA. The Kurds had undergone years of suffering. One of their goals, in an era where they felt they would have a voice and be part of the government, was to build memorials both to hold the dead but also to educate and to remind the world of what had happened to them.

I then went on to look at some of the other mass graves in Iraq on subsequent trips, even flying over for a scheduled meeting with the head of the CPA, Paul Bremer, who canceled it right as I was arriving for the meeting at the Green Zone. However, it quickly became apparent that the US authorities in Baghdad only wanted the bodies exhumed as evidence in the future trial of Saddam Hussein, who was still on the run in the summer of 2003, but who by now had been caught. That made sense, but the greater benefit that could have been achieved was similar to what was accomplished in Bosnia. Here was a chance to learn from history of the Balkans, from the progress that came from recovering and returning the deceased from the mass graves there. For the United States to be seen to be returning the missing bodies of Iraqis killed by their own despot to desperate relatives would help calm the brewing insurrection. There was one family in particular that might have helped heal those wounds. Family members of the young Shia firebrand Moqtada al-Sadr, who that summer was building his own militia, the Mahdi Army, and would for years battle US and British troops in Iraq, had been murdered by Saddam and buried in some of those mass graves. I was sure finding and returning them in addition to others would have made a difference. The coalition had maps of all the mass graves.

I really didn't care if this work was assigned to us, but it needed to be done. So I spent my own time and money on it.

I even enlisted the help of an old friend, Charlie Wilson, the former congressman from Texas who famously got the United States to supply Afghanistan's *mujahideen* with weapons to fight the Soviet Union after its 1979 invasion. Alas, there was no interest. The war was looking less like a "shock and awe" victory and more like the Soviet blunder in Afghanistan. In 2004, the American proconsul Paul Bremer quickly handed over authority to a cobbled-together Iraqi government, told them to organize free and fair elections, and then jumped on a plane.

Soon enough, new mass graves were added to the old as the country plunged into a vicious civil war, one that has since dragged most of the Middle East into its orbit.

Bosnia, by contrast, has emerged as a fairly stable state.

I cannot claim that is solely because their mass graves were unearthed, and their dead identified and returned to their families, in part because even now, twenty-five years later, some are still being identified. There are dozens of factors that determine the peace of one country and the implosion of another. But understanding and acknowledging the history, no matter how dark it is can, I believe, make a difference. There is no greater pain or sorrow than that of the unknown. It is vicious. It is a roller coaster of emotions, with no end. One day you are on a high of hope that your loved one will walk through a door. It is rare, but it does happen. Think of Steven Stayner, a seven-year-old boy who was kidnapped in 1972 and escaped and returned to his family in 1980. Other days will be those of despair and then the guilt for giving up hope and wanting to have a normal life. This is what it means for many of the families of the missing. This emotional torment is universal, not defined by religion or nationality.

Now imagine the open wound left behind on a country where tens of thousands of families suffer that collective pain and cannot move onto whatever fragile peace might follow a war. Finding and naming the dead, and laying to rest the tortured memories buried in mass graves, is at least one element that helped stabilize the notoriously fractious Balkans while pushing Iraq into an even steeper decline.

14. The Science and Emotion of Identification

Having started out in law enforcement in the 1980s, and then going on to run a company that has helped identify thousands of bodies, I have witnessed incredible advances in the process of how we make human identifications.

In real life, DNA is not generally the first go-to method for identifying a body. It is very useful for identifying fragmented remains or those without any records and we do use it, but it is not the be-all and end-all that TV shows suggest. The old-school methods of fingerprints or dental records are still our preferred first line of inquiry, especially the former. That is because it is simpler, more cost effective, and much quicker. The average police officer is trained to take a fingerprint, and most police departments have someone trained in the art of matching up the individual pattern of whorls and ridges that make each person's prints unique.

Dental records are just as effective—you can photograph the dentition of a dead body in a field morgue just as you would do with a living person, using a small x-ray machine. It is then possible to say that these records definitively match those of John Doe in a dentist's office in, say, Ohio, if you have reason to suspect that John Doe is from Ohio. Forensic dental experts can match a crown, a filling, or any restoration work to existing records. We have entire teams collecting these records once we have a list of passengers on a crashed plane or visitors to a destroyed building. Fillings have their own distinctive shapes, as they are fit into cavities drilled by a dentist. Sometimes when a body is so badly damaged, or trapped in wreckage, that it cannot easily be moved, we use a sensor that can be inserted into the mouth to capture any unique dental features, so that the process of identifying can begin even before the deceased is recovered. I once had an investigator come up to me and show me what he thought was a valuable piece of gold: it turned out to be a filling, and its real value was that the blackened tooth was still attached, allowing us to use it as an identification marker.

Fingerprints and dental or medical files are simplest because they are a matching of physical characteristics from known and verified records. Learning to lift fingerprints was one of the first things I did in forensics, back in the day when prints were stored on cards, and making a match required a trained expert to physically compare hundreds or even thousands of them. These days, it's all digitized such as on the US FBI's Automated Fingerprint Identification System, or AFIS, which law enforcement agencies can reference. Sometimes, though, even if the skin on the finger has been fragmented in a plane crash, or decayed by time, it can be rehydrated and pieced together on a very fine glove, which is fitted over the forensic expert's own finger and a print taken for comparison.

But identifications in mass fatalities are not as simple as comparing fingerprints or dentation. It is about having a process, documentation, and a way of keeping potentially hundreds of records organized; records that are often collected, reviewed, and decided on by people who have never worked together before. It is about comparing these records to those records made by interviewing hundreds of family members, and then solving the problems that arise from those interviews.

In 2010, when we responded to the loss of a plane that had crashed in Libya en route to the Netherlands from South Africa, we had to identify the body of a South African man who had fled the apartheid regime as a teenager and moved to the United Kingdom. During his time living in Britain, he had been in a car accident and had a plate in in his leg, which had a serial number on it. That is normally an excellent way to confirm an identity. But then his brother came to our family assistance center, where he informed the British police that the deceased's fingerprints would not match the fingerprints that were on his visa applications from many years before. That was when the brother admitted that, back in the days of apartheid, the deceased had been arrested by the South African police. To get out of the country, he had applied to Britain for a visa and needed to show he had a clean criminal record. So the two brothers secretly switched identities.

That presented us with an unusual problem: on the one hand, the Libyans didn't care because the bodies would not be staying in their country; the British didn't care about the old warrant because they weren't going to prosecute a dead man; and the South Africans didn't worry about someone who had died abroad and weren't going to prosecute a warrant from a regime that had collapsed twenty years before. But we could not knowingly issue a false death certificate.

I called the head of the South African police Forensic Services and explained the problem. She instructed us to send the living brother back home: we would inform him he would be detained at the airport in order to verify his identity using his original birth records, which would allow us to also verify the dead brother's identity. The brother was quite calm about it. He flew back to South Africa where he helped the police finally establish his real identity, after decades of posing as his sibling. We were able to issue a death certificate and repatriate the body to him.

Whenever Kenyon runs a morgue after a mass fatality, we immediately set up a triage station, with an anthropologist, a photographer, evidence technicians, and those comfortable working around deceased such as embalmers or pathology assistants. As we receive human remains, we record every fragment of a body that is not joined by connective tissue as separate remains. You can never assume that an arm with a white sleeve came from a torso wearing a similar white shirt. That happens, when police or firefighters are working in stressful conditions, or in war zones under fire. But it can all too often lead to a casket having three arms or three legs in it. Because after the examination the deceased are placed in refrigerated holding, and over time as DNA test results are returned, separated fragments are reassociated, often by technicians not involved in the original operations; then people place the different human remains pouches together, without looking inside each one. When the "body" is released to us, we find the additional limbs. The whole process then stops, and testing must be redone. I would like to say this is rare, but I have seen it in a lot of the events we have responded to.

Our triage teams then complete a checklist noting which further morgue examination stations may be needed and separate the personal effects to examine them for identification and to protect them from further damage. These include photography, fingerprinting/foot printing, dental, x-ray, pathology, anthropology, DNA sample collection, and if we are working with a body from a combat zone, we take the extra precaution of scanning it with an x-ray for any unexploded ordnance that might still be inside and pose a risk to the morgue team, before doing any real work. The deceased then works its way through the morgue, each section completely a different part of the examination. How detailed the examination is will depend on whether or not we are trying to simply establish an identification or conduct a complete autopsy in order to collect evidence for prosecution or trial.

Another job of our triage team is to separate human from nonhuman material. We worked on a helicopter crash where the official delegation had been presented with the gift of a sheep by the elders of a village they had visited. The first forensic team had identified some of the animal bones as human. Our forensic people did a double-check and spotted that it was not human: when we did some further inquiries, we learned about the sheep that had been aboard the helicopter.

We keep premade folders, ready with bar codes and labels already printed, so that we can start as soon as we arrive on the scene. We assign each fragment its own number. The team will also determine if a fragment looks so damaged as to be of limited usefulness for testing. We call those remains ones of Limited Forensic Value. They are still given a number, but then they are placed into holding and only examined if we can't make 100 percent successful identifications. We do that so the system can focus on the more viable remains first. When you're starting out, you don't know if a fragment is just one of many pieces you might find of a deceased person, or if it is only part of that person you'll find. DNA testing takes time, and we don't want to delay the system unnecessarily. Before we even do this, I will usually meet the medical examiner who will ultimately be in charge, and who will issue the death certificates, and ask, "People or pieces?" I need to know if the goal is to account for every missing person, or to identify every bit of human remains that are recovered. It's a question most people have never thought of or could even conceive asking. In an event in which we have a solid manifest, like a plane crash, or a building collapse with a good list of the people inside, we recommend stopping the process once all the missing persons have been accounted for. Because this meets the minimum needs of all and doesn't make it hard for people who want to bury their dead and start their transition. Otherwise, it is a process that can go on for an indefinite period. While this concept may sound simple, we responded to a plane crash with only thirty-three people on board and more than nine hundred human remains fragments were recovered. In another case one individual was identified 289 times.

The exception is when there is no list or such as terrorist attacks like 9/11, or in another case we worked on, the crash of Germanwings Flight 9525 from Barcelona to Dusseldorf, Germany, in the French Alps in March 2015. "In those cases we want to ensure there is no commingling of any of the terrorists', or murderers', remains with those of the victims." Flight 9525 plane was deliberately flown into a mountain by its copilot, Andreas Lubitz, a twenty-seven-year-old who had been concealing a longstanding struggle with depression and who appears to have had some kind of fatal psychological collapse that day.

When the captain of the flight slipped out of the cockpit for a quick toilet break about twenty minutes after takeoff, Lubitz locked the door to the main cabin and changed the selected altitude from 38,000 feet to just 100 feet. Air traffic control tried to contact the copilot but received no answer. Cockpit recordings caught Lubitz apparently breathing normally as he began his death dive with 149 innocent victims in tow. The flight's captain, thirty-four-year-old Patrick Sondenheimer, returned to find the door to the cockpit locked. He must have thought it was some kind of technical malfunction, and probably did not immediately realize the gradual loss of altitude as intentional:

planes flying across mountain ranges tend to change altitude quite frequently, and gradual loss of altitude is not the same as a nosedive. As he was still attempting to enter the cockpit the plane struck the earth.

The plane crashed into the side of a mountain not far from the small village of Le Vernet, some forty miles south of the city of Toulouse. No one survived, and there was great damage to the bodies of everyone aboard upon impact. Though we knew exactly who was on board, the condition of the remains made it impossible to say which fragments belonged to which person, without DNA testing.

While the recovery and morgue process—called the postmortem process—is underway, a concurrent program to collect records from family members is also going on, usually done at a family assistance center. The collection of records—dental, medical, etc.—is referred to as the antemortem process. As part of the antemortem process one of the things we ask families is how many times they want to be notified of a positive identification. Would they prefer just once, when the first result comes confirming their loved one died. Or whenever a new piece of a body is identified, or at the very end of the process, possibly months after the disaster, when all possible body parts have been assigned a profile. Many people are afraid to do this, not wanting to share this information with family members. But then after a family thinks the process is over and realizes more remains could be identified after they have had their loved one's funeral, they might make a different decision. When this happens, it can be devastating, and now the family is angry not because of the loss, but because of the way it was managed. And they have a right to be, because the response system should know better.

After any crash or incident in which Kenyon takes the lead in victim identification, and after we have finished the postmortem process and collected all the antemortem records, we set up what we call an identification committee, in which investigators look at all the records that exist on a person and compare them to whatever postmortem information we have gathered on a body to rule on the recommended identification. This is important, because at times the records collected from the families can conflict with what the forensic experts have found during their examinations.

For example, in one case, the deceased's next of kin was her grandfather; her parents had died in the same plane crash she had. We asked a number of basic questions such as, "Did your granddaughter have pierced ears?" He said yes. But the body we had in our morgue did not have pierced ears. Upon further inquiry we found out that the last time he had seen her was several months ago and he was not completely sure. Based on the totality of the information her identification was established. The one type of identification we never use or accept is a visual ID. There are so many cases of people, even close family members or significant others, making mistakes, and time and time again people have to learn this painful lesson. There are many reasons for these errors, not really looking at the deceased, focusing on something such as clothing that others might have. Or the fact that the deceased has been moved through the system and does not look like they did when first identified, or the numbering system used was unreliable and there is no chain of custody. This can be especially frustrating to family members in disaster zones, who don't understand the delays when they have come to recover their loved ones themselves.

At the end of this process there are four possibilities. The first of these is the deceased who are the identified. The second are the unidentified, meaning that if we receive more records, or more family members' DNA, the remains should be identifiable.

An example of this was the loss of EgyptAir 990, in which several Egyptian military personnel were aboard the flight and the families chose not to provide records at the time. So we had several remains with unique DNA profiles but nothing to match them to. Every once in a while, a family would come forward and submit DNA and we would get a match, then be able to return that deceased. The third category is those that are unidentifiable, meaning we have human remains, but with current technology we are unable to say who they are. These are usually very small fragments, and not all tissue has usable DNA. Fourth are the missing, in which no remains are recovered.

The unidentifiable and missing are the hardest for families because the perception gleaned from television is that everyone is identifiable. Without a body, some jurisdictions will not issue a death certificate. In those cases, we then petition the courts, based on all the evidence, but only after asking the families if that is in fact what they would like.

When managing a mass fatality morgue, we try to operate as if the family were standing next to us. For a long time, the forensic or identification process was done to make it easier on those doing the work, so jaws were removed to make it easier to get dental records, or hands removed to facilitate fingerprinting. It is not the way it should happen, and not the way we do it. It causes great distress to the families. It can make them feel as if their loved one was just something to work on.

When a London pleasure boat, the *Marchioness*, hit a dredger in the Thames in the summer of 1989 and sank, the coroner authorized the people doing the identification work to remove the hands of twenty-five of the fifty-one victims. His argument was that it would make fingerprinting easier as the waterlogged bodies themselves started to deteriorate rapidly. Since many of the partygoers had been gay, and no permission had been sought from the families for the dismemberment, accusations of homophobia were leveled at the police and coroner's office. The legal inquiry dragged on for almost two decades. As is so often the case, the trigger for this last-resort method of identifying the dead was because some of the key players had no experience of death on this scale before and did not understand the power of collective grief. The coroner had gone on vacation a couple of days after the disaster, and there was no effective coordination of the identification methods to be deployed. It was probably not malice on his behalf. Needless to say, the truth brought little comfort to the families, especially to the mother whose daughter's hands were discovered lying forgotten in a coroner's fridge *four years* after the disaster. Not surprisingly, the mother lambasted the coroner when she had her day in court. "He deprived me the right to my daughter, to hold her hand for the last time, to give her a farewell kiss." Nevertheless, the coroner, Paul Knapman, rejected calls for him to quit and served another eleven years in the job.

Identification can also be rushed by those who feel that it is more important to return a deceased than return the correct deceased. In May 2003, a Ukrainian charter, UM Flight 4230 was carrying Spanish peacekeepers back from a tour of duty in Afghanistan when it crashed in a thick fog during a refuel stop in Turkey, killing all sixty-two peacekeepers and thirteen crew members on board. Spain's involvement in the US-led wars after 9/11 had always been controversial. In the hurry to get the soldiers' bodies back to Spain for burial and state mourning, senior officers leaned on medical examiners to rush the autopsies and falsify some of the results. A court found almost half of the sixty-two soldiers were misidentified, and their families received the wrong bodies. General Vicente Navarro, who signed the official documents stating the bodies had been identified, blamed the Turkish coroners for the confusion, but the Turks said Spain had been in such a hurry to get the troops home that it had skipped DNA testing on the badly mutilated bodies.

After a lengthy court case, in 2009 the general was sentenced to three years in jail. Two other officers were also found guilty and jailed. Spain learned a painful lesson, one I witnessed firsthand. In 2010, less than year after the convictions, a Spanish police officer was killed in the UN compound in Haiti during the earthquake. A very senior Spanish diplomat personally asked me to check on the identity of the Spanish police officer. The request surprised me a little at the time: Spain had the officer's fingerprint records and its own forensics teams were checking up on the remains. But I realized that he wanted to be absolutely sure the same thing didn't happen again. Even more shocking was the death of the Polish president in a plane crash in Russia in April 2010; it was the deadliest aviation accident in postwar Polish history. The air disaster claimed the lives not just of President Lech Kaczynski and his wife, but also the chief of staff and other senior officers, 18 members of parliament, a former president, an archbishop, and several relatives of Poles killed in the notorious Katyn massacre. The top-ranking delegation had been due to attend a memorial to the 22,000 Polish military officers and intellectuals rounded up and shot dead by Russian secret police in a forest near Smolensk exactly seventy years earlier. The Soviets, seeking control of Poland, had tried to blame the slaughter on the Nazis.

What had been meant to be a moment of reconciliation turned into an all-out disaster when the Polish plane went down on landing, again in thick fog, killing all ninety-six people on board. The pilots may have wanted to divert because of the bad weather but decided not to because of the importance of his passengers and the significance of the occasion: there were no other viable airports in the area. Another flight that had been approaching the airport around the same time was diverted safely to Moscow, some 250 miles away. Also, the Smolensk airport was not designed to accept international flights, and the air traffic controllers were not legally required to speak English, the universal language of flight.

Then, after the crash, the body recovery and identification operation were horribly botched from the start by the Russians, who used conscript soldiers, among others, to collect the human remains at the airfield. It was later found that credit cards were missing from some of the bodies and one of them was used to make payments of more than $1,000. Russia carried out the crash investigation itself and refused to return the aircraft wreckage to Poland, angering Warsaw.

As it happened, Poland's opposition party was led by Jaroslaw Kaczynski, the twin brother of the president who had died in the crash. He and others in the party floated the idea that the plane had been deliberately targeted, although no proof was ever found. When his party came to power in 2015, they reopened the investigation and the coffins: to the shock of the Poles, prosecutors found that many of the bodies had been misidentified. Even the president's casket had the remains of two other victims inside it, while the coffin of the archbishop Miron Chodakowski contained the top half of his body but the lower half was that of a military bishop, General Tadeusz Ploski. It was an utter disaster. A mission that had been designed to smooth over a brutal history between mutually suspicious neighbors and lay the ghosts of the Katyn massacre to rest only added more. For the families, it was a double nightmare: some wanted to let the dead rest, while others were determined to get to the bottom of the complex story. The daughter of one of the dead passengers contacted Kenyon to ask if we could help ensure the remains she had been given to bury were in fact those of her father. However, since the investigation was being carried out by the Polish prosecutor's office, we lacked the jurisdiction to help her. Those families will likely never find out the truth.

Along with the importance of proper identification is the burial of the unidentified and unidentifiable, the fragments that are so often left behind after the majority of human remains have been assigned an identity. This is something that people again underestimate and that is the importance of proper planning and disposition of all human remains. The fragments—remains—are just that, human remains, not medical waste. They should be buried in a dignified manner and families should be aware of the fragments and burial. While cremation is acceptable to many, me included, it is not universally accepted and can never be undone, that is why burial is the method we use.

In 2011, US media revealed that body fragments from hundreds of US service members killed in the wars in Iraq and Afghanistan and repatriated to Dover Air Force Base in Delaware with great pomp and reverence, had been incinerated and the ashes dumped in a local landfill in Virginia. The families of almost three hundred service members had entrusted the Air Force with the respectful disposal of their loved ones' mortal remains: instead, the military bureaucracy had not known quite what to do with the inevitable tiny scraps of tissue and bone that results from the blast of an IED in some distant combat zone.

Ironically, the site of the landfill was only around thirty miles east of where the arm of the Confederate general Stonewall Jackson, shot off by one his own men in a friendly fire incident during the battle of Chancellorsville, has its own granite tombstone inscribed simply, "Arm of Stonewall Jackson May 3, 1863." It too had been destined to be tossed into the heap of mangled limbs that nineteenth-century battles and surgeons inevitably produced, until an Army chaplain found and "rescued" it.

Of course, there was outrage from the shocked families of the service members, a rage only exacerbated when the Air Force announced that it would be too expensive and time-consuming to reopen thousands of files and try to cross-reference the precise origins of these fragments. But there was also a genuine human reaction from the local residents of the area. When the news broke in the media, they clubbed together to erect a stone monument in the middle of the rotting garbage and broken household items. The plaque was unveiled to the sound of taps being played by a high school trumpeter while an American Legion motorcycle drill team carried US flags on a lap around the interior of the landfill. The message on the granite plaque was simple, and time-honored: "In memory of those American service members known but to God, who paid the ultimate sacrifice for our freedom. We are forever grateful."

15. DNA and the CSI Effect

The first case of DNA being used to help solve a murder investigation was in the United Kingdom, which was one of the pioneers of the method. Police in Leicestershire, in the center of the country, had come up empty-handed on two separate cases of two fifteen-year-old girls who had been raped and murdered, one in 1983 and the other in 1986, in nearby villages. After years of inconclusive investigations, police had a suspect, a seventeen-year-old boy with learning difficulties, who had confessed to the first killing but denied the second. For many reasons people falsely confess to crimes, especially those with less education and those with developmental difficulties, who can be easily intimidated by the prospect of police questioning.

Seasoned detectives do not just let cases go, however. Many of them spend their own time and resources checking on leads, always looking out for something that was missed or something new that can help them. This is the dedication they have for their victims and the families. As the Leicestershire cases threatened to go cold, the police decided to try out a new scientific method being developed by genetic researchers at the nearby University of Leicester. The scientists tested DNA samples from semen residue that had been recovered from the deceased. They established that both samples did indeed come from the same person, but that it was not the young man police had in custody and who had confessed. Lacking a definitive suspect but with a DNA profile from the crime scene, the police had a behavioral psychologist draw up a list of men who might be more likely to commit such a horrific crime, based on age, background, and any potential previous convictions. They then asked those men who lived in the surrounding area and whose ages fit the age profile to voluntarily submit to a DNA test.

At first, they drew a blank, but then one a night at a pub, a bakery worker named Ian Kelly confessed to friends that a colleague of his, a man in his twenties named Colin Pitchfork, had asked Kelly to submit his own blood under Pitchfork's name. He said Pitchfork didn't want to give his own blood because he had already done the same thing for another friend who feared he would be harassed by police for a burglary. By chance, a woman in the pub overheard the conversation and reported it to the police. Pitchfork was arrested and convicted. He was jailed for thirty years. The DNA genie was out of the bottle.

There have been stunning advances in DNA testing in recent years. Simply by sending off for an inexpensive test kit from a company like 23andMe, you can collect a small saliva sample, mail it off to a lab, and trace your ancestors back centuries, or discover relatives you never knew you had. On the battlefield in Syria, US special forces managed to almost instantly come up with a positive identification of the body of Islamic State terrorist leader Abu Bakr al-Baghdadi, the leader of the Islamic State terror group who blew himself up together with several of his terrified children in an escape tunnel as US Special Forces moved in on his hideout. It was announced after the raid that the Navy Seal team got their DNA match within fifteen minutes of his death, although the fastest time is generally about ninety minutes for the on-the-spot testing. That was something they simply couldn't do with Osama bin Laden just eight years earlier.

The way DNA is used as part of the identification process is similar to the way it is used in criminal investigations. It involves collecting samples from the deceased or from a crime scene, and then trying to match it. For criminal investigations the police try to match the sample to a direct reference, which is much easier than in a mass fatality where matches for identification are made through familial references. Direct referencing is matching an unknown profile against a known profile. A familial reference is not a direct match, but a match that is based on samples collected from several people believed to be related to the missing person, and where a statistical analysis indicates it is 99 percent more likely the deceased is related to those people than anyone else being tested. The more people missing, the harder it is.

For identification purposes there are two types of DNA we collect from a body: mitochondrial and nuclear DNA. Nuclear DNA is generally easier to extract because it is found in soft tissue. However, we tend to work more frequently with mitochondrial DNA, or mtDNA because it is found in bone samples, which are more likely to have survived the catastrophic damage from a plane crash or fire, or to be viable even years after the person died. However, mtDNA is only passed on through the maternal side of the family, so maternal relatives need to be available for familial references.

In the morgue, there is as previously described a station for collecting DNA samples. The person stationed there, usually an anthropologist, has to know how to collect the sample. Sterilizing tools used between each sample collection is necessary to avoid contamination. It also means ensuring that each sample that is collected is properly labeled. Most of the mistakes I see in identification are not scientific errors, but administrative errors, simple paperwork mistakes. Details are important. For example, occasionally the fragment is so small that the sample sent to the lab is all there is. An identification comes back, but there are no remains to match it, because they were consumed in testing, something that has to be explained to a family.

Every group of investigators at a disaster will have their own preferences and want either a rib or a tooth or a piece of thigh bone. That preference is generally determined by a lab's standardized testing: if you are used to working with a thigh bone sample, you generally want to collect femur samples. Also, the thicker the bone is, the better protected the DNA sample is likely to be, so thigh bones tend to be popular, as we saw in the Bali bombing, where every country wanted their own slice of femur from the missing.

The sample then has to be transported to a certified lab where a technician will prep it, either by grinding down the bone or dissolving the tissues in a reagent of special enzymes that cracks open the walls of a cell and grants access to the DNA. Once it is dissolved in reagent, the sample is amplified in a special machine that will draw out the DNA profile; this used to be done on gel sheets, but these days comes out in a printed digitized format. This is an art in itself—if the sample is not amplified for long enough, the profile will not be recognizable. You may come out with only four loci, possibly enough to say the bone came from a man, but not enough to say which man. If it is left in too long, it can damage the DNA. It is almost like baking a cake, except that every sample is different, depending on the quality of the original batch.

What you then get, or hope to get is a profile based on twenty core short tandem repeat (STR) loci, plus the Amelogenin (which is used for gender identification). Of course some countries use

the same twenty core Loci, but not all, which makes mass fatalities involving multiple countries difficult because it is not
just choice of the scientist, but of what the laws of each country
specify or allow. That result is a unique profile. It tells you these
human remains are different than someone else's, but it does not
tell you who that is. And you have to do this for every one of
the hundreds or thousands of fragments of human remains in
a crash. That is why it can take months to complete the process.

At the same this is occurring, you are trying to collect either
direct or familial references to compare to the samples of the
deceased. Direct references are preferred, but very few people
have those on file. To collect familial references is harder; we
have to identify who the appropriate family members are, get
them to agree to provide DNA, and then go and collect it. In
some places, there is mistrust of science or a fear of providing a
sample, and we must work through those problems if we want
to be successful. The location and current political state in a
country can have a lot to do with this. People are wary of giving
too much personal information to repressive regimes.

Some years ago, we were working with authorities in Australia to repatriate the bodies of refugees who died trying to reach
Australia. They had drowned when their boat overturned near
Christmas Island in the Pacific Ocean—one of the most remote
places on earth—as they tried to make it to the safety of Australia. Many had fled war and repression in Afghanistan, Iran, and
across the Middle East, and their relatives did not want to be
publicly associated with people who had broken the laws of their
countries by leaving. In places like that, simply being related to
someone desperate enough to run away can land relatives in jail.
Sometimes, there are no relatives, so we have to collect things
from homes or offices and try and generate a profile that way. In
another case we had the body of person after a plane crash, but

no good dental records, fingerprints, or footprints. This person had been adopted as young child, so there were no biological relatives that we could find. In discussing this with the adoptive parents and discussing going to their residence to collect fingerprints and material for DNA, the mother mentioned that she had collected baby teeth from all of her kids. Problem solved. The teeth were sent to the lab, DNA profiles generated, one of which was a direct match to the deceased. Armed with that information, we made a positive ID.

DNA can also bring other problems to light. For example, one time we took a cheek swab from the daughter of a man who had died in a plane crash only to discover she was not, in fact, his daughter.

Because of the intricacies of DNA testing, to get a match for the dead father, we took a swab from both the daughter and the mother. That might sound counterintuitive, since a husband and wife are not genetically related. But having identified the mother's genetic profile, we could remove that material from the daughter's DNA signature. What was left there should be a familial reference for the father's DNA. When it doesn't match, it it could be an administrative error at the lab—perhaps a technician used the wrong slide or labeled the result incorrectly. So, we run the test through another lab as quality control. And sometimes it still comes back as not a match.

That is an awkward revelation at any point in a young person's life, but especially painful in the wake of losing a loved one. We spoke to the man's ex-wife and she quietly admitted there had been a boyfriend. But it also raised the tricky question of who could make disposition of the body—by law, it is the next of kin who has that right. Since the "father" was divorced from the young woman's mother, that would have normally meant the daughter, as a young adult, would be the next of kin. But the DNA test showed clearly that she wasn't, and now the judge overseeing the case knew it, so he could not sign off on the order. Fortunately, in this case we had other relatives who had equal level of status as next of kin.

I spoke to the mother, and she said that she did not want her daughter to learn the truth at this painful moment. I told her I wouldn't volunteer the information, but warned that if her daughter asked, I would not lie to her. The mother agreed. It is a hard decision to make, but if the family is talking to each other and is getting along, then it is perhaps the best choice for them to make. After all, a father can mean so many different things, aside from being a simple biological contributor.

Following the case with the young woman, we added a line to our DNA submission forms for family members that warns: "In some rare cases, DNA results may yield a result that is unexpected in relation to paternity. If that is the case, do you want to be notified?"

Even then, people may not be ready for buried family secrets—parents who adopted a child but never told them. In the 1960s, some fertility doctors even mixed their own sperm with that of a sterile would-be father, without telling the parents, who might have lived their entire lives without knowing.

With DNA testing constantly evolving, such surprise revelations are becoming more and more commonplace, but there are still some staggering medical surprises. For example, a US man who received a bone marrow transplant from a German donor to treat his leukemia recently discovered that, four years after the procedure, the DNA in his sperm cells was that of his donor rather than his own, even though cheek swabs showed both men's DNA. Given that tens of thousands of people have bone marrow transplants every year, the potential for mix-ups in our business, or in law enforcement cases, is potentially significant.

These are issues I often have to discuss with authorities and with families when I am collecting DNA after a plane crash or other mass fatality, to explain the legal and ethical issues surrounding the issue, but also to illustrate the privacy issues surrounding DNA testing. Those can change daily and can be impacted by developments in criminal investigations. Likewise, some of the advances in identification methods have yielded advances for law enforcement. The biggest being the area of familial matches.

IN THE UNITED STATES, the FBI created a system known as the Combined DNA Index System, or CODIS, to facilitate the matching of DNA profiles across state lines. In the United States, each state has its own law enforcement systems, and there are many more people arrested for local and state level offensives than federal offenses. Many of those arrested are compelled to provide a DNA sample. However, people including criminals often move around from state to state. So for a DNA matching system to be useful, it would need to cross the state boundaries.

When the police collect a DNA sample from a crime scene, they first check against their own state database; if there is a match, the process stops. If there is no match, the state then provides the data to the FBI, who compares it to the National DNA Index System (NDIS) which is the DNA data bank part of CODIS. If there is a match, the FBI refers the state laboratory submitting the sample to the state laboratory that uploaded the profile that provides the match. Unlike on television, the FBI does not have the information about the sample, only the profiles, the generic marker.

Sounds simple right? The concept is, in execution, much harder. To begin with a standard had to be agreed upon, which loci to test and then what constituted a match. Until 2017, thirteen core loci were used, even though many labs preferred sixteen for the identification of human remains. However, in 2017, the FBI increased the number of core loci from thirteen to twenty. As the knowledge of familial DNA has increased, much of it from the identification of the deceased, the FBI was realizing that more and more results were coming back not for direct matches, but showing instead that someone in the database was a biological relative. This led to great discussion between states as to whether there were Fourth Amendment rights at stake and how to protect people against unwarranted searches and seizures, while balancing the rapid advances in technology. It is good technology; in the United Kingdom for example between 2001 and 2011 the police had more than two hundred familial searches that resulted in forty serious crimes being solved.

The issue further developed in recent years with the advent of mail-in DNA tests, such as Ancestry.com and 23andMe. Many of these sites are designed to allow people to find out which countries their ancestors came from or fill in family trees. The fact that some allow people to match up their results and track down unknown relatives also offered a historic crime-solving opportunity to an investigator in a district attorney's office in California. Paul Holes spent years comparing data from open sources sites to unsolved crime scene DNA. In 2018, in one of these sites, GEDmatch, he found a familial match for one of the most famous unsolved and brutal crimes in California history, the so-called Golden State Killer.

The killer had murdered twelve people and raped forty-five others in a series of more than one hundred burglaries in California between 1976 and 1986, just as the forensic use of DNA was beginning. The killer appeared to have gotten away with it.

But he hadn't. A seventy-three-year-old cousin of the killer uploaded his DNA profile to the GEDmatch site and Holes found a match: it was weak but suggested a familial relationship. That was enough to reopen the case, explore the man's family tree, and find any relative living in the right area of California who was also the right age at the time to have committed the crimes. One person fit the bill, seventy-two-year-old Joseph James DeAngelo, who had once been a police officer himself. Police obtained a warrant and pulled a DNA profile from a discarded item the suspect had touched. Within four hours, they had a direct match to the Golden State Killer, and the killer was finally brought to book.

Then, of course, we have what I call the "CSI effect." A generation raised on crime scene TV dramas has come to believe that DNA can resolve just about any identification issue, and within hours. As we saw with the Golden State Killer, that is possible. But what people forget is that to get to that four-hour DNA match, Holes spent *seven* years comparing online genetic profiles. In fact, it took him so long he actually retired just days before the arrest was made.

Confirming a known identity with a given DNA sample is a very different matter to saying that this piece of bone comes from 1 of the 150 people who died in a plane crash, or in the case of 9/11, taking a sample from a burned piece of flesh that could have come from any of 3,000 missing people, who may have come from anywhere in the world.

I can sympathize with the people who know about forensics from TV dramas—I grew up addicted to the 1970s show *Quincy,* all about a Los Angeles medical examiner solving unexplained suspicious deaths. Shows like that sparked my interest in forensics and law enforcement, but TV crime procedurals have vastly overstated the speed and powers of DNA testing. So I often find myself having to manage people's expectations, because in real life DNA testing can take weeks, if not months. And sometimes, it is not even possible to get a result.

My other work with DNA had to do with criminal convictions. I served on the board and later as chairman of the Virginia Institute for Forensic Science and Medicine (VIFSM), a not-for-profit organization that supported training, education, and research for forensic scientists and pathologists. One of my duties as chairman was to also serve on the Commonwealth of Virginia Department of Forensic Sciences Forensic Science Board (DFS FSB). The DFS FSB is a legislatively mandated board, which provides oversight to the Department of Forensic Sciences, a check if you will. The DFS is the state-run crime lab, the agency that provides forensic lab services to the Commonwealth's law enforcement agencies. VIFSM is probably most famous for its connection to crime writer Patricia Cornwell, who modeled her most famous character, Dr. Kay Scarpetta, on the Commonwealth's own chief medical examiner, Dr. Marcella Fierro, whom I consulted with as I was driving from Texas to the Pentagon in the harrowing days after 9/11. I also worked with her on the board at VIFSM, when I was stationed at Fort Lee and consider her one of the leaders in forensic pathology and a good friend.

In Virginia, back in the 1970s and '80s, the department had employed a very diligent forensics expert named Mary Jane Burton, who had developed the habit of cutting off the tip of cotton swabs she had used to test samples of blood, semen, and other bodily fluids—and taping them to her file records. This was highly unusual, first because the practice in those days was that all such samples were to be destroyed after a few years, except in murder cases, and also because DNA testing had not even been invented yet. But she diligently kept the samples, which were later stored away in vast repositories holding tens of thousands of cardboard boxes full of case files, where they sat almost untouched for decades while DNA testing underwent its rapid evolution.

Burton died in 1999, but two years later the Innocence Project, which works on overturning wrongful convictions, took up the case of an African-American man who had served fifteen years for a rape he did not commit. The man, Marvin Anderson, had been just seventeen at the time and had always maintained his innocence. But even after he was released on parole, he had borne the stigma of the crime he had not committed: he had difficulty finding work and was obliged to register as a sex offender. The Innocence Project contacted the forensic department's director Dr. Paul Ferrara, a pioneer in DNA studies, asking him to reexamine his files. That was when Dr. Ferrara, leafing through Burton's notes, discovered her habit of keeping cotton swab samples from all her cases. Anderson's conviction was overturned.

That left the forensics department with a huge legal question: there were thousands of case files in the repository. That meant there were potentially hundreds of people who had been wrongfully convicted, and just as worryingly, many criminals who were probably still at large, since the wrong person was occupying their jail cell.

The legal ramifications were obviously way bigger than the department itself was equipped to handle, and in 2004, Mark Warner, who was Virginia's governor at the time, ordered the department to reexamine a sample of 10 percent of the sex offender and murder files containing biological evidence that had not been DNA tested. A year later, after three more people were exonerated, he ordered a full review, and for all of the untested evidence to be tested.

Then the challenge became what to test first, and how to

notify people, especially those still incarcerated while this was going on. The DFS FSB board was made up of a lab director, medical examiner, the head of the state police, a defense attorney—Mr. Steve Benjamin—forensic specialists, a local citizen, a local sheriff, and the chairman of VIFSM, and me. Steve had proposed that all samples should be tested, and all persons convicted should be duly notified. I agreed with this method but, unfortunately, we were in the minority. We spent many meetings arguing over what samples should be tested; some suggested they be prioritized based on the crimes people had been convicted of. So I asked them what category of prisoner should be petitioning? They suggested those convicted of sex crimes and murder.

The problem with that is that some people who are arrested for sex crimes don't actually go to jail for sex crimes. Prosecutors worry that the evidence they have may not be enough to convince a jury, so they offer the defendant the chance to cop to a plea of a lesser account, like burglary—which may in fact carry a similar sentence if you already have a string of previous convictions behind you. And some defendants may still agree to that just so that they can go to jail on a burglary charge rather than be incarcerated as a rapist, which puts you at risk of being knifed in the prison showers. What also got lost in all of this was the fact that some of those test results could have been uploaded to CODIS and potentially resulted in the arrest of the actual criminal, taking a violent offender off the street.

The arguments over who to test went on so long that my time as chairman of the board actually ran out. Virginia has been building out the notification project for years now to let people whose lives may be upturned by this scientific revolution know that their convictions could have been wrongful. Many are now dead, but their families might benefit from the knowledge.

This is why I believe crime labs should always be separate

from police departments. The preponderance of testing and support always goes to the prosecution, which disadvantages the defendant who has to be presumed innocent until proven guilty. As I learned when I was a sheriff's deputy, police officers hold an enormous power: they can deprive people of their most basic liberty, which is the right to freedom. There is a dangerous and very real temptation for police officers, or disaster victim identification investigators, to try to find evidence for what they think has happened, as opposed to what the facts actually bear out. Police officers may take some evidence to a lab and say to the forensics guys, "Here, confirm this for me."

But a lab shouldn't be confirming anything: a lab should be telling you an objective fact. You should never go to the scene of a crime or a mass fatality with your mind already made up, because you will see things that don't exist and try to mold the facts to fit it. It may seem logical, but it is not fact-based, and it is very easy to follow the wrong road with devastating consequences.

16. A World of Pain

When dealing with the dead you are, to a certain extent, shielded from the living. The dead are generally compliant, though some yield their stories only reluctantly. But the other side of our work is dealing with relatives of the dead at family assistance centers, working with them to identify the deceased and returning their possessions and remains—and that exposes us to some of the rawest emotions humans can experience.

In mass fatality events, we typically hold briefings to explain the various processes to the families. The briefings should start with the CEO of the companies involved or the local government officials expressing sympathy, saying they are sorry and then moving on to addressing the needs of the survivors. However, most of the CEOs or government officials initially approach these briefings by wanting to discuss what has occurred. The survivors and families attending know what has happened, what they don't know is the why, but that is not their biggest concern. Their biggest concern is about what is next, and what does it mean for them in a practical sense. This is where most companies or governments get it wrong. In essence they are trying to defuse a bomb that has already gone off. Families know mistakes happen, and they will deal with that over time, but what they expect and what they have the right to expect is that a response will focus on managing the consequences of the incident. Yes, briefing can be very emotional. In one brief following a flight which crashed into the ocean, the father of one of the dead ripped open his shirt and starting shouting, "Who will take care of my heart? You have killed my heart!" He was not talking strictly metaphorically either: it turned out that he did have a heart condition and his late son was the one who had paid his medical bills. In his culture, it was expected that the young would look after their parents in their old age, and he felt not only sad but betrayed.

In another briefing, a woman was so distraught she blocked the door of the conference room and declared, "No one is leaving until I have answers!" And of course, no one in the world of officialdom wants to face these poor people, who are going through the worst moment in their lives. So it is something I do quite often. It is part of caring for the living and it is just one of the many things that needs to be done.

That process often starts with a phone call saying that something has happened, a plane is missing or has crashed, a bomb has gone off, or there has been a natural disaster. Sometimes I also find out from the news. One day, I was in our UK warehouse, boxing up some things to ship to the United States, when our office got a phone call from the BBC. They wanted to interview me regarding a Lufthansa flight that had just crashed in the Alps. Before I could even answer the person telling me about the call, someone else came in to to tell me Lufthansa was alerting us to the loss of one of their aircraft. Clearly, I took that call and not the BBC call.

One of the first things that should happen is that a call and data center should go live to take phone calls or receive email requests from family members or friends. While relatives and friends can get basic information, the main purpose is actually to start gathering information about the victims and their families. We have to build a picture of who is missing, and the scope and size of the event. This is something that did not happen in Louisiana with Hurricane Katrina for several weeks after the hurricane, and that created a lot of problems. There might be several call centers working, but there should only be one data center and database, and everyone should be feeding information into that.

Lots of people think there is some database that airlines or others have of all the people on board flights. The reality is they don't; they have only basic information, all the other information that might be included in a loyalty program is often a separate system and is not as easily accessed as people think. Then there is the manifest; few people really understand what is on a manifest and they are different from airline to airline. In all the crashes I have ever worked, I have yet to see an accurate manifest. For example, if I am on a US domestic flight on United, I end up as Roberta Jensen. That is because I also use my middle initial A. On the manifest, the two get combined to "Roberta." The manifest will also have a seat number and likely a loyalty status. So, no more Robert, only a Roberta. If a call center operator is asked if there was a Robert on the flight and has been working under stress or maybe not trained on the data system they are using, they are likely to tell a person there is no Robert. Conversely my family may call in also under great stress, and they call me Andrew, my middle name. That is the name I used until going into military school, when I defaulted back to Robert. They may only ask about an Andrew, not a Robert. They may ask about a Jensen, and in certain parts of the United States and the world, Jensen is a fairly common name and chances are multiple Jensens may be involved.

A big part of an initial response is trying to get a good list of those people who are directly affected (we call those PDAs) and their families. We have to build it as we track people down, or as they call in. The people who don't call in can also be a telling detail too—one of the early clues to identifying the terrorists who hijacked the 9/11 planes was that for most of the hijackers no one called in asking about these particular passengers. That is unusual, and in an incident where you suspect foul play, it can be instrumental.

The call and data center also has the role of notifying families that their loved may be involved in an incident. Notifications are inherently hard. When I was a deputy some people wouldn't open the door to me because they knew what I was going to say. On the phone it can be even harder, but the phone is the quickest way and therefore most common for large-scale events. When we have tracked down the correct relative's phone number or they have called in, we introduce ourselves and explain in a clear but sympathetic manner why we are calling. We ask the stunned person on the other end of the line if they would like someone to come to their house to be with them. Once they have had sufficient time to begin to process the news, we then inform them of the next steps. Either that someone will contact them in the near future, or if they are ready, we tell them where the family assistance center will be set up, and what information—contact details for doctors, dentists, etc.—they should bring if they can make it and are willing to travel. We then set up their travel. Often that may mean a flight. We notify the airline they are traveling on so they get special treatment— we are, after all, asking people to get on a plane to visit the site of a plane crash. This can be difficult, but most families make the flight, and I think it goes to the fact that people realize mistakes happen. I also think the fear of not going or finding their loved one is stronger than the fear that something may happen to them. If the flight provides newspapers and the incident is likely to be featured in them, we ask the airline to pull those papers.

The next step is establishing a family assistance center. It should be as close to the incident as possible, a safe place with comfortable accommodation for bereaved families. There should be meeting and working rooms and good catering facilities. So that means big hotels. We then offer to block a number of rooms, or in some cases book the entire hotel. Of course, there are cases where one branch of a family hates another branch, and they have to be identified quickly and kept separate, possibly in different hotels. Sometimes, if the event is in a small town, such as with the Germanwings crash in the Alps, the authorities themselves have already taken over all available hotel space to set up their emergency response units and house their own staff. So, it may mean getting hotels a little bit farther away. The biggest factor in deciding a location is picking an area that can support the numbers of families we expect. We may also operate smaller satellite facilities if people feel they cannot travel to the main center.

Family assistance centers serve three major purposes. First off, they are a safe and protected space for families to receive information, which is provided through a series of briefings. They should first start with the CEO or appointed official saying they are sorry for the loss of human life or injury. This is not an admission of guilt, nor is every person looking for that. What people are looking for is a human face with human emotions. They are looking for someone to tell them that there is a system in place to care for them and help them transition through this event. Sadly, people resist this because they think it admits liability. There is a palpable change in the room when the head of an airline stands up and says, "I am very sorry for the loss of your loved ones." I have seen it many times. For sure, there will be a settlement process, with attorneys and often accountants to determine the value of a life that has been lost. That is a given. But there does not have to be litigation, and it does not have to be acrimonious. In these cases, I see litigation as an extension of anger. That anger that comes from no one ever saying sorry or we are here to help. That is driven by people in charge focusing on the event, and not the response. As I have said before, you cannot control the incident, but you can control the response. Briefings are hard; they frighten people. It also means facing the fact that a system they were a part of or maybe responsible for failed. Maybe it is not their company's fault: it is most likely accidental, and certainly not intentional on their behalf. Regardless, they are now part of it, and for those that have ever taken a life, no matter how justified or accidental, it changes many things. But it must be done.

After that, the briefing should focus on practical matters, such as the process and how long it should take for the return of the deceased and their personal effects; how to access immediate financial assistance; how to start the settlement process, the investigation process, and how long it should take. All very practical matters. This allows the family to decide what level of assistance they need and to plan for how long they may wish to stay at the family assistance center. The problems often arise when deciding who should brief what and when. It's always a fight.

In Germanwings for example, on the sixth or seventh day following the accident, the French president announced that the Gendarmerie had identified 150 DNA profiles. Families at the family assistance center took that to mean that the loved ones were identified and would be released soon. Understandable, but it is not what that meant. What it meant was that the

Gendarmerie had done rapid genetic tests on the three thousand fragments of human remains that had so far been recovered from the crash site. From those fragments, 150 unique profiles had been established. We knew there were 150 people on the plane and no one on the ground was missing. That meant everyone could be accounted for. But as the antemortem process had barely started, there weren't even any familial profiles generated yet. The families didn't understand that, so someone needed to tell them what the information actually meant. The problem was who? We approached the Gendarmerie and asked them to come and brief the families. They said, "No, that's not our job. That's the prosecutor's job." So, we duly went to the prosecutor's office and asked, "Would you do it?" and he said, "No, that's not my job, that's the scientific process, that's the police."

I get it; nobody wants to tell family members that their loved ones are in pieces. So I said, "Fine. I'll do it." Because that's my job, and I know how to do it: and that is to give people the facts, painful as they may be, but with the context they need to fully understand them. At that point Lufthansa wasn't sure they should have us brief the families, which meant another discussion. I really don't mind the discussion—well, actually, I do get tired of them at times, but it is new for many people. My problem is the time they take and the delays they cause for the families.

The briefing would be in several different languages: the first thing was to make sure all the translators knew precisely what terminology was being used—that a "body fragment" wasn't a "body" or a "limb" but a general term for tissue samples of any size. I gave the translators an extensive pre-brief, then walked into the room to face the families gathered there.

"This briefing will be difficult," I warned them, "and some of you who have kids may not want them here, and some of you may not want to hear this. You may not be ready yet because

I'm going to talk about the condition of your loved ones and the identification process." I paused, and some people left. Then I began the briefing proper.

"As you know this was a high-speed impact. Which means people don't look like us and today as I understand from the Gendarmerie, they have discovered over three thousand human remains. So that means fragments of your loved ones. I also understand that because of the cold weather, the preservation, and the great forensics work by the Gendarmerie, they've been able to generate one hundred and fifty DNA profiles out of those three thousand fragments so far. As we know from the manifest there were only one hundred and fifty people on the flight, and we've not got any reports of people on the ground being killed. That means that everyone will be identified or can be identified.

"But what they have is a number, a genetic marker that says this piece of tissue is different from this piece of tissue. It doesn't give them a name; it doesn't say this piece of tissue is Robert A. Jensen. That won't happen until you, as family members, have provided your DNA samples. Now, for the individual there is a reference from the site, as collected by the police. Unless that person while alive had their DNA collected, they're going to have to tease out of the samples that they're collecting from you and your relatives a profile that will match. And that's not like on TV. That's not an hour or a day's process, that likely will take months. I would expect it to be four to six months before your loved ones are able to be identified and repatriated to you. And there will likely be many more recoveries."

Obviously, the families were disappointed to hear this, but then they were already desperately sad from the tragedy itself. At least after the presentation they could say, "Now I know what it means." They knew what to expect, how to plan, and that gave them a path forward out of this painful time.

Otherwise, you have families sitting in a hotel room in Marseilles in deep shock, not knowing what they should be doing or for how long. Some came up and thanked me for telling them afterward. It's not hard to do—in fact, it's relatively straightforward, but no one wants to be the bearer of bad news.

The second purpose of the family assistance center is to collect two types of information from the families. The first is the information that will be used to help identify their loved one, the antemortem information. The disaster victim identification working group of Interpol has developed very comprehensive postmortem and antemortem forms. Most countries use these, and they are the ones we also use. The information can take several hours to collect and should be done by a person who is trained to collect it. It is a thirty-page form. It is also very personal, and information collected needs to be safeguarded and used only for identification. To our process we have added a privacy statement, so people understand its use. There are questions like: Did the deceased have scars, tattoos, implants, pacemakers? Were they in the military, law enforcement, or ever have security clearance, something that would mean they have fingerprints on file somewhere? Some of it can seem invasive. We ask if they had ever been in jail, because that too would mean fingerprints on record. And of course, not everyone comes to the family assistance center, so we have to send people to family homes. Quite often this is done by a combination of people like us and the local police, when the deceased come from different countries.

At this time DNA references might also be collected from family members, as well as contact information for doctors and dentists. If those are lacking, then there might be the discussion about sending a team to someone's home to collect fingerprints, or items that might contain DNA—such as a toothbrush or hairbrush. A big part of this process is also understanding who to interview and who will have the most accurate information. Life is often not straightforward, and neither is death.

In one crash, we interviewed the parents of a girl who had died and whose boyfriend had come along as well to the family assistance center. The parents answered all the questions, and it was thought that someone was going to have to go to their daughter's apartment to try to retrieve DNA samples from a toothbrush or hairbrush. After the parents left the interview, the boyfriend lingered behind. He quietly confessed that he and his girlfriend had been living together, something she had not told her parents, and therefore the best items were at his place, not hers.

The second type of information we try to narrow down and collect from the family is who the legal next of kin is, or in more specific terms, the Person Authorized to Direct Disposition (PADD) and the Person Eligible to Receive the Effects (PERE). In most cases they are the same. Almost every jurisdiction has very defined lists of who, in order of precedence, can fill those roles. Unfortunately, not all families understand this and the issue of disposition—did the deceased want to be buried, cremated, have their ashes scattered at sea, or even if, as in the case of the late writer Hunter S. Thompson, fired on a rocket into the sky—can be challenging.

If you have a will or a disposition document (and I advise everyone I meet to get both) that sets out your wishes, it's not a problem. But I've had to intervene in bitter family squabbles among children who can't decide where their parent would have wanted to be buried, what kind of memorial to put up, or whether to bury or cremate them. (I have had Kenyon representatives witness the cremation of a parent's remains then deliver the ashes to three different offspring at exactly the same time, to appease feuding siblings.)

In one case I had to intervene in, a deceased man had a new wife and a very young baby, but also a very controlling mother who clearly did not approve of her daughter-in-law. She insisted that she was the next of kin, when legally that position was clearly occupied by his wife. The mother became obstreperous when I explained this to her. I took her to one side and had a talk with her. That was when she told me what was really bothering her. "He's not supposed to die before me, I'm the one who's supposed to be dead," she sobbed.

I said I understood, but asked her what would her son want if he were there now? "You have a role," I told her. "You have a year-old grandson. He had only just been married to his wife, so where is his son going to learn about his dad? Who's going to tell him what kind of a man he was when he was growing up? You're the bridge, if you choose to be part of his life, but you can't isolate yourself from your daughter-in-law. Because she's in charge, she's his wife and the mother of his child."

You have to be direct in these situations, because the problem isn't going to simply go away, and leaving such explosive emotional issues unaddressed is certainly not going to get any better with age.

Family members can also conceal other family members who might have a higher priority. It is not the norm, but it does happen. After doing a family brief one day, the Canadian ambassador came up to me and asked why no one had been in touch with the family of one of her citizens. I asked her the man's name; she told me. As it turns out, I had just spoken to the man's brother. The ambassador was unaware of the brother, and we were unaware of the family in Canada. The deceased was a dual national: he left Canada on a flight to Paris using his Canadian passport, then in Paris he switched to his Egyptian passport and boarded the flight to Egypt. To the Egyptian airline, he was Egyptian, and when the plane had crashed the family in Egypt had failed to mention the family in Canada. Naturally, we started sharing information and speaking to the deceased man's wife.

The third function of the family assistance center is to provide a place for the families to gather and process what has happened. A big part of that is going to the incident site. Again, something a lot of people—in government or from companies like airlines—try to prevent, but something we are told time and time again is hugely important to the families. These visits of course are planned; they are done after the human remains have been recovered and are supported by medical and psychological counselors. People are told what to expect, the sights and smells they will encounter. Often more than 90 percent of the people at family assistance center want to make this trip. Because it will often be months before their loved ones are returned, it is one of the first physical signs that their loved ones are dead, and this happened. Family assistance centers aren't just for adults. There was a sixteen-year-old boy, whose life is never going to be the same because his dad was just killed in a plane crash, who had a chance to sit at a site that is closed to everyone except his small group of fellow mourners. When all of a sudden he started crying, no one there judged him or thought him weak or weird, because there would be another young person who would do the same thing. Or he might start laughing, remembering some goofy memory of his dad. If he were to do the same at home, people might think him callous or unhinged, because people faced with meeting those dealing with a death often don't know what to do or say to comfort them.

The importance of doing this was underscored with the Afriqiyah crash in Tripoli in 2010. The plane, headed from South Africa to the Netherlands, had many Dutch people on board.

The Dutch government assumed that seeing the crash site would be upsetting and encouraged the families not to go. But many came anyway, and we showed them where their relatives had perished. When they returned home, some of them spoke of the moving experience to families who had not come. In response the Dutch government organized a second, much later visit. By then the wreckage had been recovered and we were all gone. It did not have nearly the same meaning as it had for the first group who witnessed the wreckage.

Family assistance is hard, and it also often means intervening with governments on behalf of the families. Possibly the most extreme measure I have had to resort to was when a government was withholding the release of the deceased.

The dispute had arisen because the plane, part of the national carrier's fleet, had flown to another country and crashed on the return leg. The president to whom I wrote was insisting that the plane had been brought down by a bomb: the country the plane had flown out of insisted it had crashed due to maintenance problems. In effect, each country was trying to shift the blame to the other. Country A said it was poor security at Country B's airport; Country B said it was bad maintenance by Country A. Neither side appeared willing to back down.

As a result, Country A was refusing to release the remains of the deceased, who came from a variety of countries. After six months of waiting for their relatives to be returned, their agony was palpable. I wrote a letter to the president of Country A beseeching their immediate release on humanitarian grounds from a medical examiner's lab in his capital.

"The unexplainable delay in this release, coupled with a lack of information and rumors about the mortal remains of their loved ones being held as part of a political battle . . . has and will continue to damage the reputation of the national carrier and the government of Country A," I wrote. I pointed out that such a long delay caused massive emotional damage to the families and was unprecedented in my twenty-plus years of experience in dealing with mass fatalities.

The letter was polite and respectful and held open the possibility that the delay was a bureaucratic error, although I knew it wasn't. I also knew that I had no reason to believe a letter from me would reach the president or have an impact, unless it could be used by the leaders of the countries who had lost their citizens, so I made sure to copy their leaders, through the ambassadors I had been speaking with. I never received a reply. But the bodies were released within a week.

17. The Wave

Imagine the largest, most complicated jigsaw puzzle in the history of the world being assembled by thousands of people who have never met each other before, and who are scattered across a dozen countries. Now, throw in hundreds of people in a deep panic rushing across the path of the investigators who are trying to put the pieces together. And now imagine the pieces of that jigsaw puzzle are dead human beings. That might give you a rough approximation of what it was like to tackle the gargantuan task of identifying almost a quarter million or so people who died in the tsunami that engulfed coastal communities from South Africa, across India and Southeast Asia, and through to Indonesia just hours after Christmas Day in 2004. The scale of the disaster was simply unimaginable to many of the people caught up in that huge wave and its aftermath. It was triggered by an earthquake that shook the ocean bed near Sumatra with a force equivalent to 23,000 atom bombs that was used on Hiroshima. The fact that it struck during the Christmas holiday break only added to the massive confusion—many government leaders were themselves on holiday, and quite a few were simply unable to grasp the scale of what had happened for several days. The Swedish foreign affairs minister even went to the theater the night after the tsunami, even though Thailand was a popular winter destination for many Scandinavians and the death toll was already starting to climb into the thousands.

I think for many it was on such a scale, a scale many found impossible to believe could happen in modern times. People just did not know how to react or even what to do. Some disasters impact a defined geographical area—like Hurricane Katrina, which was to occur later that year but with an impact to a limited number of people. That number may be in the thousands or hundreds of thousands, but it is limited. Everyone will have heard of it, but many won't be impacted by it. Because of that, until something hits home or until an issue that confronts them has a face or a name, people are at a loss. Think about the issue of apartheid in South Africa. It was a horrible system, but people in America and other countries were not sure what they could do against so pervasive a system of oppression in a distant land. But with the incarceration of Nelson Mandela, the African National Congress suddenly had a face, someone people overseas could relate to and help. You could donate money to his cause, and by helping Mandela you were helping end apartheid.

On the other hand, some disasters like the tsunami hit a large geographical area and also affect people who are spread over a much larger area—an area that encompassed thirty-three different nations, some in minor ways and others, like Sweden or Germany, significantly. Then of course there are events like the pandemic, in which almost everyone is affected. Either they were sick, knew someone who was sick and may have died, suffered job losses, lost their homes, or were challenged by fear or the endless quarantines. In effect, it causes a billion crises simultaneously.

If Haiti showed the inequities of death, the 2004 Asian tsunami—which killed more people—illustrated the enormity of treating masses of dead with some degree of equality. While the Haitian government could simply bulldoze tens of thousands of corpses into burial pits, the dead in Thailand, Indonesia, and across a vast earthquake front that included many thousands of tourists—whose governments wanted their citizens found, identified, and brought home—created complex problems.

The powerful earthquake struck Sunday morning local time; it was Christmas evening for me. By the next morning my time, the giant wave had hit all around the rim of the Indian Ocean: in some parts of Thailand and Indonesia, it wiped entire towns away, simply scoured them off the face of the earth. Divers underwater in popular Thai dive resorts said they felt like they were in a giant washing machine as the wave rolled over them. In other distant places, like South Africa, it manifested as a rather large but otherwise unremarkable wave that lapped up across seaside roads and briefly caught the attention of tourists, who only remembered it when they saw the news of the devastation it had caused elsewhere.

It was the Australian authorities who alerted us to the enormity of what was happening and requested our assistance. Initial reports were coming into Canberra: thousands were dead and missing in the beach resorts and party towns that were so popular with its citizens at that time of year. By noon on that Sunday, we were making travel arrangements and recalling staff to all our offices.

Since Thailand was the most popular tourist destination in the region, it seemed obvious we would have to be based there. I jumped on a plane myself. Christmas was over. For my family, it was to be a year that I would barely see them. Between the tsunami, major airplane crashes, trips to Iraq, and Hurricane Katrina, I was rarely home. Of course, we did not know then that I'd be away for that long, but they were used to it. Or at least they told me that they were. My attention was focused on the task at hand. I arrived in Bangkok a day or so later and went straight to meet the Australian ambassador there. Bill Paterson was a seasoned foreign service veteran but had only just arrived. He'd been packing up his home in Australia when he got the call from the Foreign Office that his job had started a week early. When he got to Bangkok, he didn't even have the chance to present his credentials to the king before he found himself on a helicopter for Khao Lak, near Phuket, where the bodies of more than two thousand foreigners had already been gathered and stored to await identification.

"We helicoptered into this village and it was hugely disturbing. It was dusty and, as you got closer, the smell began to penetrate, a very distinctive smell I have never smelled before," he told a journalist later. "They say once you smell it you never forget it, and I can believe that."

Luckily, Australian law enforcement worked well with their Thai counterparts, and had an established relationship before the tsunami struck. The country is a key regional ally in battling drugs and organized crime, and although Bill had just arrived, he started to emerge as the man in charge of overseeing operations. That was good thing, because he is not only an exceptional leader, he is an exceptional diplomat.

I don't think the Australian leadership sat well with some of the European countries. Bill understood Thailand; he knew about their internal struggles and how to get things accomplished. Most important, he knew how to help guide them and save face at the same time. This doesn't mean that the Thais were not capable or organized to undertake such an operation. Quite the opposite: they were for the manner in which they were accustomed to dealing with loss, but not in the manner that the

West deals with it. Just as it would be if the roles were reversed. In Thailand, a dead body is just that, a body. It does not have a name, it is not the person, to call a corpse by its name is to disturb it and potentially prevent the dead from resting in peace. There are no major morgues or funeral homes, except a handful to deal with the occasional tourist deaths. All other bodies are taken to temples and then cremated. Second, in European countries the police deal with deaths, and it is the same in Thailand, unless an investigation is required in which case there is a forensic institute. At the time it was led by a flamboyant, red-haired forensic pathologist, Dr. Pornthip Rojanasunand, who looked more like Tina Turner or a cutting-edge New York City fashion designer than the forensic expert she was. Her many books and her distinctive hairdos had already made her something of a celebrity in Thailand. She and the police did not necessarily get along, and in fact a Thai newspaper published a cartoon at the time showed her facing one way with the stretcher holding a body, and the deputy commissioner—Royal Thai Police General Nopadol Somboonsub, also a fine leader and good man—holding the same stretcher but facing the opposite directions. They both had different ideas on how to manage the response.

Against this backdrop, Bill and I made trips to assess different areas. The coastal region had of course taken the worst hit. We then decided to be based out of Phuket, once the jewel in the crown of the region's tourism. Now most of the town was coated in drying mud, its streets clogged with debris and its temples stacked high with bloated remains.

I've learned that it's best not to dwell on the devastation all around you: people with that inclination tend not to last too long. However, just a few days before I arrived, these Thai coastal resorts had been full of happy families with young kids enjoying their dream vacation, paddling in the sea on white beaches or lounging by hotel pools with cocktails and best-sellers. Young backpackers had saved up for months to be able to get here and have the adventure of their lives.

That their heaven had become hell in an instant was clear when we arrived and set up our first working meetings in the conference room of the beachside Hilton: it had survived relatively unscathed. But there was an odor, one most of us knew; that of a decomposing body. After a few days of looking, we located it. A body that the wave had wedged into a crawl space between the shops below and the conference room where we were working.

Initially, the bodies were being collected in temples. Instead of incense, the open-air shrines smelled of dry ice, which was being rushed in to prevent the rapid decay of so many deceased in the heat. We would walk to the temples and see hundreds of bodies lined up in ragged lines outside them. Some were in crude wooden coffins, but most were just wrapped up in plastic or grubby linen sheets hastily pulled from the hotels where the dead tourists had slept because the Thais had long since run out of body bags. Quite a few were uncovered except for the blocks of dry ice that the army trucked in to slow putrefaction: the contrast between the deceased lying in the dirt and the clean white blocks of ice perched on their chests and legs was striking, especially as the dry ice emitted wisps of fog that added to the otherworldly effect of the scene. And from the point of view of identifying a body, putrefaction can be a major hindrance, obscuring fingerprints and making distinguishing tattoos harder to see.

Soldiers had been deployed to keep order, and friends and relatives of the dead—many of whom had only just survived the horrific ordeal themselves—were scouring these grim depositories for any sign of their loved ones, opening up body bags and lifting soiled shrouds, handkerchiefs clutched over their mouths.

The walls of surviving hotels were covered in desperate handwritten notes in Thai, English, German, Swedish, Chinese and other languages along with descriptions of the missing and reports of where they had last been seen, often accompanied by heartbreaking photos and a contact email address. We had use of an Australian Defense Force helicopter for aerial surveys and to search for bodies, and relatives would often plead to be allowed on board to look for their missing.

Our goal was to start the process as soon as we could. The first hurdle was the battle between Dr. Rojanasunand and General Nopadol. It was an internal Thai issue, but it had a huge effect on the international operations, because we could not start until it was settled as to who was doing what. In the end, those deceased that were believed to be Thai were taken care of by Dr. Rojanasunand and those believed to be foreign by General Nopadol's teams, supported by international teams.

Next came solving how the international team would work together. With a job of that size, two things are key: first, working out the process and then assigning the right people to the right part of that process. This might sound easier than in fact it was. People wanted to carry out work on their own people, which meant cherry-picking the deceased and which areas to focus on, because different resorts tended to be more popular with different nationals. For example, there were some areas around Phuket, like Khao Lak, that were more popular with Germans and Austrians; others which tended to attract more British people. I had seen similar national claims in the Bali bombings, and from the outset the group focus was that we couldn't have people saying, "We think this is a German person, so we are sending them to Germany for testing." I understood the pressure from families and politicians, and the pressure on the politicians.

It took time. More than it should have. For most, if they are not in on the takeoff, then don't count them in on the landing, so you need agreement and buy-in. Here we needed for everyone to agree to a process, what samples for DNA would be collected, how would records be shared, what team would work where, and who would provide overall support. Initially, some of the teams said they would only focus on their citizens. They were under enormous pressure back home to start repatriating their people. Families were desperate for information on their missing loved ones. When a tsunami hits, it sweeps its victims out to sea and can dump them miles away, depending on the powerful and erratic currents in play at the time. Or it can sweep them miles inland and leave them in trees or in collapsed buildings. The victims are likely to have been wearing beach shorts or swimsuits when they died, and therefore lacking most of the common identifying markers we could use—wallets, ID cards, or keys. Of course the action of the waves and being tossed around also removed personal effects from the bodies. And when each country announced it wanted to retrieve its "own" citizens, how could we tell what nationality or even ethnicity a water-damaged body might be? Even the Thais had problems identifying their own victims in their own country, because even if someone could, by some miracle, be identified as ethnically Thai, they might still be a citizen of another country, like Canada or the United States, for example. Ethnicity does not equal nationality. At this point more than five thousand international visitors were missing and feared dead.

In one frustrating, stifling, and un-air-conditioned meeting, I said it isn't as if you want to walk into the temple and say, "Everyone who is Swedish here, put up your hand," and you think that will work. The police understood this, the diplomats not so much. That helped illustrate the futility of that line of pursuit, and eventually everyone agreed instead that all the bodies would be considered simply as tsunami victims, therefore potentially the citizen of any country. Only when postmortem data had been positively linked to antemortem data by members of a multinational forensic team could that body be considered as having a name and nationality. It did, however, make sense for different countries to take the lead in areas where they had the most victims, such as the Germans in Khao Lak, but they would be supported by other countries there, and all the data collected after the autopsy would be sent to the central Thai Tsunami Victim Identification Centre.

Not understanding this—nor I think how uncomfortable it was for the Thais to even think about having this many bodies not being cremated—some of the European diplomats, decided on what is known in diplomacy as a "démarche": a representation from one country to another announcing that unless you comply with our request, there will be serious consequences. This did not go down well with Thai officials, understandably enough. The foreign ministry threatened to throw everyone out of the country: the Europeans shot back that they could stop sending their tourists there, gutting the Thai economy. No one gets what they want with such actions. Most of all the families. Bill was able to smooth things over and by then we were moving equipment into place with the plan being to establish three main collection areas/morgues, the Thai Tsunami Victim Identification Centre (TTVI) mentioned above, and a Repatriation Center. The collection areas/morgue and TTVI would be staffed by Kenyon support teams, including forensic teams, and led and supported by other international teams. The teams aligned along typical patterns; for example, you could find the United Kingdom, Australia, and New Zealand in one area. Even in death people align.

By this stage, it had become clear that massive amounts of

equipment would be needed. So, we set up an office at Phuket airport, eventually supported by Qantas, one of our clients that we had worked closely with in the Bali bombings. It became the main hub for the operations and we started sending in charter and commercial flights, at one point moving over fifty tons of equipment. Not having anywhere near the number of body bags we needed in our warehouses, we called the companies that make them and asked them to reopen their factories—they were closed for the holidays—and work overtime on the mass production of body bags.

After getting the three collection/morgue areas set up, the next step was to set up the Thai Tsunami Victim Identification Centre. This was located in part of the Thailand Telecommunications building. This would be where the records gathered from the three morgues would be compared and identifications made. Leadership of this operation would rotate every two weeks among the countries involved. I understood this, but at the time it made things difficult as each person had their own way of doing things. I believe it must have been the largest and most complex multinational Disaster Victim Identification data operations in history. Kenyon alone deployed nine hundred people to help identify and repatriate the dead over the many months we worked on the project, with two hundred in the field at the peak of the job.

There were many long days there, and although we moved to a very nice resort, the Marriott, which had been chosen by the Australian government, few of us ever enjoyed the facilities, or in my case even knew they were there. One day, several years after the tsunami, I made a visit to Phuket, and stayed at the same Marriott. The manager remembered me and was showing me to my room when we walked by a very nice pool. I asked him when the pool was added, and he looked at me kind of funny and said,

"It was there all along." I had just never noticed it going back and forth to my room during the days of the tsunami response.

⟶

EVEN THOUGH WE AGREED that no work would be done outside the centralized system, national politics still interfered. Some foreign forensic experts were caught at the airport one day with a batch of bone samples, trying to get them home to carry out their own independent testing. The Thai authorities and some of the other countries made their displeasure clear to the country's ambassador.

Interpol also joined in, as did other international organizations, and sent a team to work inside the TTVI. Slowly but surely, order was emerging out of chaos. Remains started making their journeys home. Similarly, the living who had been separated by the rushing water were being reunited.

Some of the dead, especially the foreign tourists, could be identified through dental records, but a lot of the work had to be done by DNA searches. Even though taking DNA from the living usually just involves a cheek swab, collecting samples from thousands of relatives who had someone missing was a time-consuming process, and the rate of DNA identification was slow at first. Dental records played a key role in our task of putting names to bodies: in the end, it was estimated that some 80 percent of the successful identifications were carried out using forensic odontology, as the process is technically known.

These days, those still missing and unidentified have become cold cases, unlikely to ever be given names. Their possessions—wallets, keys, electronic gadgets, watches, and jewelry—are stored in containers at police stations across the arc of the tsunami. Their bodies lie in unmarked graves or have vanished at sea. Someday, some of them may be given names and graves where their families can visit them.

While operations in Thailand were successful, thousands of others remain unidentified, especially in Banda Aceh, the area of Indonesia that bore the brunt of the wave. Memorials have been held in coastal towns completely rebuilt after the tragedy, and fishermen refrain from taking their boats out on the anniversary. In some places, the memorials are overshadowed by fifty-feet-high concrete "tsunami towers," which people can flee to and climb in if another massive wave hits. The tops are open-air platforms to ease airborne evacuation, and more than $400 million has been spent on developing early detection and warning systems across the region. The tourists have returned, bringing much needed investment, but the region is still regularly rocked by earthquakes and tsunamis, a constant and sometimes deadly reminder of the big one that brought death on such an unprecedented scale.

18. Another Day at the Office

We had only a few days to recover the bodies. Bad weather was moving in on the remote area of northern Peru where a helicopter flying for the Rio Tinto mining company had slammed into the side of a mountain. We needed to get to the precarious crash site, an impressive rock face where the jungle rose up to meet the western cordillera of the Andes. I had my team, which included several mountain park rangers, volunteer search and rescue climbers, and members from a state Office of Emergency Services. This team included several regulars on Kenyon operations including a friend I call "Mother Matt," formerly a deputy chief with a state Office of Emergency Services, and head of Search and Rescue Teams in California. He serves as our safety officer and seems to always be on my case on about something or another; that is, he feels I do things unsafely, such as failing to remember to clip in on a rope! We also had an expert climber and medic. His name was Keith but I call him the "Tent Slob" because he is so messy to bunk with in the field, which I have had to do twice. There is no other climber/medic I would rather have with me, though. Then there was Bob, also formerly a deputy chief within the Office of Emergency Services, a genius at logistics and someone I gladly take on any operation when he is available. These were some of the climbers responsible for getting the rest of the team on site. Then there was the forensic team, including a young skilled anthropologist—who was probably a tad bit afraid of heights and working on ropes—the crash investigators, and the two Peruvian police officers who came with us. All of them were ready and waiting for the order to hike to the site and scale the cliff. It was already getting dark and I wanted to hit the trail at dawn.

That was when the company rep insisted that the rules governing all contractors for Rio Tinto stipulated that we had to attend a mine safety training day in order to carry out the job.

"But we're not going into a mine," I pointed out. "We're going up a mountain."

"I'm afraid that doesn't matter," the rep said. He was sympathetic, a good guy, but his hands were tied. In any other circumstances, I might not have cared—my team could sit through a dull and irrelevant corporate presentation, if that's what it took. And I respect Rio Tinto's strict health and safety guidelines when applied logically. But this was not the moment. We had just arrived from the United States: had flown to Lima, then to Chiclayo, and gotten all of our gear ready. The next day we would drive east from the town of Chiclayo—fording swollen streams in a convoy of our pickups—to a point ten miles west of Santa Cruz de Succhabamba to begin a trek/climb to the crash site. We had a four-day weather opening and the job was already physically strenuous and fraught with hazards.

"Either we skip this, or the mission is scrubbed and the team goes home," I told the rep. A few hours later he came back and said he could take the night to teach us the class. Again, I explained that it didn't seem very safe to have the team up half the night listening to a mine safety briefing, and hitting the trails exhausted before they even began. Finally, the decision was made that we could skip the mine safety class. We set off at first light for the crash site, unbriefed on the mysteries of mine safety.

While the big crashes and disasters tend to capture the headlines, they are not the only ones we respond to. Nonetheless smaller missions like this one in Peru in the spring of 2008 also carry their own risks. They are in remote, inaccessible spots and you are pretty much on your own if something goes wrong. I knew we would have to scale a perilous rock face and hack our way with machetes through thick jungle, so before we left the United States, Keith had researched the different types of poisonous snakes we might encounter and tried to track down the relevant serums. Unfortunately, there were twenty-three different types of venomous snakes in the hilly jungles around the copper mines of Chiclayo—where the ill-fated helicopter had been ferrying the company workers—and he could only find antivenom for three. So I told the crew that if they were bitten, they should get a good look at the snake before they passed out. Our mission is to recover the dead, not add to the total.

When the crash had occurred a month earlier, we had sent teams to work with the families, the authorities, and the Rio Tinto personnel. Immediately after the crash, the Peruvian police had made a very brief and hazardous helicopter landing on a nearby rocky outcrop and had managed to recover some of the deceased and the flight data recorder. Rio Tinto felt that more could be done and wanted to recover all the deceased and support a fuller investigation. Our job would be to pick through the debris and thorny undergrowth to locate the remains.

Getting to the crash site would have been easier with a helicopter. But the only one flying in that region belonged to the same company that had lost the first one, so we agreed it would only be used as a last resort. We loaded our equipment on our backs and started hiking. It was exhausting slogging through the jungle and up to our base camp, one thousand feet above the valley floor on a ridge close to the near-vertical rock face. The air was hot and sticky, with frequent heavy rains, and we had a lot of kit to carry—machetes to clear the brush, ropes, shovels, and markers to outline the areas where we would dig and sift. The flora and fauna seemed to work against any human endeavor in such inhospitable terrain—I still have a piece of thorn in my hand that went right through two pairs of gloves and embedded itself impossibly deep in my finger.

Normally, you would send a scout team ahead to make routes and get a better understanding of the terrain. We don't often get that opportunity, because we are working against the clock. The first night the lead team, with myself, made it halfway to where we would set up base camp before stopping because of darkness. The next day, as we started, the follow-on team or main body was to start. Their team leader Jerry Novosad, head of our operations and one of the best men to ever work for us, made the smart decision that for some of the people it would be too hard to make the terrain. He would wait until we had set up and could clear a proper landing and use the helicopter. It took us about eight hours the second day to reach the area we would set up and operate from: a flat area on top of a cliff, surrounded by a valley and river on three sides and the high mountain that the helicopter had crashed into on the back side. We cleared a spot for the helicopter and set up tents and arranged for the rest of the team to come the next day. To reach the crash site we would first hike up the ridge. Then, using ascenders, we would reach another flat area, rope in and work on the main debris field, where part of the engine and fuselage were tangled in the wiry scrub of loose scree. The first day, Mike, a Marin County firefighter also on our team, and I moved the heaviest section of wreckage, what had been the engines, by bouncing up and down on the section until it was loose enough to crash into the valley below. We could not take the chance that it would fall on its own while we were working in that area. We then set up a sifter on the nearest patch of level ground and passed bags of earth via a human chain to one of the forensic anthropologists who was mastering his vertigo enough to be able to go through the dirt looking for human remains.

At one point, I had to rappel down the sheer rock face to where some human remains had become tangled in a tree sticking out over the precipice. We would work the site during the day and return to our camp at night. Because the helicopter only flew daylight missions, that meant any human remains we recovered were buried each night to prevent wild animals from scavenging them. Every night we would inter whatever we had found and say a few words over them, out of respect for the victims and to remind ourselves that these had been people like us, each with their hopes and fears, just a short time before. Then early in the morning we would disinter the remains and load them onto a stretcher for the flight out.

After four days of being on site, we flew out and then retraced our route back home. We were successful in that we recovered multiple human remains, found the cockpit voice recorder, and a number of personal effects. And everyone we brought came home.

FOR MANY ON THE team, it was an exciting operation, for some a once in a lifetime. For me, it was almost just another day at the office. It had all started with a phone call. There is no normal in my job. One day I can be meeting with the CEO of a multinational corporation, dealing with lawyers or accountants, facing families going through the most painful moment of their life, or be deep in the wilderness searching for human remains and the possessions of the dead.

A few years before that trip to Peru, Kenyon was hired by the United Nations to recover the bodies from two UN planes that had been shot down years before, one within a week of the other, by rebels in the Angolan bush. What made this particular search mission all the more poignant was that the son of one of the pilots who died in the first crash was killed in the second plane: the son, himself a young South African bush pilot, was desperately looking for his missing dad when he was killed in an almost identical strike. Some bodies had been recovered but no one had been identified: no one knew for sure who was dead and who might still be alive. There was lingering speculation that they might have been captured and held by the UNITA antigovernment rebels for all that time, although after almost a decade such hopes were slim. Finding their bodies and bringing them home would be a huge balm for the family.

The UN is a vast bureaucracy that ordinarily I find difficult to put up with. But I work with them because the work they do is so important. Everyone likes to talk about their failures and shortcomings, but I always like to look at the successes, which have been many and often overlooked. I can't imagine what the world would look like without them. Since the end of the war in Angola, Dr. Christen Halle, a Norwegian doctor in the Department of Peacekeeping Operations had made it his mission to bring these people home and our goal was to help him. The Angolan countryside is still littered with landmines from forty years of war, when four centuries of Portuguese colonial rule abruptly came to an end and a full-blown civil war began. The late Diana, Princess of Wales had made removing landmines there a personal crusade before her death. In fact, Angola is still one of the most heavily mined places on earth, with an estimated one billion square feet "contaminated" by hidden ordnance. It is not somewhere you want to be just wandering around, looking for wreckage from planes that crashed almost a decade before.

The country is deeply scarred by conflict: between 1975 and 2002, the guerrilla groups who had once fought the Portuguese turned on each other for dominance in what became a proxy for the Cold War itself—the Soviet Union and Cuba backed the communist People's Movement for the Liberation of Angola (MPLA), who claimed power in the capital Luanda, while the United States and South Africa threw their weight behind the anti-communist guerrillas of the National Union for the Total Independence of Angola, or UNITA. The stop-start war cost the lives of half a million people and displaced another million, destroying the country's economy and infrastructure and leaving it strewn with the debris of conflict.

The conflict survived the end of the Cold War in large part because in the 1990s, the trade in blood diamonds kept UNITA going after Western backing had waned and its leader, Jonas Savimbi, had rejected his loss in elections to the MPLA. South African government troops were replaced by South African mercenaries, including those supplied by the security company Executive Outcomes, who fought on the side of the MPLA and against their old allies UNITA.

By 2005, though, the messy and complex war in Angola was finally over; UNITA's leader Savimbi had been shot dead on a riverbank three years earlier by government troops, and the one-time guerrilla groups had become political parties. Now the United Nations deemed it safe enough to try to recover the bodies of the men who died flying their aid workers and humanitarian deliveries through Angola's hot zones.

UN Flight 806 was brought down on December 26, 1998,

just a day after Christmas. The plane belonged to a company called TransAfrik International, which was contracted by the UN to fly staff around the war zones of southern Africa in light aircraft. They also used heavy Hercules C-130 planes to carry food, blankets, and other supplies to displaced people—which at that time was around a third of Angola's population. The pilots were often experienced South African bush pilots looking to make a buck or airmen seeking a life of adventure. Many of the crews were Filipinos or Angolans, with the occasional Russian or American. Since the roads were far too dangerous to use trucks, C-130s had become the preferred method of moving people and goods for the United Nations, although even in the sky, there was still plenty of risk involved.

The captain on UN Flight 806 was one of the most experienced fliers in the world. Johnny Wilkinson was a fifty-one-year-old South African who had racked up 23,000 flying hours, mostly in Hercs, and in some of the world's most dangerous places—his plane had been strafed by gunfire over Somalia, and he had flown missions in Mozambique, Sudan, and Rwanda before being deployed in Angola for eight years. He would spend two months at the TransAfrik base in Luanda, flying five or six days a week, and then have a month's leave to spend with his wife and two daughters back home on the outskirts of Johannesburg. His son, Hilton, who was twenty-five at the time, worshipped him and had followed in his footsteps, getting his commercial license in South Africa and then spending several years flying for a different outfit in Angola. In late 1998, his parents had just managed to persuade him to return home and fly for commercial airlines there, where they knew it would be safer.

That day, Johnny Wilkinson and his crew were scheduled to fly from Luanda to Huambo, the third largest city in Angola and some three hundred miles southeast of the capital, where they would pick up UN personnel. From there, they would head to the garrison town of Saurimo to the northeast before heading back to Luanda. Huambo was under siege by UNITA, which claimed the city as its capital. It was surrounded by guerrillas, some of them armed with the highly effective Stinger surface-to-air missiles which the CIA had supplied to the rebels—the same kind of shoulder-launched missiles my friend Charlie Wilson had delivered to the Afghan *mujahideen*. It was likely a strike with one of these that brought down the UN plane shortly after it flew out of Huambo on the second leg of its journey that day. The plane abruptly vanished from radio contact with the base in Luanda, but that was not unusual in a war zone or even today. When other planes flying in the area failed to make contact, concerns started to grow.

When Wilkinson's son heard that his father was missing, he scrambled to get back to Angola. Since there was no news of the plane whatsoever, the family, the UN, and the flight company had reason to hope that a skilled pilot like Wilkinson might have managed to crash-land safely, opening the possibility that the crew were being held somewhere by UNITA forces. When Marie Wilkinson dropped off her son at the airport in Johannesburg to catch the first available flight to Luanda, Hilton reassured her, "Mum, I'm going to bring Dad home."

Hilton already knew many of the bush pilots flying in Angola from his own time working there. He managed to talk his way onto a TransAfrik flight a week later that was scheduled to fly into Huambo. The captain, a seasoned Filipino pilot called Ramon Dumlao, had been scheduled to spend New Year's Eve with his wife and kids in Nairobi, Kenya: despite being just a few months shy of retirement, Dumlao had returned to join the search for his missing colleagues. He also agreed to sneak the distraught Hilton Wilkinson onto the flight to Huambo, promising to fly low to look out for any sign of wreckage from the missing plane.

Then their flight, UN 806A, also disappeared in the exact same area.

A week or so later, the UN managed to negotiate a fleeting visit to the first crash site for its own air-accident investigators: a couple of weeks later, UNITA allowed them to visit the second site. They found that the wreckage had been plundered and covered with branches to disguise the sites from the air, which had hampered the search. The black boxes had been removed. They concluded the first plane had been shot down by a missile, at a height of around 18,000 feet, the second hit by artillery at a much lower altitude—it had been flying low to look for the first missing aircraft. Some bone fragments were recovered, but not enough to account for all the missing crews and passengers. They were handed to the South African police's forensics unit, but no further tests were done to establish the identity of the remains. In part that was because Angola was technically supposed to issue the death certificates, as the country where they died, and also because not all the dead were necessarily South African. They were also UN employees, which further muddied the jurisdiction.

And so the remains of the missing were left in the Angolan bush, among the landmines and rusting military hardware, until 2005, when we were asked to bring back the final remnants.

As in Peru, my first task was to assess the main danger we would face: in the jungle it had been snakes, in the Angolan bush it would be landmines. I had a bit of experience with landmines from Bosnia and other combat zones I had been in, so I made a list of all the unexploded ordnance we were likely to encounter: there were more than seventy different types of landmines originating from twenty-two countries used in Angola, and they ran the gamut from Russian antitank mines, which a person on foot might inadvertently step on without necessarily having the weight to trigger, to horrific bounding antipersonnel mines such as the PP-Mi-SR, one I really dislike, and made in what used to be Czechoslovakia before the Berlin Wall came down and designed to spring up to waist height when detonated, then blast shrapnel in a deadly radius of up to sixty-five feet, enough to wipe out my team.

Our brief from the UN was to recce the area and see if it was possible to recover human remains. It was meant to be a two-trip mission. However, if we could do the operation in a single trip we would, but on paper it was trip one of two. The terrain was so hazardous that we didn't want to risk two trips, and secondly, because once we had shown interest in the sites, that was more than likely enough to trigger locals to go back and see if they could find anything of value. In any case, the kit was not extensive on a job like this: we carried digging trowels and surveying markers and human remains pouches.

We flew first to South Africa to pick up our security team who would accompany us: they were the same company that worked with the US government and were fully vetted, some of them were members of the now-disbanded 32 Battalion—an apartheid-era unit that had been commanded by white officers—South Africans, Rhodesians, and Australians mainly—but whose ranks were largely filled by Black Angolans who had fled their country after fighting on the losing side of the war. They carried out covert ops inside Angola for years and were also eventually deployed inside South Africa's own townships against anti-apartheid groups, earning themselves a highly controversial reputation. In fact, their team lead had actually been to the sites years before, but that was something we did not share with others. They were disbanded in 1993, after apartheid ended and Nelson Mandela's ANC came to power. I was slightly worried that some of them might get stopped by the border police when we flew into Angola, but fortunately, they were all cleared without incident. We had our luggage searched and were waved through, chartering a private plane to Huambo, which we had to reach before nightfall because the airport still didn't have any lighting. The plane, a Beechcraft 1900D, or Dash 1900 as I called them, was like many models I had flown but which I had also been called to recover human remains from after crashes. Something I can't help but think about every time I board a plane!

Huambo was a neat little town, though you could see the bullet and shrapnel holes in buildings, and there were red triangular signs everywhere warning *Perigo Minas!* or Danger Mines! It was dangerous to drive at night because the roads were unlit and many of the cars were so beat up that their headlights didn't work. They would loom out of the darkness like sharks from the depths.

We checked into a hotel, readied our kit, and met with the provincial police commander and the governor to go through our operation. When we were ready to go, we drove in a convoy along rutted, dusty roads, keeping in constant contact by radio. The main obstacles were trees that had fallen across the road: it was too dangerous to simply go off-road to get around them since there were still mines everywhere. I could tell when we were getting close to the wreck sites because I'd spotted parts of the crashed aircraft that had been looted and incorporated into houses, mainly for roofing. It was good metal after all.

The village headmen came out to meet us dressed in an unusual military uniform, but clearly dressed for the occasion—a Cuban military cover and raincoat. That made sense because Fidel Castro had sent twelve thousand Cubans to Angola to fight with the MPLA against the South Africans and UNITA. Although this was in territory held by UNITA, they had effectively lost. While the Cubans were long gone, their uniforms remained. We also bought gift of palm wine, chickens, and salt as an offer to the village elders when we got to the crash sites, as a token of our friendship.

The headman remembered the days when the planes were shot down, but was curious as to why we were there since the UN had sent their crash investigators years ago. I explained that the families of the missing crews needed answers, and he said he was happy to accompany us to the crash sites and would allow us to work there. He told us to beware, though: a farmer had been killed just a few days before when he stepped on a landmine in the same area where we'd be going and suggested we exercise caution. As an ex-Army officer and team leader, I scouted out the crash sites myself to check for hidden mines and was very strict with my team about where they could go beyond that.

The crash sites themselves still had visible craters. We spent two days digging up the soil and sifting for human remains. By that time, it was all bones: a rib, a patella, a femur, and some teeth. There were only four or five bone fragments at the crash site of the first plane, but almost ninety at the second site. We also found some personal effects and an empty safe box. Even a new wedding ring! Our pilots, who had flown us in, were remaining with us for the entire trip and had asked if they could accompany us into the field, after a proper safety briefing on mines. (No irony at all from our time in Peru.) One of them was newly married and noted as were getting ready to leave that he had lost his ring at a crash site, while helping dig in the dirt. Explaining that he could not go home without it, we all went back in and fortunately found it very quickly.

Everyone had told us the Angolans would never let us take

any human remains out of the country and would want to keep any human remains to test them themselves, as part of a political maneuver. But when we asked them, they agreed that we could take them back with us to South Africa. We put them in a body bag and draped a UN flag over them, in honor of the cause they had died for.

And that should have been that. Except there is a local expression—"TIA," which stands for "This Is Africa," and which refers to the fact that there is always some unforeseen circumstance waiting around the bend when you operate anywhere on the continent.

Usually when you move human remains across borders, you need permits and death certificates and a whole host of other documents. But what we had were unidentified skeletal remains, which carried no chance of transmissible disease, and since there was no cadaver, there was no chance of it being used for smuggling or containing any unexploded ordnance. Our cargo consisted of very fragile bone fragments, which could be crushed into powder if mishandled. You could still get DNA results from them, however, which is what we ultimately wanted. I had coordinated with the brigadier general who headed South Africa's police forensic services as well as the chief pathologist, and the plan was to bring the remains and turn everything over to the pathologist's staff on our arrival.

So we flew into Lanseria International Airport in Johannesburg: it was the evening when we arrived in an aircraft chartered from a company called Executive Air, but the forensic experts who were supposed to collect the remains from us were not there. We thought they had gone home because it was so late, but as we later learned, were sent home by intelligence officers. No problem, I thought, we'll take the bags with us and hand them over the next morning. So we went to the villa we were staying at, cleaned up, and just having a celebratory dinner when the police raided the villa. The police said, "Give us the bodies." Not knowing what they meant I asked again, and they just repeated themselves: "Give us the bodies." They then explained that they knew we were smuggling bodies of mercenaries into the country.

"I think there's been some confusion," I said. "What we have are skeletal remains from two plane crashes in the 1990s that your forensics people were supposed to pick up." They started to insist we were lying to them, so I showed them the bone fragments. I could tell from their expressions that this was not at all what they were expecting. Rather than admit there had been some mistake, though, they ordered us to accompany them to the police station.

Our host got really pissed at that point and laid into the police. South Africa was still horribly crime-ridden back in those days, and she made no small point about them for wasting their valuable time on us. "My daughter was just carjacked and now you're coming in and harassing my guests . . . !" she yelled.

As the police took flak from our host, I pulled the senior person aside, who it turned out was not police, but part of the South African Intelligence Services. He confessed that the police suspected us of being mercenaries. This was partly due to the fact that some of our security had been in the 32 Battalion and partly due to confusion over the name of the plane charter company we had used. The authorities had apparently confused Executive Airlines with Executive Outcomes, the private military company (the modern euphemism for "mercenaries") set up by a former senior officer in the South African army called Eeben Barlow, and who had actually been contracted by the Angolan government to fight against South Africa's old ally UNITA.

Normally in such a mix-up I would refuse to go, citing the

Vienna Convention governing the treatment of foreign nationals on diplomatically sanctioned missions—such as working for the UN—and insist that they had to notify our embassies and the United Nations itself. After all, our party included a UN diplomat. But one of our guys was South African, a former deputy police chief in fact, so that protection would not apply to him. Since another of my rules is to always keep my team together, we went.

"Do you want us to come to the station for an hour or two?" I asked. "Oh no, this is going to be three or four days in jail," said one of the arresting officers. They wanted us to get into their police van, but it wouldn't start. Embarrassed, they asked us to push it. We refused, of course, and eventually they got it started. I rode with the intelligence guy in his vehicle: he realized something was going badly wrong and advised me I should start making phone calls. By then the villa owner had already notified our head office, who had started alerting the UN, US State Department, and UK Foreign and Commonwealth Office.

When we arrived at the police station, the custody sergeant refused to take us. Eventually she did agree to allow the police officers to keep us in the holding area. And there we spent a majority of the night on the phone and being visited by the security team and the head of Police Forensic Sciences. Also, the wife of our South African team member managed to get in touch with some senior police officials who issued a swift order to release us.

I later asked around to try to understand what had happened. I was told there was a power struggle between the police force and the intelligence services. The police controlled the intelligence services, but they wanted to be separate, not under the police. So, the intelligence service, which was trying to exert its independence from the police, had decided that bringing in a bunch of mercenaries stealing the bodies of fallen comrades working with the police, would embarrass the police and give the intelligence service case for independence a boost to its credibility. Alas, their intel wasn't quite up to their ambitions. It's possible that the police deliberately moved slowly in getting us released, because they hoped we would create an international incident and embarrass the intelligence chiefs, which is almost what happened. The police apologized profusely for the mix-up, and I received a letter of apology from the Minister of Intelligence. Nice, but not important; what was important was we managed to get the human remains to the forensics department.

When Johnny Wilkinson's widow, Marie, finally got the phone call to tell her the remains of her son had been identified, her first thought was that she was about to be told they were alive and coming home. Such is the persistence of hope. Instead, she got to bury her beloved son in a grave where she could finally visit him. She got a marker for her husband and the others. Out of the twenty-three people on board both aircrafts, DNA profiles were generated for eighteen of them. Sadly, not all the victims were identified, but enough to convince people that there were no survivors. All the remains were later buried in a ceremony attend by many of the family members in Pretoria.

19. London's Towering Inferno

Bratish prime minister Theresa May's government was already in trouble when a fire broke out one warm summer's night in 2017 in a London tower block full of working-class residents, some of them immigrants from less developed nations.

The United Kingdom was as deeply divided as it had ever been following the Brexit referendum on whether to leave the European Union just a year before. In an astounding complete lack of leadership, May's predecessor, David Cameron, who had overseen the referendum, quit. Failing to secure support on the hugely divisive issue, May misread the political tea leaves and called an early election to shore up her standing in the Houses of Parliament on June 8. Disastrously, she instead lost her majority and had to form a narrow, fragile coalition with the small ultraconservative Democratic Unionist Party of Northern Ireland.

Less than a week later, on the night of June 14, the fire station for Kensington and Chelsea received an alert of flames in a 1960s concrete tower block, a government-subsidized housing development in a wealthy west London borough. I imagine the initial responding firefighters thought it would be a simple matter to deal with, since fires in concrete buildings were usually easily contained: after all concrete does not burn easily.

This crisis surrounding the Grenfell fire was like many crises. It was not the result of one incident, or one bad decision, or an error in response. It was a result of several different things coming together at one time. Sound decision-making was probably the thing I saw most lacking. Somebody should have made the decision to evacuate the burning tower block long before it was finally made. Today too many organizations have regimented the process of decision-making, through fear of prosecution, of losing one's job, or being attacked by a social media lynch mob, that people often feel their hands are tied. The United Kingdom has great fire prevention through a system of safety standards, inspections, and zoning rules: in US cities, you hear fire trucks all the time, but very rarely in Britain. The downside of that is they don't gain experience, and in a job like firefighting there is no replacement for experience.

Fire is a living, breathing thing. It follows a pattern, but that pattern changes based on the fuel, the building structure, weather, and various other factors. Any firefighter learns that in training: I know because I served as a volunteer firefighter while stationed in Virginia. When an experienced firefighter sees a fire on the roof of a building that didn't start there, and they know it has not come from inside the structure, then it means there is a chimney of some kind, a column of heat and flame that is rising along the edge of the building. Experience of other fires would have told them that it was likely behind some type of cladding. They also know that once the fire is on the roof, that's it. Heat rises, but once it can't rise any farther, it goes outward, left and right, and in a square building it will eventually meet in the middle and consume the edifice. And once it's at the top, what equipment do you have to fight it? Most apparatuses can reach between seven and ten floors: Grenfell was twenty-four stories with very little room around the building to maneuver big trucks.

If you think you've put a fire out and then half an hour later you see it's on the roof, you know how fast it has climbed and ought to be thinking there is a serious problem.

But the policy in Britain was to "shelter in place," which in 99 percent of cases would be good idea. It is designed for blazes where the fire is on the inside of the building and will take time to work its way to the outside. But the outside of Grenfell was covered in aluminum cladding, designed to protect it from London's inclement weather. That created a chimney between the concrete outside the building and cladding. Without any fire breaks built in, it funneled the flames to the roof and turned the tower block into a vast Roman candle that burned at 1,800 degrees. Residents who listened to the fire brigade's advice saw their corridors and flats fill with deadly black smoke. By the time they decided to make a run for it, it was too late: they would not have been able to see a hand in front of their face, and would have quickly succumbed to suffocation before they could hope to find the one narrow stairwell that might have led them to safety. The heat was so intense it cracked the concrete, exposing the reinforcing rebar to water, which caused it to expand over time, a process known as spalling, rendering the entire structure unstable.

It took the fire brigade several hours to realize that their established shelter-in-place policy was not right for this type of fire. But that was their training, so drilled into them that they had little flexibility to make a different decision on the spot. People should have been empowered to make decisions based on what they saw, not what was written in a book.

I believe, that had the fire happened a week earlier, it would have changed the course of British politics, and maybe the future of Europe. May would have lost to the Labour Party, and Brexit might have never happened. Not just because of the fire, but because of the response.

Mass disasters can rock societies to their core: they can bring down governments and even trigger conflicts. In 2003, Spain suffered its worst-ever terrorist attack when an Al Qaeda cell blew up a train in Madrid, killing 193 people and wounding 2,000 more, just three days before national elections. The ruling conservative party of prime minister José Maria Aznar tried to blame Basque separatists, fearing that the backlash from an Islamist attack would highlight Spain's controversial military involvement in the unpopular US-led occupation of Iraq. But the true story quickly emerged, and fury erupted both over the bombing and the attempted cover-up. Aznar's party suffered a stinging defeat.

Similarly, Bangladesh achieved independence from Pakistan in a bloody war in the 1970s that was triggered in large part by the Islamabad government's halfhearted response to a deadly hurricane that tore through what was then known as East Pakistan.

Theresa May and her Conservative Party were already in trouble when the disastrous fire broke out in Grenfell Tower. Prime Minister May and council leadership of the Royal Borough of Kensington and Chelsea (RBKC) Council had problems from the get-go. The frustrating part is that had the fire department ignored "their book," the fire may not have resulted in so many deaths and had the prime minister and the RBKC followed their well-written book, their own government manual on humanitarian assistance, they would have had a much better response.

Of course, not everything was bad about the response. The central government created and staffed the Grenfell Recovery Organization. The GRO was created to oversee the recovery actions within the tower, because the building owner, effectively RBKC, was potentially party to the investigation and therefore could not be on site. The GRO consisted of great, hardworking people from emergency services, community service offices, and the London fire brigade, all headed by a chief executive also brought in from another council. The police also did a fantastic job, especially considering the hours needed to conduct fingertip searches of burned out flats. Fingertip search means each room is searched by hand and every surface is touched by a police officer's hand. The care that they showed to the family members was also impressive, as was the fact that they positively identified every deceased person. It is often the case that the work done by the rank and file is overshadowed by decisions and actions of people far removed from the event.

The worst fire in the United Kingdom in decades was made even worse by some who wanted to spread the perception that this was a tower block full of people who were somehow "lesser than," or in some instances even involved in criminal activity, yet were living in one of the richest parts of the country at the exact time when Brexit was whipping up nationalist, anti-foreigner sentiment. Absolutely unconscionable and undeserved. The fact is, like in any tower block in London, most of the residents were simply hardworking people. People who kept their homes clean and well maintained: there may have been some who were on the wrong side of the law, but the same could be said of just about any community.

When the prime minister finally visited the scene, she congratulated the firefighters but was reluctant to meet the confused and traumatized survivors. That may have been because they were already angry at being so badly neglected and ignored, and their rage was boiling over in public encounters with any authority figure. Maybe it is British thing: I remember that at the family assistance center in Bali, Australian prime minister John Howard came in, rolled his sleeves up, walked around and talked to people. More importantly, he listened to them. But then a diplomat from the UK embassy came in, wearing a double-breasted suit, and with security staff who keep families away from him. Not very approachable nor conveying the message of "I am one of you and here to help." The residents, the survivors, and the families of the dead desperately needed to be heard, and, more importantly, to understand what would happen next.

The police had investigated and cleared some of the flats where they suspected there had been a loss of life. But a lot of the other apartments were still full of the possessions of residents who were barred from entering the unstable building. So, they called Kenyon to get the property out and return it to its owners.

As soon as I arrived, I went to the tower, which was close to one of the main routes into the capital. With my camera in hand and a hazmat protective suit and mask on, I began my assessment. The first thing I came across was the fire brigade's makeshift command post inside a stairwell on the ground floor. The scribblings in board-marker on the grubby wall were a testament to the chaos of that terrible night: "flames @ window 0215"; "people on roof"; "9–people waving"; "11–people hanging from floor (EXTERNAL)," the latter probably indicating that people had been spotted in their windows trying to get attention on the eleventh floor. Adding to the confusion, the floor numbers in Grenfell had been reordered because community floors had been converted into flats.

Quite a few of the rooms and spaces had been untouched by the flames, despite the ferocity of the inferno. Ironically, that only added to the confusion and anger of the residents, who could not understand why they were not being allowed back in to get their possessions. Some had even been shown pictures of their almost-pristine flats by police investigators shortly after the fire.

But even apartments that had not been damaged by smoke or fire were already starting to suffer from mold. The fire brigade had pumped something like 600,000 liters of water into the upper floors to douse the flames, and where did all that water go? Down, into the lower floors. Some residents I met were worried about asbestos, but mold was actually a far more toxic threat to the health of anyone working inside the building. In addition, firefighters had smashed through walls and brought down ceilings with axes, hooligan tools, and pikes to make sure there were no smoldering pockets of fire hidden out of sight: that rubble had settled on people's beds and furniture, adding to the mess. Cabinets had been pulled off walls for the same reason, often smashing the crockery inside. Because of the severe damage and the need to shore up the upper floors and scaffolding, builders had put in what are known in the United Kingdom as acrow props. Basically, these are adjustable poles that connect to each other to create a support skeleton to hold the weight of the floor above. The connecting rods went right through apartment walls and windows to reach the outside scaffolding. It was mayhem; even the places that, at first sight, looked to be okay. That was the first thing the residents needed to know. Yet nobody had bothered to spell that out to them.

When I told the council that the residents needed to be briefed properly, they suggested that I do it. There was clearly a lot of simmering anger in the group I faced, and I could see they were wondering why an American private contractor (me) was being allowed into their homes when they weren't. I could understand that and I stood there and took it, even from one woman who spent what felt like half an hour laying into me. I then explained to them as clearly as I could what was going to happen, and why, because people need to be given facts they can act on.

One of the first things we try to do before starting any response is build a picture of who the people directly affected are, where are they from, what are their cultural norms, religion, and background. That way we can try to meet their needs. It doesn't matter what I think or want, because it is not about me. What I learned was that for some time, residents had been complaining about the fire safety and felt nobody cared if they died. I learned that some had fled to Britain from countries where it was only natural to distrust a government, and where it was not safe to use the banking system. I learned that most identified as part of Grenfell and that they would work together to help each other. All of this was important.

While most of our jobs involve plane crashes or buildings destroyed by bombs, earthquakes, or floods, this was an oddly intimate act, going through the homes of people who had been forced to flee in the middle of the night. Much like in Hurricane Katrina. The fridges were still full of rotting vegetables, potatoes sprouting in pantries, and coins from different countries scattered where they had been left on sideboards; children's stuffed toys still strewn on bedspreads from the last night of playtime in the flats. It was a snapshot of lives abruptly interrupted. It was also painstaking work.

We started by going into flats and collecting as much as we could. We had limiting factors, such as the number of people we could have in the building, and the fact that there was only one way in or out, a very narrow stairwell that terrified residents had escaped down on the night of the fire. We could not risk blocking it by moving heavy items, so as a rule of thumb we decided that we would remove nothing larger than a microwave. We could only carry boxes out when there was no one working on the floors above us, to make sure we would not do anything to trap people if there was an evacuation. While we were clearing flats, the police were working to search apartments that still had human remains, reduced to bone fragments by the fire. Not every flat had the support scaffolding yet and we were working against the clock. The workers were coming but had not reached every floor. In the meantime we went in and conducted a quick inventory, took photographs, and removed whatever we could: no cooking utensils or clothes; no bedding that was already covered in mold. Daily we had trucks bringing people's property to our warehouse, where a different team began the process of drying things out, trying to save photographs, and completing much more detailed inventories. We also focused on trying to separate for quick return things like purses, wallets, passports. Things that people needed for their daily lives. While we first asked to recover property from a limited number of flats, that quickly increased to eventually most of the flats. The higher we went the more damaged it was and the more work to restore items. This went on for several months.

I give slack to people who are trying to manage, even if they do not do it well. However, I have none to give to the Royal Borough of Kensington and Chelsea (RBKC). To say they were unhelpful in all of this would be an understatement. The residents were not being informed as to the basics—what they could expect to retrieve, and when and how. We would not be party to that, so Kenyon set up a website to explain all this vital information: how the recoveries were being done, risk from mold, things to consider; along with several video Q&As that I personally did. We were getting calls from residents and their solicitors who had no idea what was going on, people desperate to find out if anything had survived.

RBKC asked us to take the website down. We did not. Their

reason: it went beyond our remit. They literally just wanted us to bring possessions out and store them, without telling people where we were holding it. Yet they themselves were doing nothing to inform the residents where their belongings were. Eventually, working through the Grenfell Recovery Organization we were able to get contact information. That enabled us to have the residents come to our offices to go through their things. One man came in to look at his property. We had placed it all in boxes that were open, but in a very large training room. His first comment was why were we showing him everything from the entire building. We told him it was just property recovered from his flat. He was floored at how much he had and how much had been recovered. We then showed him the amount of property in our warehouse and he asked if we had his neighbor's things, and we did. He said he would tell him to contact us, because his neighbor was unaware anything had been saved. That is the way it went.

Meanwhile, I drew up some suggestions at the strategic level to help the government weather the political storm it was going through. I urged the authorities to first clearly identify the stakeholders, to form a panel or a commission with legal recognition to coordinate all actions with the building when the police were finished with it, to get the residents involved, and let them take the lead. Transparency was the key, I warned, and they should study previous cases of devastating fires to see how long the process of technical investigation and inquests would take, because I knew it would last years. You cannot leave people in the dark for that long without telling them why. I suggested that a mediator be appointed to manage the claims, as was done following the 9/11 attacks.

However, politicians were acting like this had never happened before, even though a quick online search showed me that there had been a number of similar fires, one of them in another London tower block as recently as 2009, when the Lakanal House blaze killed six people in a fourteen-floor apartment building in Camberwell. I wanted to demonstrate to everyone involved just how long the process was likely to take, since the Southwark council was only just pleading guilty to criminal negligence in 2017, eight years after the fire and right as Grenfell itself was happening.

"This is a minefield, and you are navigating without a map," I warned.

As far as I know, the government paid little heed. We carried on with removing and restoring the people's belongings, doing whatever we could to help the residents salvage whatever they could, finally finishing in early 2020.

Theresa May lasted another couple of years, trying and failing to push through her Brexit plan. Grenfell was not quite done with her, though: in her resignation speech, she cited the response to the fire as one of her successes. That unleashed a new storm of anger from survivors and from the firefighters themselves, who said that they had borne the brunt of the blame (the London fire commissioner eventually resigned over the response to the Grenfell fire in 2019) rather than the Tory government, which they accused of having dangerously deregulated safety codes for building contractors while May had been serving as Home Secretary. Clearly, these safety regulations are something that should be looked at. A representative of the survivors' group Justice4Grenfell slammed her comment and the fact that no one has been charged for the tragedy, drily noting: "72 dead and still no arrests is something no one should be proud of." What she should have said: "72 dead and the only arrests so far were of those living in the towers for unrelated crimes, and still no changes to processes—prevention or response—is something no one should be proud of." Whether anyone will face charges remains to be seen. In the United Kingdom, there will first be public hearings, they will likely last years, and then if there is criminal prosecution that will come next. If the Grenfell response follows the pattern that will be sometime around 2023 or 2024.

The Grenfell tragedy emphasized the need for effective leadership at every level and the devastating consequences of having people in charge who are simply not up to the job. A crisis quickly reveals who is a leader, capable of making hard decisions under pressure and facing up to people who have lost everything they have, and who is merely a manager, relying on focus groups, rigid rules, or popular opinion to guide their actions.

As for the tower itself, as I write this, it is still standing like a tombstone on London's skyline, abandoned and clad in plastic sheeting. There are often workers in there at night still, and the light behind the sheeting can give off an eerie glow, as if the building itself was on fire again. One day it will come down and if the United Kingdom does not choose to learn from this response and the investigation, there will tragically be another Grenfell, something almost completely preventable.

20. The Resilience Factor

Being prepared for a disaster is really not that hard. It means accepting that bad things will happen, building up resources, and when things *do* occur, reacting appropriately. Some people argue that as a society, we have become rather soft. If we want something, we only have to click a link on our phone, and it is delivered to our doorstep. We complain and post bad reviews if our food delivery is a few minutes late. Psychologists have even identified a nervous disorder—"phone separation anxiety"—that people suffer from when they are parted from their cell phones for even short periods. Our problem is not that we are soft or hard, but that we have a lack of patience and confidence, a lack of leadership and a lack of self-responsibility, a lack of discipline and the inability to use knowledge, while at the same time ignoring facts.

Today, more people have access to more information than at any other time in history. But in the sense of understanding history, of studying the past and learning what may await us in the future, people generally don't have the discipline to read beyond the headline or take the time to understand what it all actually means.

Days after Hurricane Harvey hit Houston in 2017 and

flooded my company's headquarters, I sat in on a conference call with about sixty different organizations, from private to government at the local, state, and national level. One of the topics that came up was the supply level of anxiety medication in the city. I have some reservations about doling out addictive medicines such as benzodiazepines in the middle of an opioid epidemic so severe that the average life expectancy of Americans is dropping for the first time in living memory. It's not that I'm against medicine for any condition that requires it—it's just that I think there are maybe some better options. There is a cultural anxiety around crisis management, but the best way to alleviate anxiety in such events is better preparation, not just at the government level but at the individual level, and then with good consistent information once the event has occurred.

When Hurricane Harvey hit Houston, my husband and I were in Key West. Just as we were preparing to leave for Texas to help out there, Hurricane Irma was headed to Key West where we had spent two years building our home together, and which was now in the direct path of a category 5 hurricane. A hurricane that had just ripped apart the island of Puerto Rico. We didn't freak out: we knew when we moved there of the risk of hurricanes. I had studied the maps to see which areas of Key West were prone to flooding and we prepared our property accordingly: we took down the fan blades and outdoor speakers, we put up the storm shutters, wrapped the tailpipes on the car so floodwater wouldn't get in. I trimmed the trees because the wind can turn coconuts into dangerous projectiles, I sandbagged and taped the doors, and put the furniture up on the end caps of pipes we got at Home Depot so it would spare us from water damage if at all possible: if floodwater comes in and goes out again quickly, it does a lot less damage than if it washes in and stays. I already had my hurricane kit, which includes tarps, roofing nails, ropes, and sealing calk. We also had boxes of food and a generator. True, it's a pain in the ass to do all that, but it limits the damage and allows me to have some control over a potentially catastrophic situation. I can't stop the hurricane, but I don't have to just sit and be a passive victim as my home is battered or wait for someone to come rescue me. Even if you can't control the event, you can control the response.

Anxiety, the fear of what is going to happen, can be debilitating. Stress can have very serious health impacts and medication doesn't treat the core problem. Actively working to mitigate the damage can help reduce that stress, because it makes you feel more empowered and less like a helpless bystander. And of course, the things you do can actually help the recovery effort after the event.

Likewise, with terrorism, we can't prevent every terrorist attack. Terrorists will try thousands of times to attack, and they only have to get lucky once. The good guys have to get lucky every single time, and statistically, that is not going to happen. There are also always going be earthquakes, hurricanes, and wildfires: that is just a simple fact. The threat is no greater than in the past—in fact, we are in a much better situation to monitor and predict them than ever before. But that constant awareness of the threat can make people freeze with fear or confusion. The massive amounts of information out there can make people feel overloaded—as if drinking from a fire hose. Paradoxically, too much information renders people incapable of making informed decisions, becoming task saturated.

Disastrous events are always stressful. But just because you are stressed, staying up all night to see if the storm hits or the floodwaters rise does not mean you are *not* resilient. Resilience comes with time, experience, education, and preparation. There is also a big difference between stress and panic: you see a bear in the woods and your body goes into fight-or-flight mode: but if you have bothered to look into how to deal with bears before you headed out into the wilderness, you have an idea how to respond to make sure you get out alive. Running screaming through the forest is not necessarily the correct response. That doesn't mean the encounter is not stressful: of course, it is. If you see several bears over the years of hiking trips, your stress will naturally go down.

Look at it this way: exercise stresses your muscles and your cardio system. You will sweat and feel stiff after the first few workouts. But it makes you fitter over time and better able to cope with future physical challenges.

When the United States invaded Haiti in 1994, I saw how incredibly resilient the people were. You could tell the good guys from the bad guys; the former were skinny and the latter were fat, in a country so divided between the corrupt "haves" and the honest "have-nots." People could build a working water pump out of leftover car parts because of the embargo on their country. You had to be resourceful just to get by. Fast-forward to when I went back for the 2010 earthquake, when the country had become aid-dependent after sixteen of UN missions, and I saw people sitting in plastic chairs outside their collapsed homes with signs that said, "Help me," instead of picking up and clearing the roads so the aid trucks could get through. After World War II, when English and German cities were bombed flat, war-hardened residents formed human chains and cleared the streets by hand, one brick at a time. That was how the World Trade Center was cleared in the very first days, bucket by bucket.

One thing politicians, planners, and ordinary people need to remember is this: we don't control nearly as much as we think we do. Mass fatalities and crises expose that fact like nothing else. We have to learn to accept that fact in a way that we generally don't at the moment. But we also have more ability to respond than most of us realize. Don't fight the things you can't control. Focus on the things you can.

Our cultural norms right now tell us to forget bad things, to move on. Dust yourself off and get back to normal life. If we don't honestly acknowledge our mistakes from the past, or bother to understand the lessons, not just noting that the events occurred, we will just repeat them.

These days, everyone is talking about the 1918 Spanish flu pandemic as a historical precedent for the COVID-19 pandemic ravaging the planet. But how many people are aware of the 1957 H2N2 pandemic that began in Singapore and Hong Kong and killed 1.1 million people worldwide, including 116,000 Americans? Or the 1968 H3N2 avian influenza that killed a million people around the world, 100,000 of them in America? They are far more recent and comparable to what is happening in the United States during the current coronavirus outbreak. Yet we think we are living in a once-in-a-century pandemic because we don't want to remember frightening events, because it makes us think we are not in control. We conquered the moon, we guarantee life, liberty, and the pursuit of happiness. In fact, there are no guarantees.

That is a reality that we as a society are reluctant to acknowledge, and it saps our self-reliance. When I was a young deputy sheriff in California, they were starting to introduce personal safety devices, the locator beacons that lost hikers or climbers can activate if they got into trouble. All of a sudden, the number of rescues spiked. People started to think they could head out into Yosemite without all the extra gear they needed for any eventuality, or without basic skills for surviving a day or two lost in the woods, because they could just flick a button and out of the blue a helicopter would come and get them, no matter the risk or cost to the rescuers. I'm not knocking the technology; it certainly saves lives. Technology was never supposed to be a replacement for common sense, training, or preparation. The unintended consequence was a diminution of the self-reliance you need to face adverse circumstances. Today for example, far fewer people can read a map than when I grew up.

My long experience has taught me this: it is not anyone's job to bail us out. If a grease fire breaks out in our kitchen and we have a fire extinguisher, I can probably put it out. But if I call the fire department and wait for them to arrive, my grease fire is by now a house fire and I'll probably lose a lot more. I will still call the fire department—they are on their way in case I can't control the fire—but the first attack will be mine. Or put it this way, if we are out sailing and our boat sinks, the Coast Guard will come get me, but not in five minutes. We need to have a life jacket and know how to stay afloat until they can find us. It's not the government's job to bring you water within an hour of a hurricane. You have to have some basic skills and self-reliance initially.

Being prepared is a burden, I know. It's a pain to have a hurricane kit; you need to spend money on it and find the space to store it. But think of the Mormons and their emergency supplies next time you stand in line outside a supermarket during an outbreak of a deadly disease, trying to buy toilet paper.

What the media generally gets wrong in its coverage of storms and natural disasters is that it's not the storm that is actually the worst part. It's the recovery, and no one ever plans for that. When I started writing this book, large parts of North Carolina were under water from Hurricane Florence. Hundreds of thousands of people fled the storm, but they didn't know where to go because it's been years since such a large hurricane slammed the coast. So, they arrived, exhausted and bedraggled, in shelters and hotels inland, and their temporary accommodations quickly burned through their savings.

Typically, hurricane survivors have to wait several weeks before they can go home: How many of them plan in advance where they could stay in the event of a hurricane, even if they live in a historically storm-prone region? And when they get home, will it be habitable? Probably not. Same thing for wildfires, which are affecting more and more people as population growth pushes urban development into areas that would have been considered off-limits in the past. That's why you need a contingency plan—if you have kids, you may want to think about them staying with a relative for a semester, because you'll probably have to gut your house, throw out ruined furniture and fittings, and find builders to carry out repairs in an area where such skills are suddenly in very high demand. We are talking months of expense and disruption and maybe years before any government compensation actually gets to you. How are you going to pay for that? Millions of Americans live paycheck to paycheck. Where are you going to put your family? Having a plan is a big part of being resilient.

Now here's the thing: hurricane survivors live in areas where there may be a devastating storm every twenty years. So for twenty years you live there and nothing happens. Then the one year when it does happen, it makes up for all twenty years. That doesn't mean these people are reckless for living there. My husband and I live in a hurricane zone. It means we understand the challenges and the risk versus reward, but many forget about the risk. It's human nature, in a way, but it seems to have gotten worse in recent years.

Even if you can handle that kind of disruption—if you have the physical, mental, and financial resources—necessary to stay

264   Robert A. Jensen

in an area like that, you still need to plan. And if you won't plan, you really need to go somewhere else.

Everyone has different tolerance levels to stress and loss. On just about every job that I go out on, someone hits that wall: they either ask to leave, or we send them home. Trauma is like holding a jug of water at arm's length: every incident adds a few more drops until you simply cannot hold the jug out anymore. For many people, it's some tragedy in their personal life that makes them unable to deal with death—I asked someone to work on the site of a bus crash once and he said he had recently been in a traffic accident where two people died, and he simply couldn't face it. He needed time to recover, mentally and physically, and I respected that.

I encourage everyone I work with to be self-aware and to assess their mental state with clarity. Even people who are used to everyday hardship can react irrationally to trauma: in the Haiti earthquake, there was a woman who had lost her daughter. All she could find was a severed leg with a sock and shoe on it. The mother took the leg home, washed it, and put it to bed. She wasn't crazy: trauma makes us do strange things, can turn us into people we don't recognize for a period of time.

Resilience can be learned and passed on. People who have been through violent hurricanes, floods, or fires need to warn newcomers about the risks. Because if you haven't been through it, how can you really know? You may have seen some shots on your television, but that won't convey the smells or sounds; it will leave no visceral memory attached to it. But often even those who have experienced such things firsthand don't pass on their experience: they think maybe it won't be so bad, or that people will laugh at them for being fearmongers. Am I going to uproot my kids for six months and live somewhere else? These are real decisions we have to face, and which we, as a society, tend to suck at that. The media circus moves on after the storm, and people forget about the tens of thousands of people still stuck in shelters and motels or houses infused with black mold or no roof.

And scientists predict that hurricanes, wildfires, epidemics, and flooding are only going to get worse as the climate heats up. Now you can debate the causes of that warming until you are blue in the face—man-made, geological, God-given—but if it is happening, you had best be prepared.

As Gavin de Becker, one of the world's leading experts in threat detection and avoidance said in his classic book *The Gift of Fear*, denial "has an interesting and insidious side effect. For all the peace of mind deniers think they get by saying it isn't so, the fall they take when victimized is far, far greater than that of those who accept the possibility." If you have not read his book, I would encourage you to do so. It is a seminal piece on human nature.

We can build soap bubbles to live in, believe that we are the exceptions, and that history will be kind to us: or we can be more rational and soberly assess the risks we face. As de Becker notes, "denial is a save-now-pay-later scheme, a contract written entirely in small print, for in the long run, the denying person knows the truth on some level, and it causes a constant low-grade anxiety." No Xanax is going to ease that angst away.

We often fall into the mistake of expecting people in times of crisis to respond either logically or emotionally. In truth, you have to see things logically but also understand the very real emotions involved—your own included. When people suddenly realized in March 2020 that the new coronavirus, COVID-19, was a potentially massive and deadly threat, many rushed to their local supermarket and panic-bought toilet paper, clearing the shelves. It wasn't logical, and people were told to stop hoarding it. Did they? Of course not. But they were doing it out of fear, trying to control what they could control but not really understanding what their real needs were.

The same thing with face masks: scientists will tell the population that some form of face covering cuts contagion dramatically, and it does, but some people resented being told to wear them and saw it as an infringement on their personal freedom. But it isn't just that. Masks are an annoyance. They fog up your glasses, they're uncomfortable, some people think they make it harder to breathe. But that is not the real reason. On a deeper level, they are also an explicit acknowledgment that things are bad, and we don't like that. Not wearing a mask reminds us of normality, of life as it was and as we want it to be again. Just like the shocked relative who won't open the door to a police officer bringing the news of the death of a loved one in a plane crash, we try to shut out death and disaster. Or imagine that it will happen to someone else. Having some leaders and media outlets downplay or politicize the health guidelines only added to a sense for many people that the threat was overblown, or the price of self-isolation not worth it. And that cost tens of thousands of lives, and it got worse.

The coronavirus challenged our society in ways it hadn't been challenged for decades. It should not have come as a surprise, as epidemiologists have been constantly warning of the threat. But we were not prepared, as a society, either mentally or practically. But how resilient were we? Well, society didn't collapse. Hundreds of millions of people around the world followed their governments' shelter-at-home instructions and flattened the curve of infection that prevented hospitals from being overwhelmed in the initial outbreak. Our economies proved to be far less resilient, and within weeks had collapsed into deep recession. Overextended supply chains, the rise of protectionism, and a lack of any social safety net in many countries meant that businesses folded, and desperate workers were forced to go back to work even if that meant exposing themselves to the risk of infection. We had wanted cheaper and cheaper things without understanding the risks of having everything on the cheap. We had families, whose income was based on two incomes with kids at school, and all of sudden there was no school.

Needless to say, Kenyon was quickly enlisted to deal with the massive spike in excess deaths. New York hired us to remove the bodies of people who had died of the disease in their homes, because as we saw in Katrina, the active military or National Guard under federal control are not legally allowed to enter private citizens' homes. The police were reluctant to do it because they lacked the personal protective equipment to enter enclosed spaces where surfaces were certain to be contaminated and losing officers to disease could also lead to problems in combatting crime. So, we went in and recovered some 1,400 bodies in the epicenter of the disease, without suffering a single infection. We advised hospitals on the correct way to adapt standard refrigerator trucks to cope with overburdened morgues, which means installing racks to hold the deceased and making sure the bodies do not cover the refrigeration units at the front, which would lead to some bodies being frozen solid and others not being cold enough to avoid decomposition.

We also had to remove dozens of bodies that an overwhelmed funeral home had been storing in rented U-Haul trucks, a case that triggered outrage in the city. Workers at a nearby business had alerted police to the unpleasant smell coming from the trucks parked in back of the funeral home, which had been taken by surprise by the sheer volume of bodies coming through its doors. Running out of storage space, it resorted to using un-refrigerated rental trucks.

Meanwhile, we were helping county councils in the United Kingdom set up emergency storage areas for coronavirus fatalities, one at Birmingham airport with a capacity to hold 2,300 bodies, and another in a car park in Essex, just north of London. At first, we were flooded with requests from a whole variety of local authorities. I had to tell them we would not work at such a local level, since it was not clear how badly hit any given area might be, and to do so would lead to waste and duplication. Instead, I advised the authorities to organize on a regional level, since it would be much better to move bodies to a central storage point than to have dozens of smaller ones, some of which might be empty, and others overwhelmed. Just as in New Orleans during Hurricane Katrina, some authorities were wildly overestimating the death toll and wanting facilities that could hold ten thousand bodies or more. I advised them to start with a capacity of a few hundred and scale up as needed.

It is too early to say what all the long-term effects of the pandemic will be, but two things are clear already: the psychological impact will be felt for years along with the impact of the disruption to the education of an entire generation of students. The inability to say goodbye to loved ones will also be hard to overcome. Many people had no chance to say their final goodbyes, because their relatives were taken to hospitals that were under strict quarantine orders to prevent the spread of the disease. For some, their last encounter with their relative may have been a quick FaceTime chat on a cell phone that was being held by a masked nurse as they prepared to be sedated and intubated, knowing the chances of them ever waking up again were slim. The relatives at home would then be ordered by the same health authorities to isolate themselves for two weeks because they had been exposed to the disease, then sit at home waiting for news of their loved one's condition. As a final blow for many there were no, or only limited, funerals, family gatherings, or memorial ceremonies held because of the risk of transmission. All the rituals of death, designed over millennia to pave the way to a new reality, were abruptly stripped away, leaving the bereaved feeling angry, guilty, or depressed and frequently looking for someone to blame, usually themselves.

It is a mental health crisis waiting in the wings of the pandemic.

21. What I've Collected

In addition to all the images I have in my head, there are the case files and the physical reminders, such as the piece of thorn that is still lodged in my right hand from my time in the Peruvian Amazon. Sometimes before a file is archived or destroyed, I will go through it. I recently came across an old contact sheet of photos. The first three pictures were of my daughter at a Thanksgiving party when she was about four years old—a cute little girl, smiling at the camera.

The next picture is of a woman's corpse, bruised and swollen. She died in the 1996 plane crash in Croatia that killed US commerce secretary Ron Brown. The plane went down in heavy rains as it approached Dubrovnik's notoriously difficult airport: I had left home, just before Thanksgiving and I had taken some quick photos before leaving Fort Lee in Virginia, then used the same camera to capture the aftermath of crashes. I feel bad for the poor Army technician who developed the contact sheets: it must have been jarring to see such a juxtaposition of images.

The sequence of images is a stark reminder of the proximity of life and death, and the ease with which they crisscross the paths of my own life. In the midst of life, we are in death, says the *Book of Common Prayer*.

There is a line written from a Civil War soldier in a letter home that sticks with me to this day: "Mother, may you never see the things that I see." But it is not just the visual memories. All my senses can trigger powerful associations with the past. I hear a jackhammer and for a split second I am back in Oklahoma City, in the ruins of the Murrah building. I smell jet fuel while waiting for a connection at an airport and I am transported back to any one of the dozens of plane crashes I have worked on. A huge truck reminds me of the vehicle that ripped apart the Canal Hotel in Baghdad. And so on and so on.

Even holiday trips come with their own reminders. In 2019, I returned to Dubrovnik to go sailing and scuba diving. Of course, it was very different than it was in 1996. But as I landed, my mind drifted back to the days following the crash of CT-43. When I closed my eyes, it was all right there.

My "normal" is probably very different from most people's normal. When I check into a hotel room, I always make a mental note of how many doors stand between my room and the staircase. In fires, people often run past perfectly good exits because they instinctively seek the same way they came in. Usually, they have come in via the elevator, which won't be working in a fire. When I enter a movie theater or concert, I can't help scoping out the people around me for any suspicious signs. I'm not paranoid: I'm not afraid that something bad will happen to me. It has just become standard practice, like washing your hands has become in the coronavirus pandemic. It's what the people now call "the new normal." Only for me, it's been the norm for years.

There is also a paradox to my life. In general, people don't like to talk about death. Most people don't like to even think about it. But when I am asked at social gatherings what I do, suddenly everyone is transfixed by the subject. It's not great for me: usually I don't want to talk about it anymore than I already have to every day. As I said earlier, constant exposure to death has taught me to really appreciate the joys of everyday life. But I understand why they ask. We need to talk about death. Not obsessively, or morbidly, but sometimes—and with open eyes. It is something momentous that happens to us all.

The fact is that the dead have incredible power over us. We will all die, and that is hard to come to grips with. When we lose people suddenly and unexpectedly, we need something to fill that void, to momentarily stand in for the person we knew until we can come to terms with the new, painful reality of our lives. When people are lost in large numbers, that need becomes an issue that affects whole communities, whole societies, and can rock us to the core.

The American psychologist Pauline Boss argues that there is no such thing as "closure," at least outside of real estate deals. Certainly, it is a term I don't use. Boss has written extensively about what she calls "ambiguous loss," where a person abruptly disappears—in a plane crash or natural disaster, for instance—and is physically missing but emotionally still present. You don't just stop loving them from one day to the next. The flip side is even more common these days, as dementia and Alzheimer's spread among our older generations, and where someone is physically present but mentally absent. It is a particularly difficult type of loss to grapple with, especially in a modern society that demands quick fixes to problems and insists that people "get over it" or move on. Boss, who started out studying the impact of MIA soldiers in the Vietnam War and who later worked with families affected by the Asian tsunami and 9/11, argues that with sudden, unexpected death there simply is no quick fix, and that ambiguous loss is the hardest form of grief to deal with. It is normal to be sad over long periods of time—the sadness pulsates for years, coming and going, and may eventually ebb but will never go away entirely. In the absence of a body to mourn over, memorials, rituals, and possessions of the dead are vitally important to offer some tangible mastery over your sense of loss, some driftwood to cling to in the violent storm of emotion.

How we treat the dead reflects how we treat the living. If we treat them and their possessions as disposable, as trash to be dumped in a landfill, how can we deal with the knowledge of our inevitable demise? Society is, at its heart, about where we fit in as people—communities, families, lines of ancestors marching back in time. To shrug and say we are just meat that can be left for the vultures, without acknowledgment of loss or life, would be to undermine something vital about how we function in life.

People sometimes ask me how I don't get nightmares—how come I haven't become a miserable person, a wreck locked in my house alone and angry? Well, first of all, *there's still time.* As I said earlier, trauma can be a cumulative process. Yes, I am tired, but I think the reason I have been able to compartmentalize is that out of the bad, my work brings some element of meaning to chaos, provides people in pain with the symbols and tools to navigate through the darkest of days. At least I hope so. To tell people that no matter where they end up, they will not be forgotten. I feel I am actually helping in some way: helping the dead return home, helping families ease their suffering. I hate to see people suffer; it is a waste and so unnecessary. And on a practical level, helping companies restore some level of trust in their services, which like any other risky endeavor can fail spectacularly at times.

Some people who do dangerous, high-stress jobs become addicted to the adrenaline. That is not me. I don't miss my work when I'm not doing it. It is tiring, the battles, explaining things over and over, and not knowing if, when you get home from a job, the phone may ring within the hour and you will have to head out to some other disaster that has taken hundreds, possibly thousands of lives.

I do, however, have what is almost an addiction to adventure sports. I like skydiving, climbing, kiteboarding, scuba diving, biking in my spare time. Most of these are solitary sports, because I spend so much of my working life in abnormal proximity to people, sharing their most painful or terrifying moments. But even in these high-risk solo activities, I still mitigate the risk: I scuba-dive alone, even though that is frowned upon in diving circles. However, I am a dive master and as well as the computer I use; I have the backup on the watch; I still monitor my dive time, depth, and air and I still know my dive tables. I have a secondary regulator, and I carry a big orange inflatable tube that says "Diver" in case I get too far from the boat I dove off, which has happened at times when I get absorbed swmming after some shark or turtle I can get my rush, but with managed risk.

What is hardest is the price my family has had to pay. I am sure I am not easy to live with—everything always ready, phone calls that have to be answered regardless of the time or other things going on. Missed plans, and then I'm gone, out the door with no idea when I will be back. I know it was hard on my first marriage, and I am sure it's no easier on the second. Sometimes I think I have spent so much time on other people's problems, that I don't have enough left in me to give time to my husband. That is not what he signed up for. So I have spent a lot more time on training people and trying to make sure that the next generation is ready. I don't want them to do only as well as me, because a lot of the time I have got through by sheer luck. I do not want the people who follow me to depend on luck or learn what I have learned the hard way, I want to make it easier to learn and people not have to learn at the cost of someone else. I want and expect them to do better. I want to be known not for my job, but for being a good father and a good husband. In the end I don't want people to say it was my job that took my life and soul.

Although I have a low tolerance for stupid, and I have seen a lot of the bad in life, that doesn't mean I'm jaded or don't enjoy life. It just means I think I've missed some of the good. When I do stop retrieving the dead, it won't be because I am tired or can't do it anymore, it will be because others are ready, and I want to see more of the good and be normal like everyone else.

Epilogue

One hundred and sixty-eight empty chairs made of glass, bronze, and stone sit in lines across the green lawn. Nearby, a reflecting pool is bookended by two huge metal doors, each marked with a time code: 9:01 and 9:03, the former representing the last minute before Timothy McVeigh's truck bomb detonated, and the latter commemorating the minute afterward, when the people of Oklahoma City emerged into a bewildering new reality, suddenly tasked with mourning, recovering, and rebuilding their shattered lives.

Part of that recovery is represented by the peaceful park that now occupies the land where the Murrah building once stood. Every tragedy sparks its own spontaneous memorials—those neat rows of World War I graves in Belgium started out as inverted rifles in the Flanders mud, each one topped by a tin hat, or a glass bottle turned upside down and a scrap of paper inside bearing the slain soldier's name and serial number.

In Oklahoma, the fence that police erected to cordon off the wrecked federal building was quickly festooned with wreaths, teddy bears, poems, flags, and key chains. The fence stood for four years as workers demolished the smashed building and built something new in its place. A section of it was eventually incorporated into the permanent park memorial, alongside the empty chairs representing the people who died at their desks that day.

There is another poignant symbol at the park: an elm tree that had stood in what had been the federal building's parking lot and had most of its limbs ripped off by the force of McVeigh's bomb. It was slated to be cut down, in part to retrieve body parts and other evidence that had been caught in its branches or embedded in its trunk. But when survivors, rescue workers, and mourners gathered for a memorial on the first anniversary of the bombing, they noticed that the wrecked tree—which had stood on the site since the 1920s—had begun to bloom again, and they insisted that it be spared. Seeds from the Survivor Tree are now grown every year into saplings and distributed around the nation's parks as a symbol of hope, endurance, and regeneration.

I visited the park once, several years ago. It was unrecognizable as the place where I had labored to pull bodies from the wreckage pile, but one thing remained that I could easily recognize: the bell tower of the First United Methodist Church, where we had set up our emergency morgue. It is still standing, its new altar made from church stones damaged in the explosion.

At Kenyon, we have built dozens of monuments. They are often modest stone edifices: messages or lists of names written in a mixture of English, French, Spanish, or Arabic—the languages of those who died, and those who mourn. Some of these monuments offer thanks to the people who looked for the missing, or who cared for the grieving families at difficult times. They usually cover the last human remains from a disaster— those final shreds of human tissue that are just too small to be identifiable, and which are gathered and buried near the site of the tragedy. Whenever I put one in place, I say a quiet "May you find the peace you didn't in life," because the people I encounter in my work have usually met extremely violent ends. That silent prayer also serves to remind me that all these fragments I am burying were once people: mothers and fathers, brothers and sisters. Because in my work, it would be easy to lose track of that.

Some monuments have become part of the local geography: landmarks on a seaside hiking path that tourists might look out for and briefly contemplate the tragedy that once occurred there. The Swissair monument in Peggy's Cove, Newfoundland, is a large, beautifully finished round stone among the rocks that are strewn on the rugged coastline. It has several lines carved out of its rounded back, pointing out to sea: "In memory of the 229 men, women and children aboard Swissair Flight 111 who perished off these shores September 2, 1998. They have been joined to the sea and the sky. May they rest in peace."

Exactly 3,340 miles away, on the Pacific Coast, is a sundial on the beach at Port Hueneme, commemorating the eighty-eight people who lost their lives on the Alaska Airlines crash. Bronze dolphins leap into the air next to the arm of the sundial, which represents the passing of time and the healing of pain. The statue was designed to be both monument and artwork, a thing of beauty arising from tragedy.

These scenic monuments serve as markers, triangulating the difficult terrain between life and death, the transition points for those who go on living. It can be a shocking transition: you say goodbye to your husband or wife as they head off in an airport taxi for another routine business trip, and then days or weeks later you find yourself on a windswept beach, coming to terms with loss and the random, fleeting nature of human life.

As time passes, and time is the single universal measurement in the world, the monuments themselves undergo a transformation, from a memorial to the recently deceased to a local landmark, a turn in the coastal path or a weathered artifact from a time long ago, the names barely legible but still a thing of powerful significance, a monument to the dead and a totem for the living. They are also the reminder that no matter how bad things were, we can recover.

The Staten Island landfill of Fresh Kills, where thousands of scraps of human tissue were commingled with the rubble of the World Trade Center, is being transformed into a wetlands park, New York City's largest green space, full of wild birds, cyclists, and kayakers. No doubt the mound of debris still contains the tissue of some of those who were murdered on September 11, but the transformation of the spot into a peaceful park seems a fitting tribute to those who were swallowed up by the insane violence of that day.

New Orleans, a city already full of famous landmarks, sprouted a slew of Katrina monuments, ranging from a formal garden on Canal Street with marble slabs bearing 1,300 names, to a bronze dog commemorating all the abandoned pets that died. There is also a tiny artisanal altar on the side of a restaurant dedicated to Vera Smith, the woman whose body was left covered on the sidewalk during the storm, her makeshift grave adorned with the handwritten message, "Here lies Vera, god save us all."

Interestingly, the owners of St. Rita's—the nursing home that became a death trap in the flooding—were acquitted in the lawsuit that was later brought against them for criminal negligence. They argued, successfully, that they were adequately prepared for the hurricane that they were warned about, and that evacuating their elderly charges could have caused more death and suffering than leaving them to weather the storm, in normal circumstances. What they weren't prepared for—and no one was—was the breaching of the levees that caused the devastating floods. Instead of building a monument on the site, in 2018, they opened a new assisted living facility on the same property.

As for me, I have left instructions with my husband as to how I would like my remains to be handled: I want to be cremated and my ashes scattered at sea. I know this will mean my husband and daughter will have no physical place to visit, so I have also asked for a bench to be erected by the sea in Key West or in Monterey, California, bearing a small plaque with my name on it. That way, even if I die in a plane crash or one of the natural disasters that are my stock in trade—and if no recovery is made, she and my husband will have somewhere to sit and remember me as they look out on the waves where I vanished, if they wish. Similarly, one of my sisters has also asked to be cremated and spread in the Pacific, noting that Native Americans believed that the blue of the Pacific Ocean erases sorrow and pain. I don't know if that is true or not, but the idea of it is nice.

The end, but for me the end is always the beginning and if I am lucky, this will be my beginning.

Peace Out.

And God shall wipe away all tears from their eyes;
and there shall be no more death, neither sorrow, nor
crying, neither shall there be any more pain: for the
former things are passed away.

—REVELATION 21:4

Acknowledgments

I never planned to write a memoir or anything about my life and work. I've written technical books and had planned to do more of those, but never a memoir. In fact, I am not sure it is all that noteworthy or interesting. I have a job like most people, and I try to do the best I can, again, like most people. I know I'm different and not what people typically expect, so maybe that is what makes people interested. I know when I meet people, I am often much more interested in what they do than what I do.

Nonetheless, after a profile in *The Telegraph* by Sally Williams, and another in *GQ* by Lauren Larson, Anna Sproul-Latimer approached me and said my story was a book waiting to be written, and that I should write it and she would get it published. I agreed—on the condition that we could do it in a way that didn't sensationalize the incidents or take away from the deceased, and would help others. She liked that and so here we are. Therefore, a lot of thanks goes to Sally Williams and Lauren Larson, both excellent writers and journalists. I would love to write like them. They can so expertly share complex subjects in a compassionate and informative way. I hope I haven't embarrassed either of you with my writing!

Writing a book involves so many people, all of whom play such a key part. To begin with, there is Anna, my agent, who worked so hard in getting me to agree to write the book and then found James to help me write it. Then she helped pick the perfect editor and publishing team at St. Martin's, led by Michael Flamini. Their advice and direction are without fail, spot-on, and I am very lucky to work with them. Michael is supported by Hannah Phillips, who I am sure will be as happy as me to have the book off to the print shop. She has been a great help. Kudos also to Ervin Serrano for the jacket design, not an easy task. I hope I have not damaged them with my stories or been too late on my submissions.

There is, of course, James Hider. James and I spent many hours going over text and drafts. He has his own stories and I hope mine have not added to his own burden. Needless to say, James, we wouldn't be here without you. Thank you, brother. Awesome job. You're a great writer.

There were many drafts and proofreads of the manuscript, and to that I owe my enduring gratitude to Donald Steel, Andy Luckey, and Mike Seear, all very busy people who have served as sounding boards, proofreaders—reading and rereading drafts, and providing feedback, as well as great attention to detail and fact-checking! To give you an idea of the caliber of these three, if you have read a newspaper article about the BBC, you have seen Donald's influence. He's an expert on honest communication and a great person. If you watched *Toy Story,* you would have seen Andy. He is the epitome of a great friend, one who drops everything for others, honest, caring, and a hard worker. Mike, a fine friend who has written several books about the 1982 Falklands-Malvinas War, an expeditionary joint war in which he fought as a British Army Gurkha infantry officer.

Beyond proofreading, I also wanted to ensure that the tone

and stories were ones that would not cause sorrow or pain. To that end, I owe my thanks to Destiny Torres and Victoria Hardwidge for reading the drafts and edits.

As a kid growing up watching *Police Story* and other military movies, I saw examples and read about people who acted as mentors or leaders and always wondered if such people really existed. As I got older, I realized they did, and I have been very lucky in life to have found so many of them, people who have taken an interest in me and given me their time, shared their experiences with me, and made sure I knew right from wrong. In many ways, the work I have done is, I hope, an extension of their accomplishments. Thank them for the good you see and me for the bad, my faults are my own. Some have passed, most I have lost touch with (the sad hallmark of always moving on to the next problem). If any of you read this, I hope you see the good and feel proud of it.

In high school at Admiral Farragut Academy (AFA): Captain Orie T. Banks, Commander Edward Lillich, Commander John Rhoda, Major James Harris (I probably still have not learned the proper use of the comma, despite your best efforts to teach me), Commander James Dunning, Chief Edgar J. Maus, Mrs. Evelyn Dayo, and Captain Edward L. Gilgenast. All gave freely of themselves and their legacy stands in the graduates of AFA. I could not have asked for a better cadre of people at that important age in my life.

In college with the Army ROTC cadre, with my coworkers in the California State University Police Department and Fresno County Sheriff's Department, again, I was fortunate to have the help, direction, and, at times, a kick in the pants and support of so many fine people.

Teaching real leadership and service was a hallmark of some of the key cadres in the ROTC program and Captain James R.

Shellington, along with SGM McClendon, MSG Robert Pavia, and SFC William Reynolds, filled that bill by personal example, dedication, and always having time to help a young man: me, even when I didn't know I needed the help. An officer in the military has great responsibility and authority. They give directions and make decisions that have real-life consequences for those they lead and those they serve. It is far too easy to see rank as a privilege, when the real privilege is the ability to lead and serve. That is learned and honed, teaching it is no small skill. I hope I have done your efforts proud while wearing the uniform.

Law Enforcement was also a great teacher. As a peace officer, you have incredible power, the power to deny a person liberty by arresting them or to take their money by issuing fines. You learn the law, tactics, and techniques in school and the academy. But you learn compassion, temperament and the will to survive on the streets. I was fortunate to have some of the best people to learn from. They not only gave of their time, but they also made an effort and cared. Officers such as Raymond Mendoza, Drew Bessinger, John Moseley, and Deputies Julio Chacon and Tom Klose: I know I was not always the easiest to work with, and I am sure I drove you all nuts at some point, but you made a difference for me and I am sure for others. Thank you.

When I graduated college and spent the next ten years on Active Duty in the Army, I was very fortunate to first always have some great noncommissioned officers, the true backbone of the US Army. For some reason, I always seemed to get along with most NCOs, and as a result, I was, I am sure, saved from a lot of trouble and chewing out from above. Officers outrank NCOs, but NCOs have a lot more experience—both technical and with people, so they are great to learn from and depend on for support; in return, an officer's job is to make sure the NCOs have the support they need to get their job done, the resources.

It is a great relationship and one that can pay dividends. At least it did for me. I will miss many names here but some standouts among the many are (ranks at the time I knew them) SGM Rivero, 1SG Chappel, 1SG Brundy, SFC Whitfield, SSG Hampton, SSG Carpenter, SFC Napoleon, SSG Posey, SGT Riggins, and my Section NCOIC, who also became a good friend and my daughter's godfather, MSG David Rich.

While I did not share the same relationship with the officer corps I had with the NCO corps, I was lucky enough to serve and learn from some of the best officers, those you see as the heroes in the war movies and the ones I hoped I would end up being like and could follow. That wasn't in the stars, but one of the reasons I can do what I do today is because of what I learned from them. So, CPT S. Brown and CPT J. Stewart, from my time as a Pershing Officer, and LTC T. Leeman, who helped me navigate the halls of the PERSCOM and Pentagon when summoned there to brief, I thank you. There were also four bosses who really made an impact and I'm sure were often in front of their boss (not in a good way). On my behalf and to you all I am forever grateful: LTC Marilyn Brooks, LTC Dean Tarbet, COL Terry Clemons, and MG Kenneth Guest. Dean and Terry I still get to talk to these days, and that is good thing. As a bonus, I don't think they get in trouble because of me anymore.

I also had the privilege of serving with some of the best civil servants, the constant in the ever-rotating military, the ones who have seen everything and yet will, with each new commander, smile as they start to reinvent the wheel. They are the guardians of history and the go-to resource: David Roath, Jackie Lockhart, Tom Bourlier, with whom I worked at the US Army Mortuary Affairs Center. I was also very lucky working with a Public Affairs team who, because of the Oklahoma City Bombing and Bosnia, had their small one-of-kind and little-known US Army unit thrown into the spotlight—Joy Metzger, Anne Harrison, and Phil Connelly Williams. Your training has served me well. Who knew how much I would use it after leaving the Army? Not me.

As I joined Kenyon, I've been again very lucky to have access to meet and work with some of the most caring people in the world. There are far too many to mention. So, I simply put here, to all who have responded and stopped what you were doing to care for a deceased, to sit with a family member, or take time to explain this process: Thank you for doing that. It means more than you will likely ever know.

There are those who have worked to make the system better for families, who saw anguish and didn't turn away but, instead, chose to work to change the system and make things better. And they have, both for the system and for me: Dr. Marcella Fierro, Robert Gerber, Jim Hall, Sharon Bryson, Matt Ziemkiewicz, Gail Dunham, Ambassador Bill Paterson, Howard Way, Mary Schiavo, and Sean Gates. Never underestimate the good you have done for so many.

Most importantly, I have a debt of gratitude for my husband, who I think may have worked in concert with Anna to urge me to write the book, and my daughter. Both have borne the cost of the job they didn't take or ask for. I do not know what the future holds for me; sadly, I expect more loss and disasters. I hope I don't bring those home with me, because you don't deserve it and I am grateful for you.

Index